D0324024

CHICAGO PUBLIC LIBRARY

CAREERS AND IDENTITIES

CAREERS AND IDENTITIES

Michael Banks, Inge Bates, Glynis Breakwell,
John Bynner, Nicholas Emler, Lynn Jamieson
and Kenneth Roberts

OPEN UNIVERSITY PRESS
Milton Keynes • Philadelphia

Open University Press
Celtic Court
22 Ballmoor
Buckingham
MK18 1XW

and
1900 Frost Road, Suite 101
Bristol, PA 19007, USA

First Published 1992

Copyright © The Authors 1992

All rights reserved. No part of this publication may be
reproduced, stored in a retrieval system or transmitted in
any form or by any means, without written permission from the
publisher.

British Library Cataloguing-in-Publication Data

Careers and identities.
  I. Banks, Michael
  305.23

  ISBN 0-335-09715-4
  ISBN 0-335-09714-6 (pbk)

Library of Congress Cataloging-in-Publication Data

Careers and identities / Michael Banks ... [et al.].
    p. cm.
  Includes bibliographical references and index.
  ISBN 0-335-09715-4. – ISBN 0-335-09714-6 (pbk.)
  1. Identity (Psychology) in youth–Great Britain. 2. Occupations–
Psychological aspects. 3. Youth–Great Britain–Attitudes.
I. Banks, Michael (Michael H.)
BF724.3.I3C37 1991
305.23'5–dc20   91-21346
                                                                                   CIP

Typeset by Stanford Desktop Publishing Services, Milton Keynes
Printed in Great Britain by Biddles Limited, Guildford and Kings Lynn

CONTENTS

& HISTORY DIVISION

REF

AUTHORSHIP

This book was collectively authored but individual authors had responsibility for particular chapters: Chapters 1 and 2, John Bynner; Chapter 3, Michael Banks; Chapter 4, Lynn Jamieson; Chapter 5, Inge Bates; Chapter 6, Glynis Breakwell; Chapter 7, Nick Emler and John Bynner; Chapter 8, Ken Roberts; Chapter 9, Nick Emler. In Chapter 5 the ethnographic studies were provided by Inge Bates (YTS 'care' girls and BTEC fashion designers); George Riseborough (YTS building operatives and BTEC hotel and catering management); John Quicke (sixth-formers). John Bynner produced the final manuscript.

The book draws heavily on analysis and reports produced by Initiative team members through the life of the Initiative, especially working papers in the 16–19 Initiative Series produced at City University. Rather than refer to these repeatedly throughout the text a full list is printed in Appendix 3.

16–19 INITIATIVE
TEAM MEMBERS

City University

Professor John Bynner	National Co-ordinator
Dr Pat Ainley	(Young People Leaving Home)
Dr Sheena Ashford	Core study

University of Sheffield — (Sheffield Project)

Dr Michael Banks	Co-ordinator
Dr Inge Bates	(Core Study)
Dr Steve Evans	(Core Study)
Professor John Gray	(Core Study)
Dr John Quick	(Core Study)
Dr George Riseborough	(Core Study)

University of Liverpool — (Liverpool Project)

Professor Ken Roberts	Co-ordinator
Mr Ray Derricott	(Core Study)
Ms Glennys Parsell	(Core Study)
Dr Janet Strivens	(Core Study)
Ms Michelle Connolly	(Afro-Carribean Youth)
Dr P Torkington	(Afro-Carribean Youth)

University of Surrey — (Surrey Project)

Dr Glynis Breakwell	Co-ordinator
Dr Angela Dale	(Core Study)
Dr Karen Evans	(Core Study)
Dr Chris Fife-Schaw	(Core Study)
Dr Evanthia Lyons	(Core Study)
Ms Kathy Clayden	(Video Project)

University of Dundee	(Kirkcaldy Project)
Professor Nick Emler	Co-ordinator
Dr Dominic Abrams	(Core Study)
Ms Sharon Hall	(Core Study)
Dr J Martens	(Core Study)
University of Edinburgh	(Kirkcaldy Project)
Dr Lynn Jamieson	Co-ordinator
Dr Helen Corr	(Core Study)

Associated Studies

University of Durham	(Young Entrepreneurs)
Professor Frank Coffield	Co-ordinator
Dr Rob McDonald	
Plymouth Polytechnic	(Rural Labour Markets)
Professor David Dunkerley	Co-ordinator
Dr Claire Wallace	
Teesside Polytechnic	(Family Socialisation)
Dr Pat Allatt	Co-ordinator
Ms Claire Benson	
University of Ulster	(Political and Social Identities)
Dr Peter Weinreich	Co-ordinator
Mr James Doherty	
Ms Sheena McGrellis	

Linked Study

Vocational Preparation in England and West Germany

University of Surrey	
Dr Karen Evans	Co-ordinator
Mr Alan Brown	
University of Liverpool	
Professor Ken Roberts	Co-ordinator
Dr Stan Clark	
Ms Michelle Connolly	
University of Bremen	
Professor Walter Heinz	Co-ordinator
Mr Peter Kupka	
University of Bielefeld	
Professor Klaus Hurrelmann	Co-ordinator
Ms Martina Behrens	

PREFACE

This book is about the ways young people approach adulthood and the kinds of adult they become. It focuses on the influences that mould the choices they make and the dilemmas they have to resolve. And these, in turn, point to the kind of support they need through the education system, the workplace and in their leisure lives to help them make the transition successfully. Our evidence comes from the ESRC's 16–19 Initiative, a programme of research on young people conducted by research teams in the Universities of Surrey, Sheffield, Liverpool, and a combined team from the Universities of Dundee and Edinburgh. At the core of the programme was a longitudinal study of 5000 young people growing up in four labour markets (Swindon, Sheffield, Liverpool and Kirkcaldy) in which two groups aged 15–16 and 17–18, respectively, were followed up for two years, with data collected in 1987, 1988 and 1989.

We wanted to discover how young people find their niche in the economic and occupational structure and how they form political judgements and make political choices. Social scientists refer to such developmental processes as 'socialisation': the means by which the adult personality or 'identity' is formed. An earlier ESRC Initiative, Young People and Society (Beloff, 1986; McGurk, 1988) launched a number of studies of different facets of adolescent socialisation, ranging from delinquency through occupational socialisation to politics. Their research approach was novel in drawing together theoretical perspectives and methodological strategies from across the social sciences. Quantitative data collected through surveys were combined with qualitative data generated by ethnographic study, including account gathering and observation. The research we report is an integrated study of young people which builds on this earlier work and adopts the same interdisciplinary approach. The aim of this book is to take some steps towards unravelling the processes and mechanisms of economic and political socialisation among young people aged 16–19.

Our purpose is not to cover all aspects of the subject. Limitations of the research design we were able to employ ruled out the pursuit of some of topics in the depth that was needed. Many of these are the subject of special investigations mounted as associated studies in the Initiative and reported separately. Thus the experience of young people in rural labour markets in the South West of England, Afro-Caribbean young people in Liverpool, young 'entrepreneurs', in the North East, families in Teesside, political and religious identity in Northern Ireland, and young people who had left the family home were all the subjects of associated studies. There was also an associated study in Swindon on the use of video in the study of young people's identities.

Even from within the core research which constitutes the material for this book, the scope of our analysis has been fairly limited. Our intention has been to share our understanding of the broad patterns of young people's experience, to elucidate the form and content of their developing identities, and to relate these to personal circumstances and to local and national economic and social conditions. We demonstrate the variety of teenage careers, how economic and political understanding becomes part of young people's conceptions of themselves, and how they come to terms with disadvantage and failure.

The book examines, at this quite basic level, careers and identity formation in the spheres of education and work, domestic and social life, and politics. It also looks at the context of identity formation and explores its relation to behaviour and attitudes. The book concludes with an attempt at a synthesis directed at social scientists, policy-makers and those who work with young people. In later books we plan to take the work further in each of these areas, exposing in more detail the socialisation processes in each domain while developing with much greater precision our model of adult identity formation.

ACKNOWLEDGEMENTS

The research reported here was supported by grants from the Economic and Social Research Council as part of the 16–19 Initiative. Four teams were involved, from the Universities of Sheffield, Liverpool, Surrey, and Dundee and Edinburgh (combined). In addition to the 'core research' reported here there were seven associated studies which are reported separately: on young entrepreneurs, at the University of Durham; young people in rural labour markets, at Plymouth Polytechnic; political and social identities, at the University of Ulster; Afro-Carribean youth, at the University of Liverpool; young people leaving home, at City University; the use of video in the study of economic and political socialisation, at the University of Surrey. There was also a linked study on vocational preparation in England and West Germany based in the Universities of Surrey, Liverpool, Bremen and Bielefeld. The work was co-ordinated initially from the Open University and subsequently from the Social Statistics Research Unit, City University. The names of the members of the teams involved in the core research and the associated studies are given on pages vii–viii. We would like to acknowledge the help of the working group comprising Harry McGurk, Duncan Gallie, and David Ashton, who formulated the first plans for the Initiative and who formed the nucleus of the Advisory Group which supplied us with valuable guidance as the research progressed. John Gray, of the Sheffield research team, read the manuscript and made helpful editing suggestions. Sharon Clarke of SSRU at City University typed the final manuscript. Sheila Young and Kevin Dodwell also provided valuable help in getting the manuscript ready for publication. Debi Roker from Sheffield University compiled the index.

Chapter 1 CONTEXTS AND ISSUES

Choices and dilemmas

More than any other period of life, youth is the time when critical choices are made. But what is youth, and what significance does the period from age 16 to age 19 have within it? Youth is essentially transitional and preparatory, characterising young people on the threshold of adult life, not yet having access to all its advantages nor having to take on all its responsibilities. The biological changes associated with puberty (average age 14.5 for boys and 13.5 for girls (Tanner, 1962)) and the onset of adolescence mark the beginning of youth; and the social status changes designating full entry to adult roles and responsibilities signify its completion. An adult typically has an established occupation, has financial independence, has left the family home, is likely to have developed political preferences, may be married and may have children. Youth is the period when young people are preparing the ground for adulthood. In Britain the process is, for the majority, fairly compressed, with adulthood considered to have begun by the age of 21. In most continental European countries a more protracted period of transition extends youth to 25 or beyond.

Although many of the foundations of adult attributes are laid early on in life, the critical pathways to them open up in the teens. Education, employment and leisure offer options and opportunities which have to be appraised. The period from age 16 to age 19 is when past experience and achievements in education and in social life are consolidated and crucial choices about future directions made.

But these choices are not made in isolation. The young person is subject to 'structural' influences stemming from the social and cultural groups to which he or she belongs. Thus social class, gender, and ethnicity will all play a part in shaping aspirations, as do the characteristics of the locality in which the young person lives. These influences are mediated via social relations which change as maturity approaches. The dominance of the family as the source of advice, guidance and values gives way to the influence of the peer group, which itself gives way to the influence of a single partner; however, for certain choices, such as what job to do, parents' views continue to prevail. Other adults, such as relatives, family friends, youth leaders and teachers, may also have a role in the decisions taken. Good careers advice offered at school from a sympathetic teacher may be critically important. How to respond to this range of often conflicting advice and pressure, while holding on to personal preferences and inclinations, presents a series of dilemmas which have to be resolved en route to adult status.

Probably the most important of these dilemmas in the mid-teens is what to do at 16: whether to stay on in the education system or leave to get a job. The former brings with it the possibility of enhanced career opportunities later in life; the latter offers the prospect of adult wages and a degree of early independence from the family and autonomy, especially for girls. But those who stay on are still faced with choices: what subjects to pursue after age 16, whether to take vocational courses or academic ones, whether to mix study with part-time work, whether to go on to university. Outside the education system, choices are between jobs or, more frequently, between training schemes; some settle for part-time work interspersed with unemployment. By age 19 the resolution of most of the dilemmas associated with occupational choice has been achieved. Career patterns have crystallised into the routes to permanent destinations in the labour market.

Parallel to the world of work is that of leisure, which presents another set of choices sometimes complementing but often at variance with those in education. In the early teens, as Hendry (1989) reports, leisure activity for young people is concentrated in adult-organised settings, such as youth clubs, scouts and guides. These give way to casual pursuits with, initially, a single-sexed teenage group with much time spent in each other's houses or in group activities such as sport. In the late teens increased income, brought about through full-time or part-time work and the lifting of age restrictions, gives the young person access to commercially organised activities in mixed-group settings, such as the pub, the disco and the pop concert. Every step on the way from one type of activity to the next confronts the young person with dilemmas to be resolved, involving, for example, changes of allegiance from one group of friends another; while all the time ties with the family are loosening. Leisure time previously spent with the family is increasingly spent with friends. The family holiday is finally dropped in favour of one with one or more peers. Running through this changing pattern of social relations is the increasing importance of sexuality and partnership: the group gives way to partners and ultimately to a more stable relationship with one other person, including, for some young people, marriage. Through the late teens, sizeable minorities leave home – 27% of 19-year-old girls and 15% of 19-year-old boys in 1987 – and some of these have set up house and started families of their own (Roll, 1990). For them, we might say, youth is over and adulthood has fully begun.

Leisure life is also the forum for other kinds of choice: what football team to support, what style of music to prefer, what clothes to wear are important features of teenage identity, expressing solidarity with the peer group. These are among the easier choices to make. The decision to smoke, to drink, to take drugs represents a more difficult set of dilemmas that all young people have to face; those participating fully in the activities of the wider 'teenage culture' are under pressure to try them, especially if associating with a group where such activity is the norm and where the young person is keen to gain acceptance in it (Bynner, 1969). Similarly, relations with the opposite sex will be motivated as much by pressure to conform with group values about the appropriate routes to social and sexual maturity as by individual interest. Various types of delinquent act, from petty theft to vandalism, hooliganism and fighting, may also be engaged in, not because the young person needs to satisfy some pathological criminal need but because delinquent activity represents a form of bravado which certain peer groups demand of their members (Emler *et al.*, 1987).

Targets for hostile adolescent attitudes provide a basis for another set of choices which start to become important. In the arena of adult politics, interest may be low and party loyalties weakly formed at this age. What exists will be strongly influenced by parents' preferences. But some of the social and political issues that find a place on the party platforms, from the endorsement of 'green' values to trust in the police and politicians, do arouse strong feelings. To make sense of politics in teenage terms requires a broader definition than that which would apply to adults. In the words of Schaffer and Hargreaves (1978), it needs to include 'the adolescent's conception of himself and relevant social relationships, his understanding of his local community and the wider society and his ideas about the relationships between self and society'.

Contexts

One of the difficulties in studying young people in the 1980s has been the rapidly changing contexts in which their socialisation occurred. At the end of the previous decade, Schaffer and Hargreaves (1978) were able to write that 'most adolescents join the labour market at 16 years of age: it is the normal life experience of the adolescent'. By the time our research was carried out nearly half of those aged 16 were staying on in education and direct job entry for school leavers was restricted to a minority of less than 20% (Courtenay, 1988). The rest of the leavers entered a variety of training schemes, often interspersed with part-time jobs and unemployment. But even training itself underwent a change while the research was in progress. At the time our older respondents became eligible to leave school, the national Youth Training Scheme (YTS) was a one-year scheme and much of it took place in the form of community provision. This was the training available to our older cohort of 17–18-year-olds. In 1986, when our younger cohort aged 15–16 first became eligible to enter training its duration had been extended to two years, and most of it, at least in theory, became employer-based (Department of Employment, 1986). Similarly, at the beginning of the project, unemployment and living on social security was a serious option for school leavers who failed to find jobs. During 1988, legislation took effect to prevent most young people under 18 claiming social security and to stop young adults up to the age of 25 gaining state benefits when living away from home. In consequence, unemployment could only be a viable option if parents were prepared to provide support.

To find the origins of these developments, we need to go back to the beginning of the decade. Throughout the 1970s and early 1980s, industrial decline, concentrated particularly in the manufacturing areas of the North of England, the Midlands, Wales and Scotland, brought in its wake a dramatic growth in youth unemployment, leading Ashton and Maguire (1983) to refer to a 'vanishing youth labour market'. In 1973, 60% of males and 55% of females aged 16–17 were in employment; in 1985, 20% of males and 25% females were employed (Junankar, 1987). Traditional industries were also being replaced by new ones, requiring different kinds of skills. New technology was coming to play an increasingly important part in manufacturing and there was a massive expansion of service industry. Training schemes, originally offered as an alternative to unemployment, soon became the means of bridging the gap between what school courses were able to offer and what employers were now demanding; though some critics also saw them serving the function of social control (Edwards, 1983). Craft apprenticeships, which had always largely been the province of boys (120,000 boys to 20,000 girls at their peak), steadily declined and those that remained became absorbed into YTS or regular employment (Raffe, 1990). At the end of the decade YTS went through a further transformation. The government's 1988 White Paper (Department of Employment, 1988) heralded the setting up of locally based Training and Enterprise Councils (TECs) which were given the responsibility of administering youth training to fit local employers' and young people's training needs. The national programme was over.

Paralleling the growth of 'training', attempts were made to reform the school curriculum. Many of the early initiatives, such as those based on the Hargreaves Report (Inner London Education Authority, 1984), stemmed from local education authority concerns to improve the quality of secondary education and strengthen the links between school and work. These were soon overtaken by the government's plans to reform the school curriculum, initially using the Manpower Services Commission as a means of injecting new money and new ideas into the education system (see, for example, Ainley and Corney, 1990). The Technical and Vocational Education Initiative (TVEI), aimed at 14–18-year-olds, began in 1983 in this way as a pilot project, and in 1986 became a universally available scheme, even extending to Scotland where education is administered quite separately and organised quite differently than in England (Department of Employment, 1986). TVEI laid the foundations for the Certificate of Pre-Vocational Education (CPVE), an examination syllabus based on a one-year modular course in the sixth form inspired by the Department of Education and Science (DES). It also dovetailed with Scotland's earlier post-16 modular educational programme, the '16+ Action Plan'. These developments paralleled the establishment of the National Council for Vocational Qualifications with the task of rationalising all vocational qualifications in terms of a single record of vocational achievement certifying six levels of skill. Together with the traditional pre-vocational courses offered by the British and Technical Education Council (BTEC), the Royal Society of Arts (RSA), and the City and Guilds of London Institute (CGLI), about a third of those staying on in education were engaged in vocational preparation (one-tenth in combination with O levels) at the time the 16–19 Initiative began. The other two-thirds had embarked either on A-level courses, often with the aim of gaining access to higher education (54%) or were retaking O levels (14%) (Clough et al., 1988). These initiatives, which culminated in the Educational Reform Act 1988 and the establishment for the first time of a national curriculum in England and Wales, have also not been without their critics (see, for example, Bates, 1984; Ainley, 1988). Vocationalising the curriculum has been seen as reinforcing the divide between young people pursuing academic as opposed to vocational tracks and diverting attention from the proper task of education, the development of the whole individual.

Economic transformation affected all European countries, though the responses of young people to it varied. The most striking change in the countries of Western Europe was the virtual disappearance of a youth labour market, and its replacement up to the age of 18 (and beyond) with extended education and training, including a steady rise in the number entering higher education. At the time the research began in 1985, 43% of 18-year-olds were in full-time education in France compared with 17% in the UK (DES, 1990). By 1988, the gap had widened with 52% in full-time education in France and 20% in the UK.

One of the reasons for the expansion of education and training had been recognition of the need to equip the next generation of workers with a much wider range of vocationally relevant skills than was needed at a time when a substantial market for unskilled and semi-skilled labour existed. (France had gone so far as to set a target of 80% of its school leavers achieving its higher education entrance examination, the *baccalauréat*, by the end of the century.) The main difference with the UK was the stronger commitment of Continental employers, parents and young people to the education system as a means of bringing about the desired changes. The value placed on vocational preparation – through the 'dual system' of work-based training and part-time vocational school in German-speaking countries, and through full-time education in most others – is stronger on the Continent and there is acceptance of a longer route to achieving adult worker status in all types of occupation (Bynner and Roberts, 1991): in 1987, the average age of graduation from West German universities, for example, was 28 (Federal Republic of Germany, 1990). In contrast, Britain's 'mixed' system of jobs, training and full-time education continued to offer adult worker status and near-adult wages to a sizeable minority (20%). In consequence, over the whole decade, the staying-on rate in education only increased marginally: from 40% in 1978 to 47% in 1988. From 1981, unemployment remained fairly constant at around 10%, and YTS participation increased steadily, reaching 24% in 1988 (DES, 1988).

With the advent of a single European market in 1992, it remains to be seen whether Continental patterns of extended transition to employment will finally take over in the UK. If they do, then some of the concerns of Continental commentators about the 'post-adolescent' life phase may come with them. The German writer Baethge (1989), for example, saw the growing separation of the individual from the socialising effects of the workplace and the 'individualisation' of work and leisure brought about by the microchip as potentially damaging to the social fabric. Work values declined and social mores concerned with co-operation and support were weakened. Others, such as Heinz (1987a) and Mahler (1989), took a more optimistic view. Heinz saw extended education as producing an ambivalence about work, but not fundamentally affecting its centrality in adult life. Mahler saw advantages in a situation where the age-gap between teacher and taught narrows, and 'anticipatory socialisation' in place of socialisation in the workplace gave individuals greater opportunities to influence future forms of education and work.

In the UK the upheavals in the labour market, concentrated in the industrial heartlands, were having an effect on domestic and social life as well. Youth unemployment had the consequence for boys of extending dependence on parents, and replacing early marriage by what Wallace (1987) described as 'a form of perpetual adolescence'. The consequence for girls was to be absorbed back into a domestic role in the family, with finding someone to live with or getting married the only escape. The longer a girl remained unemployed the more likely she was to take this step.

As unemployment has been replaced by training or staying on at school, the consequences have similarly been postponement of settling down. This has led to a renewal of interest in 'youth culture' (Roberts, 1987) with its variety of forms and supposed concomitants: drug-taking, sexual promiscuity and delinquency (Brake, 1985). Much media attention was directed at the time of our study to the more flamboyant and challenging forms of youth lifestyle, of which 'punk' at the beginning of the decade and 'acid house' at the end were two examples. The rise of new and particularly threatening kinds of drug such as 'crack', and the apparent 'breakdown in civilized values' associated with soccer hooliganism also aroused much media concern and indignation; though to what extent they impinged directly on the lives of the vast majority of young people was debatable.

Changes in teenage styles, tastes and interests were part of a longer process of growing consumer strength among young people, which the new electronic media were serving. Developments first in audio communications, then in video and more recently satellite and cable television, both internationalised the music tastes and entertainment on offer while at the same time, in a sense, individualising the means by which they were received. The microcomputer, too, not only transformed much work practice, but also dominated leisure life for large numbers of young people, particularly boys (Bynner and Breakwell, 1990).

A major issue confronting young people was the positive and negative benefits of technological change. Concern about nuclear power and nuclear defence strategies was being joined by concern about environmental damage and pollution. At the end of our data-collection period the penetration of 'green' issues into the electorate's conciousness was evident from the level of support gained by the Green Party in the 1988 European Parliament Election, the bulk of which came from voters aged under 30. The risk of biological catastrophe was coming to the centre of the political stage. Young people, as the inheritors of the 'poisoned planet', had a growing stake in shaping the politics of the future. How far these values signified the adoption of a 'postmaterialist' world view (Inglehart, 1977) was more debatable: commitment to the idea of employment remained undiminished, especially among young people with working-class backgrounds. Finally, the AIDS epidemic cast a shadow over social life, challenging the sexual liberalism prominent at the beginning of the decade.

In the wider political context, this was the decade of heightening party polarisation to which, despite their general political apathy, young people were not immune. The 'enterprise culture' promoted by the Conservative government as part of the broader ideology popularly described as 'Thatcherism' was in continual conflict with the 'liberal establishment' that preceded it and the remaining bastions of 'socialism', most notably in Labour-controlled town councils. Labour was in office at local, if not at Parliamentary level, in all the towns where our young people lived. The battles over restriction of local government expenditure, or 'rate-capping', reached their peak in Liverpool where our research took place. In Scotland the early introduction of the community charge or poll tax gave our young people in Kirkcaldy another exposure to a major political controversy with a direct impact for them. The wider attack on Labour councils' promotion, through the education system, of such causes as anti-sexism, anti-racism and gay rights, and the treatment of sex education in the curriculum also brought these issues into young people's conciousness. The question was raised by political scientists whether these changes in the political terrain and the wider effects of Thatcherism as a set of political beliefs were detaching voters from their traditional class allegiances – a process referred to in this book as 'class dealignment' (Robertson, 1984). Were young people being politicised in the same way and in the same direction as their parents' generation. Certainly, early indications at the beginning of the decade of the politicisation of young unemployed people in the direction of fascism (Cochrane and Billig, 1982b) failed to materialise. Political participation of any kind remained rare, and what existed of it tended to be restricted to a relatively small educated minority. In so far as there was political affiliation, it was strongly related to that of parents.

Careers

To make sense of teenage socialisation against this backcloth of turbulent economic and political change, we need to distinguish between two types of influence which shape progress and determine ultimate destination. Structural influences concerned with social group membership and cultural inheritance are one set of pressures on young people; developmental changes concerned with the move towards sexual and social maturity are the other. We can see their impact in the two critical areas of life on which this book focuses: careers and identities. What do we mean by them? Let us look first at the concept of 'career'.

In this book, the notion of 'career' is defined not only in the narrow sense of entry into and progress through the labour market, but also in the wider sense of entry into adult domestic life, leisure and politics. Careers differ between different social and cultural groups, between males and females, and from one area to another; most become more stable with age. The term 'career trajectory' (Roberts, 1987) sums up effectively these two major aspects of life chances: variability across different sections of the population and change with time. At any one point in time – the snapshot which a single survey can provide – an individual in the 16–19 age group will show any one of a number of levels of economic status (in education, in training, at work or unemployed). The individual may be living at home or have already left, may be a member of a mixed teenage group going to discos or a single-sex group engaged in delinquent acts, or 'going steady' with a partner. Across the 16–19 age group, individual statuses are likely to be changing, often erratically. By the twenties options and opportunities are beginning to narrow and trajectories are beginning to level off.

One of the important goals of our research was to chart teenage careers and to derive a classification which could be used to direct later stages of the design and serve as a major basis for analysis. We also wanted to unravel their origins and discover what shapes them across the teens.

What did we know already about careers? Roberts's (1968) opportunity structure theory stressed the importance of social class, gender, race and educational attainment in determining destinations in the local labour market. Thus although personal choices have a role in occupational socialisation, there is a high predictability about the form of an occupational career and its ultimate outcomes. The segmentation of the labour market stressed by Ashton *et al.* (1990) is another factor in job entry. Broad groups of occupation have specified entry points attached to age, gender and qualification. Opportunities for young people to enter them as early school leavers or at later ages are therefore severely curtailed, and at times of economic slump barriers against entry become more difficult to surmount. This leads to an important distinction in teenage socialisation: 'protracted' versus 'accelerated' transition. Those jobs, especially in the professional sphere, demanding extended education and training, postpone entry to employment and financial independence and consequently marriage and family formation. Early entry into employment via unskilled or semi-skilled jobs removes these barriers accelerating the transition to full adult status.

Locality

In comparing young adults' (aged 18–24) prospects in four areas of the country (St Albans, Leicester, Stafford and Sunderland), Ashton and Maguire (1986) demonstrated the significance of labour-market opportunities in shaping occupational careers regardless of educational qualifications. For example, among males with no qualifications, over three-quarters were unemployed in all areas except St Albans, where 62% were unemployed; for those with A levels, less than a fifth were unemployed in Leicester, St Albans and Stafford, but over half in Sunderland. The value of training schemes was also shown to be related to labour-market opportunities. In Leicester and Sunderland, four-fifths of the young people who had been on training schemes were unemployed, whereas about half of those in Stafford and less than half of those in St Albans were in a similar position. These differences were far less marked for females, which suggests that in the economic climate prevailing at the time their opportunities were being less affected by major changes in the labour market than were those of males.

Differences between labour markets in offering prospects to young people did not extend to differences within them. Garner *et al.* (1987) showed, for example, that once the characteristics of young people living in particular parts of a city were taken into account, variations in opportunities between one part of the city and the next were minimal. This underlines the importance of the labour market as a totality which shapes prospects. It also highlights the considerable differences between the opportunities offered in labour markets in the North and the South.

Gender

Men and women's prospects diverge sharply after the age of 18. Despite more females than males staying on in education after the age of 16, fewer females go on to higher education, the route to a professional career (Redpath and Harvey, 1987). Those who do leave and get a job or go into a training scheme enter a quite different and more restricted range of occupations. For example, Raffe and Courtenay (1988) report that more than half of the girls in Scottish and English school-leaver surveys worked in just two occupational categories (clerical and personal services), and two more (selling and materials processing) accounted for most of the remainder. In contrast, boys' occupations were spread over all 12 categories of the occupational classification.

Early work on young people's occupational socialisation, stemming particularly from the Centre for Cultural Studies at the University of Birmingham, tended to focus exclusively on young men. Willis's (1977) classic study charted the ways in which young men become socialised through their peer group into adult occupational roles, distinguishing between what he called 'the lads' who leave school at the minimum age and end up in unskilled employment, and 'the earoles' who fill white-collar jobs. In a similar study Jenkins (1983), working in Belfast, distinguished between the socially immobile 'lads' and what he called 'citizens' and 'ordinary kids'. And more recently, Brown (1987), in a study in South Wales, drew attention to the irrelevance of secondary education to 'ordinary' (that is, working-class) boys and girls. Willis's work assumed implicitly that girls' employment was of secondary importance or that much the same process of occupational socialisation occurred for them. But a number of writers later set out explicitly to challenge this view.

To see female careers in the same terms as male careers is to overlook the central importance of domestic life and childrearing in the experience and career aspirations of most girls. Although in the middle and late teens there is a degree of overlap between male and female progress to the labour market, from the early twenties onwards male and female career paths diverge sharply. Writers such as Pollert (1981) and Griffin (1985) exposed the pressures girls are under to fulfil traditional female occupational roles in factories and offices and the great difficulty they have in resisting male dominance in the workplace, or in breaking through the barriers around 'male' occupations such as engineering. Other research by writers such as Allatt (1986), Allatt and Yeandle (1986), Breakwell (1986a), Wallace (1987) and Cockburn (1987) amplified the picture further. Allatt and Yeandle, for example, identified the key role of the mother in ensuring that work habits and attitudes were inculcated in the young and that jobs were held. Wallace demonstrated the dominance of female relatives in determining the young girls' occupational aspirations and values. Cockburn drew attention to the rigid gender segregation of much of YTS. Breakwell, studying a YTS programme for girls in engineering, exposed the obstacles confronting girls in trying to pursue a traditionally 'male' career and concluded that they could be successfully surmounted only if feminine identity within the job was preserved.

Social class and race

As we might expect, the effects of social class on prospects are mediated mainly via examination performance, especially in what at the time of our research was the GCE. The national Youth Cohort Study (Courtenay, 1988) showed that young people from non-manual and professional homes make up the bulk of those who do best in the education system, and that those from unskilled manual homes make up the bulk of those who do worst. Training schemes were similarly stratified, with the best-qualified tending to get the best 'employer-based' offers. Where employment fails to materialise after training or where unemployment has been the main experience since leaving school, prospects in declining economic areas can be grim. Ashton and Maguire (1986) estimated that up to 10% of the population who enter adult life without qualifications or early employment experiences are likely to spend most of their lives in part-time unskilled jobs or on the dole. Such young people were poignantly described in the far-reaching ethnographic study of unemployed youth in the North East of England by Coffield *et al.* (1986). Though some had achieved exam passes, many had not bothered to find out what they were, and all of them had left school at the minimum age in order to get work. Since then all they had experienced was drifting in and out of government training schemes and part-time semi-skilled and unskilled jobs. Training for them was often no more than exploitation by unscrupulous employers looking for cheap labour.

Race also affects prospects. In a two-year follow-up study of West Indian, Asian and white school leavers, Sillitoe and Meltzer (1986) found that black young people's commitment to and positive appraisal of education and training was stronger than among whites, but that they were less likely to get permanent work at the end of it. In a study by Clough *et al.* (1984) in Sheffield and Bradford, it was found that among the best-qualified young people (those with four or more O levels) blacks were three times as likely to be unemployed as whites, and among the unqualified 1.5 times as likely. Black YTS trainees were less likely to get jobs because they tended to get taken on in mode B (community-based schemes). Another study by Banks and Ullah (1987a) confirmed that continued difficulties in finding employment impelled young black people to seek less-skilled employment or ultimately to give up the search for employment altogether.

Identity

Structural factors dominate the development of careers. Developmental factors come into prominence in the other major outcome of socialisation:

identity. Identity, as we conceive it, embraces the individual's own perception of himself or herself generally and in specific domains – for example, occupational identity, political identity, domestic identity (Breakwell, 1986b). Its development is fundamental in relationships with others and, consequently, the ability to function in the social world, including the world of work. Its evaluative aspect, self-esteem, is also central to social action. The shattering of expectations and aspirations typifying many adolescents' occupational experiences brings with it a diminution in self-esteem and, consequently, the need to find ways of shoring up identity. Solidarity with the peer group provides an important means of doing this and at the same time helps shape future identity. The young person shares in 'group' or 'social' identity with respect to interests, tastes and fashions and a wider range of norms and values. But this is not a passive absorption of influence. The idea, which we endorse, of the individual as an active 'agent' implies purposive choices and actions following them – a 'productive processor of reality' (Hurrelmann, 1988). Perceived success in achieving personal goals (self-efficacy) will be manifested in confidence about ability to influence the course of events in all spheres of life and is typically accompanied by a sense of 'internal' as opposed to 'external' locus of control (Rotter, 1966).

Thus research carried out by the Social and Applied Psychology Unit (SAPU) of the University of Sheffield showed that failure to get a job after leaving school or subsequently losing one was likely to be accompanied by a temporary reduction in self-esteem and emotional stress, but no further worsening of psychological health as the period of unemployment extended (Banks and Ullah, 1987a). Most young people found a means of coming to terms with unemployment, by seeking satisfactions and achievements in leisure life or by placing less value on the goal of work. How well they were able to resolve the conflict was, of course, affected by the importance they attached to work in the first place: such values as work commitment or subscription to the 'Protestant work ethic' (Furnham, 1984) mediate the effects of experience on personal action and consequently the developing identity (Warr *et al.*, 1985).

Another important aspect of identity is how the individual views the social and political world, and how he or she attributes cause and effect within it. Intersubjective understandings and meanings lie at the heart of group life and underpin the formation of social and political values (Moscovici, 1981). In relation to attribution of cause and effect much attention has been directed to how young people perceive the causes of unemployment. Most young people attribute the national economic situation to political causes, but perceive their own position and that of other individuals in terms of personal failings (Heinz, 1987b). This gulf between the general and the personal and the way group processes mediate and reinforce the contradictions is central to identity formation.

What do we know about the socialisation processes involved in identity formation and their interaction with physical and social development? Hendry (1989) specifies six developmental tasks for adolescence:

1. Developing a self-identity in the light of physical changes.
2. Developing a gender identity.
3. Gaining a degree of independence from parents.
4. Accepting or rejecting family values.
5. Shaping up to an occupational or unemployed role.
6. Developing and extending friendship.

It is in leisure life particularly where these tasks are accomplished and the necessary socialisation is achieved.

Coleman's (1974) focal theory, drawing on Erikson's (1959; 1968) stages of personality development, presents the whole period in terms of a series of conflicts which need to be resolved if a mature and adjusted adult identity is to be achieved. At the beginning of adolescence conflicts centre on the growing awareness of heterosexual (and homosexual) relationships; later on, acceptance or rejection from the peer group is critical; later still, conflict with parents over autonomy and independence hold centre stage. At any one age young people will be at different developmental stages in relation to these conflicts but ultimately all will pass through them.

The dominance of these conflicts in the mid- and late teens largely cuts out interest in adult social concerns, especially in the realm of party politics. But this does not mean that young people are apolitical, merely that their political world is defined in different terms – more, for example, by attitudes to authority in the home, the workplace and in leisure. 'Teencentrism' (Meus, 1989) expresses the extent to which young people feel hostility to all groups outside their immediate peer group, including all manifestations of adult authority such as the police, and other teenage groups. Thus to understand teenage identity and especially its function as a basis for adult political identity it is necessary to understand teenage leisure behaviour and values, and their relation to the wider youth culture.

Youth culture and lifestyle

The manifestation of youth culture for a particular generation is dominated by the media response to young people as consumers. This means that the extent of participation in youth culture will be affected by the financial resources available to the individual and this in turn places a structural constraint on the form youth culture takes for particular groups at particular ages. The degree of teencentrism exhibited is similarly affected by structural factors: hostility to outgroups, including adults, generally is likely to be strongest among those who have left the education system earliest and performed worst in it. Willis's (1977) work suggested that many working-class boys under strong peer-group pressure make a conscious choice around the time of puberty whether they are going to play the game of educational achievement or to treat it with a degree of contempt. In order to supply the young unskilled labourers that the labour market of the time demanded, it was in society's interests that many of them chose the latter course. Teachers aided this selection for working-class careers by deciding who was worth making an effort with and who should be written off. For these young men, life in the youth culture outside the school gates was where satisfactions and achievements were to be found. Most obviously success with the opposite sex, toughness, bravado, style, and achievements in sports, provided a means of achieving status and maintaining self-esteem, not only with the immediate peer group but also with the others committed to remaining in the education system. This is because these activities represent the values of 'subterranean adult masculinism' to which most young boys aspire (Matza, 1964; Brake, 1985). The counterpoint in female terms has been described as 'bedroom culture', making the point that much of teenage girls' social life takes place privately in the confines of their homes (McRobbie, 1978; Griffin, 1985). The ideas of glamour and romance were formed there and, nurtured through the fiction and magazines directed at girls, easily replaced the less exciting goals of school and occupational achievement. Again family and community pressure on girls to conform with the expectations of motherhood and domesticity helps speed the process.

Smoking and drinking are an important means of expressing peer-group solidarity and are very common among the school-leaver age group. In a national survey, Dobbs and Marsh (1985) found that among 15-year-olds, 70% of boys and 74% of girls smoked. The slightly higher percentage of girls trying smoking points to an interesting reverse trend across the generations. Studies conducted twenty years previously on smoking showed consistently higher percentages of male smokers (Bynner, 1969). While boys were abandoning the habit, girls were taking it up. Drinking among young people is even more prevalent in both sexes. Coffield *et al.* (1986) noted, for example, the importance of regular nights out accompanied by heavy drinking in the lives of the unemployed young people they studied. From the mid-teens onwards, the pub is the most important social centre for young people and drinking alcohol is an integral part of young people's social life. Aitkin and Jahoda (1983) showed, from observations of adolescents in Glasgow pubs, that girls' drinking differs from boys in form if not alcohol quantity; that each member of the group needs to establish a drinking 'identity' ('heavy drinker', 'light drinker', 'non-drinker'); and that 'round buying' and its associated rituals provides the means of ensuring group recruitment and conformity.

Research on drug-taking has naturally been much rarer. But what has been done points to the same function in relation to cementing group identity. Pearson *et al.* (1987), for example, found that heroin addiction was intimately tied to the world of young, usually unemployed adults, whose lifestyle came to revolve around the habit. The form the addiction took – injection or smoking – differed from one town to the next or even from one housing estate to the next. Identities became so intimately tied to the habits and values of the group that the chances of any one individual giving up the drug were very low, unless, of course, the friendships and the lifestyles that went with them changed as well.

Politics

The values reinforcing the lifestyles and behaviour just considered, provide the framework for youth politics. There has been little study of its interface with those facets of identity concerned with political party values and allegiances – including the issue of class dealignment (Robertson, 1984; Franklin, 1985). Although many issues, such as dealings with the police, the judiciary, local services, drug-taking, sexual behaviour, unemployment and YTS, raise strong 'political' feelings in young people, few young people show much interest in party politics and most express distrust of politicians. Even among sixth-formers, Furnham and Gunter (1983) found that knowledge of political institutions was limited largely to the local council or to other state institutions of which they had direct experience.

The school curriculum in Britain is largely devoid of political education, which may provide part of the explanation. This has been seen as laying young people open to the attractions of extreme right-wing political beliefs, which are typically presented as an antidote to economic hardship. Coffield *et al.* (1986) noted the racist views held by many of the young people they studied, even though they lived in an area where there was hardly any minority ethnic population. Cochrane and Billig (1982b) observed, at a time of rising unemployment in the West Midlands, increasing support for the policies of the fascist British National Party. In 1979, just under 7% of their sample listed the British National Party as their first political choice; by 1982, the figure had risen to 30%. These effects do not appear to have been repeated in other places and the indication from election results is that what exists of them does not carry through into adult voting patterns. Apathy is the more dominant stance, as Billig (1986) reports: even an ostensibly political organisation such as the Young Conservatives, which Cochrane and he studied, was used by its members largely for social purposes.

In so far as young people have party-political allegiances, evidence suggests that these tend to be transmitted through families across the generations. Himmelweit *et al.* (1983), for example, showed that children tend to adopt their parents' political preferences, especially when the parents' politics conform with that of the dominant allegiance of their social class. They also found that of the two parents the mother had the most important influence. The international Political Action Study (Marsh, 1990) also emphasised the importance of parents in young people's political preferences, and pointed to greater political awareness and interest among young people in Continental countries than in Britain, but similarly found that party allegiances were strongly related to those of parents in all of them. This would point to changes in the political allegiances of adults being reflected in those of the next generation.

Questions and approaches

The earlier work we reviewed when designing the research reinforced our view that relatively little was known about identity formation in the late teens and how this related to teenage career patterns. This is especially the case in relation to young people's political understanding and beliefs but extends to a range of other facets of occupational and political identity as well. More generally, we need to know how local cultural and economic circumstances interact with the major socialising influences from the home, the education system, the workplace, and the peer group in shaping adult identity.

This brings together what has typically been a concern of social psychologists – identity formation – with the focus on careers and opportunity structures that typifies the work of sociologists. The central thrust of our research strategy embraced this interdisciplinary perspective. First, we needed to construct a typology of teenage careers and map out the broad differences in transition patterns between different groups of young people. Second, we needed to elucidate the effects of economic and social structures and the socialising influences stemming from the family, the education system, the peer group, and the workplace on entry into and subsequently progress through a teenage career. Third, we needed to unravel the processes of identity formation and to find out how these relate to political values and action.

Such a model of socialisation processes is of necessity not static in the sense that certain conditions and experiences lead inevitably to certain outcomes, but, in line with the idea of 'agency', needs to be dynamic. At any point in time, current behaviour and attitudes both are a product of past experience and exercise an influence on future experience. For example, entry to a training scheme may enhance status in the family, possibly improving relationships there; whereas in the teenage group entering a training scheme as opposed to getting a job may reduce status with the consequence that either the group may need to change its values or the individual may need to prove himself or herself to the group in other ways. Disentangling such dynamics is wellnigh impossible with a single cross-sectional survey, which made the case for longitudinal research (Bynner, 1987). As we shall see in the next chapter, it also pointed to the need for case-study methods including extended interviewing and ethnographic investigation.

Why try to model teenage socialisation at all? Besides enhancing our understanding of how young people get to where they are and where they are likely to go next, we also get pointers for policy and practice. Most obviously, the ever-changing situation of young people demands continual re-evaluation of the education and training and the advisory and support services that will best enable them to make the transition to adulthood successfully. Those suffering particular forms of disadvantage in education, at home and in the labour market will need targeted help, including, for some, financial assistance. The curriculum for all, especially in the areas of vocational preparation, needs to be continually updated to meet the requirements not only of the labour market but also of the social and political world. Knowledge of how careers develop and how identity is formed is the base on which successful attempts to enhance young people's prospects and improve their effectiveness as adult citizens, will grow.

Chapter 2   STUDYING YOUNG PEOPLE IN CONTEXT

Rationale

As we saw in Chapter 1, economic and political socialisation embraces most facets of teenage life. 'Careers' express young people's progress through the domains of education, employment, leisure and domestic life. 'Identity' is the sum total of their perceptions of themselves. Their 'politics' emerges initially through the attitudes they adopt towards social issues of immediate concern such as sexual and racial equality and adult institutions and authority, and later through their allegiances to political parties.

Young people's careers and identities vary in form between different sections of the youth population, at different ages and in different parts of the country. How can we chart their development in the late teens and elucidate their interactions with each other? More specifically, how are adult occupational and political identities established?

In designing our research there were a number of options open to us. To describe the characteristics of all British teenagers, we could have undertaken a representative sample survey. This was the approach adopted in the Training Agency's major studies of school leavers (Courtenay, 1988). Large representative samples of young people in their last year of compulsory schooling were surveyed by self-completion questionnaire and followed up at annual intervals. These surveys give the best overall picture of the destinations of school leavers. Of particular value to policy-makers, they also enable precise estimates to be made of the numbers in the total school-leaver population pursuing different career routes and entering particular occupations.

At a certain level these studies can also tell us about the conditions in the lives of young people that accompany certain outcomes: whether girls enter different occupations from boys; whether family background characteristics such as social class are correlated with young people's occupational statuses, and so on.

It is when we want to go deeper into the way institutions such as schools, training establishments and workplaces, and the social processes that go on within them, shape young people's occupational and political careers, that the inadequacy of the national survey becomes apparent. Young people relate to particular schools, training establishments and jobs within a particular locality. Besides having its own education system and labour market, each locality has a distinctive economic and political culture which mediates the influence of the national economic and social systems on young people's development. Young people are socialised by a particular set of local agencies in relation to a particular set of local opportunities. How significant these local effects are for the young people will, of course, also depend on where they are located in the social structure: whether they are male or female; whether they are from minority ethnic backgrounds; what social backgrounds they come from; how well they have performed at school; in what direction their vocational ambitions lie.

The importance of locality, as stressed in the studies by Ashton and Maguire (1986), and Roberts *et al.* (1987), led to the decision to locate the 16–19 Initiative core study similarly in particular areas of Britain. An earlier ESRC initiative, Social Change and Economic Life (Gallie, 1988), had been based in six British labour markets: Kirkcaldy and Aberdeen (in Scotland); and Coventry, Northampton, Swindon and Rochdale (in England). The 16–19 Initiative took two of these areas, Swindon and Kirkcaldy, and selected two more, Liverpool and Sheffield, in which to locate the study.

The decision to undertake area studies was strategic. The next questions to resolve were what information to collect from the young people in each area and how to collect it. Reflecting the multi-disciplinary nature of the Initiative, it was decided to adopt a variety of different methodological approaches as in the earlier initiative, Young People in Society (Beloff, 1986).

To assess the characteristics of the young people in each area, a representative sample survey was carried out in each of them. To uncover the way choices were made at crucial transition points, what led up to them and what followed them, subsamples in each area were interviewed using a combination of structured and unstructured methods. To expose the processes of socialisation in group settings and the shared meanings of particular life events, ethnographic studies were carried out with groups of young people, and more extensive information was collected from a few individuals.

These different methodological approaches were complementary in the sense that the statistical picture produced by the survey could be extended, reinforced or challenged through individual case study. It is at the level of explanation of particular social phenomena such as entry to particular occupations that the payoff from a combination of methodological perspectives is most clearly seen. Surveys deal with regularities and discontinuities in observations of populations in terms of the relationships between variables. The holistic nature of case study allows the causal complexity in the life of an individual (or group) to be revealed. Setting up a 'dialogue' between the two approaches (Ragin, 1987) provides a form of validation which the 16–19 Initiative was in a particularly strong position to exploit.

The ways in which these different methods were implemented are described in Appendix 1, which also provides a pen-portrait of each locality in which the research was conducted. In this chapter we describe the broad features of the research design.

National and local contrasts

As we hope to demonstrate in this book, our choice of areas in which to locate the study proved particularly advantageous. The areas not only encompassed the main economic and social contrasts prevailing in Britain, but also enabled us to study national differences. As noted earlier, two of our areas, Kirkcaldy and Swindon, were also studied in the earlier ESRC initiative, Social Change and Economic Life, which concentrated on adult employment prospects and experience. The data from that initiative enabled us to build up a much more detailed picture of labour-market characteristics in these two areas than would otherwise have been the case. In addition, the long tradition of research on the economic, cultural and political character of Sheffield and Liverpool could be drawn upon to contextualise our data collected on the young people there.

Kirkcaldy was distinctive in being an economic area, rather than a town, albeit one that on many indicators came close to the average for the whole of Scotland. Its mixture of urban and rural experience for young people broadened the picture of transition to adult life. Its location in Scotland also allowed us to study the effect of the Scottish systems of education and training, different from those of the rest of Britain, on young people's progress into the labour market and also the distinctive character of their political development, with 'nationalism' being a particularly important feature.

At the beginning of our study, parts of Kirkcaldy had levels of youth unemployment similar to those of Liverpool and Sheffield, two of the most depressed areas of England. But the latter two cities themselves could hardly be more different, as we found by the end of our data collection. Liverpool's long-term decline was merely accentuated by the economic problems stalking the whole of industrial Britain in the early 1980s. Sheffield's economic collapse was of much more temporary duration. With the high skill levels in its unemployed workforce, new industry to replace steel was established relatively easily, and, by 1988, Sheffield City Council, orginally the leading light in promoting its variant of YTS, was no longer operating it. Liverpool, meanwhile, was still offering various forms of training scheme to large proportions of its school leavers as an alternative to unemployment.

At the other end of the economic spectrum, Swindon exemplified the economic boom of the South of England. A town with strong traditions originally in one industry, the railways, it was transformed with relatively little difficulty into a 'new tech' town. In such a setting, YTS, except in highly specialised forms such as the Information Technology Education Centre (ITEC), was never seen as more than a stopgap for school leavers.

Swindon also exemplified the political trend of working-class allegiance shifting from Labour to Conservative. The defeat of Labour in urban Parliamentary seats throughout the South of England provided the basis of the Conservatives' hold on political power at Westminster. Though many such towns were electing opposition parties to run their councils – the Labour Party in the case of Swindon – they were also electing Conservative MPs. Our northern cities in England showed little evidence of such ideological shifts. In Liverpool the Conservative Party had lost virtually all hold on power, while the Liberals and, at the time, the Social Democratic Party (SDP) provided the main challenge to Labour. In Sheffield the Labour complexion of the city barely changed, but the form of Labour politics was different from that of Liverpool. Liverpool City Council for a time was run by the Militant faction of the Labour Party, and the defiance of central government over local government finance was at its strongest there. Sheffield's approach became conciliatory much sooner and its stance generally typified more the politics of the new urban left, with much concern with local enterprise, cheap transport and equal opportunities. With Kirkcaldy we had another striking political contrast. The strong Labour traditions of Kirkcaldy, rooted in mining, were challenged by the attractions of Scottish nationalism. With the collapse of the Conservative Party in large areas of Scotland, the political battle was increasingly becoming one between the Scottish Labour Party and the Scottish Nationalist Party, with the former having to adopt many elements of the nationalist ticket to stay ahead.

Collecting the data

Questionnaire survey

To chart the development of young people over the 16–19 age range, data were collected from samples of young people selected from school records in each area. Two 'cohorts' were sampled, those in the final year of compulsory schooling, aged 15–16, and those who had passed this point two years previously, aged 17–18. Samples of the order of 600 in each cohort in each area completed questionnaires in their own homes in May of successive years, 1987, 1988 and 1989 (which we refer to as waves 1, 2 and 3, respectively, of the survey). In addition, in the autumn of 1987 and the autumn of 1989, subsamples representing the main types of post-school career pattern were interviewed.

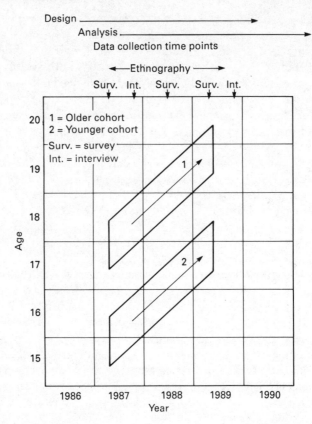

Figure 2.1 Longitudinal cohort design

Figure 2.1 shows the overall design and the sequencing of data collection. The two-year span for data collection with each cohort meant that over the whole survey the age range from 15 to 20 was covered, with an overlap between the two cohorts at age 17–18 who were separated by a two-year interval.

How successful were we in retaining the young people's interest in the project over the three years when data were collected? Response rates averaged out at 60% of the target sample of each wave for the older cohort, and close to 70% for the younger cohort, though of course over the whole two-year period the response rate based on the original sample was substantially reduced (see Table A1.1 in Appendix 1). The lower response for the older cohort is almost certainly due to the less accurate address lists for them. Many were also away at the time of the survey, some having left home altogether, and were very difficult to contact.

Response rates also varied between areas, with Kirkcaldy having the best rates at all three waves of the survey, and Liverpool having the poorest rate, especially in wave 1. In fact we lost over 200 more potential respondents in Liverpool than in any other area simply because they had gone away, a sign of the pressure on young people there to leave.

Surveys of each area enabled us to build up a statistical picture of young people which could be compared and contrasted with that of other areas. For many purposes we could also aggregrate the data across samples to produce a single sample of young people. We recognised, of course, that this would not be representative of the whole teenage population of Britain. The sample tended to be slightly more working-class at wave 1 than the national population, but became slightly more middle-class in successive waves. The proportion in the older cohort at wave 3 was also slightly less than at wave 1. In each wave the sex, cohort and social class proportions were reasonably comparable, except that in Liverpool there were disproportionately more male and older cohort dropouts and that in Swindon there were more middle-class families than anywhere else (Table A1.2 in Appendix 1).

The questionnaire employed was designed to cover young people's work, leisure, political activity and domestic life. Four-fifths of the questions were asked in all four areas and the other fifth met the special interests of each area team. At each new wave of the study, some questions were carried forward from the previous wave; some were dropped and new ones were added. Certain questions to do with self-perception and occupational history were asked in all three waves of the survey.

The questionnaire was fully piloted in wave 1 using a separate pilot sample of 200 randomly selected respondents. This enabled us to test fully all the proposed field procedures and the question design. For later waves, piloting was based on the same sample but inevitably involved much smaller numbers, especially at wave 3.

Besides providing directly much information on young people's circumstances and experience, for the purposes of analysis the questions were also used in combination to form derived variables indexing key characteristics. For example, the information from the past occupational record collected at each wave of the survey was used to construct a 'career trajectory' variable, charting five different patterns of post-16 progression through the education system and the labour market: academic (A levels); vocational (post-16 non-A-level education); school to job; school to YTS to job; and YTS or unemployment (no career) (see Appendix 1). A large number of opinion items were included in the survey, inviting respondents to express their views on particular topics such as employment and social and political issues. From the results of factor analysis these were combined in groups to index more general orientations towards each topic. Thus the 'support for training' attitude scale comprised four items, expressing opinions for or against training, such as 'Youth Training Schemes are better than the dole' and 'Youth Training Schemes are just slave labour'. Full details of the constituent items of all such scales used in the analysis reported here are given in Appendix 2. Finally, many of the questions generated information that required coding. Types of examination taken, subjects studied and occupations of self and parents were all coded into sets of broad categories. In the case of pre-16 examination passes, English and Scottish educational attainment scores were produced which were subsequently grouped into four broad bands, each containing a quarter of the sample (Appendix 2). In the case of types of occupation, a multiple classification using the Cambridge Occupational Coding Scheme was employed (Stuart *et al.*, 1980; Prandy, 1990). This generated a number of standard classifications including the Registrar-General's social class classification of occupations which is used in all the analyses reported here.

Interviewing

Besides constructing a statistical picture from the surveys, we also wanted to know what happened to young people individually in making post-16 transitions, especially in relation to the choices they were making in work, social and domestic life and politics, and the influence on these of family and friends. For this purpose we used the survey data as a framework for selecting 110 young people in each area for personal interview, first in the autumn of the first year of the study and then following up in the final year. Young people from the older cohort, all two years past the compulsory school-leaving age, were selected to represent the five career trajectory patterns described previously. Those from the younger cohort were selected at random (Appendix 1).

The approach adopted for the first interview involved a combination of structured and unstructured methods. Certain questions were standardised in all interviews, but there was plenty of scope in the latter half to extend the questioning to elicit qualitative information, if the individual team wanted to collect it. The interviewee was also asked to complete a short questionnaire adding to our data on leisure activity and work values. The approach had the advantage of yielding data which could be analysed quantitatively, thus extending the main survey analysis, while at the same time each interview constituted a case study in its own right.

The same subsample was followed up with a second interview two years later in the autumn of 1989. Because the sample was much depleted, largely qualitative methods were employed this time, except that an 'event history' grid was completed for each respondent and the wave 1 self-completion questionnaire was also used. The respondents were also asked to complete a 'spending patterns' diary for the week following the interview and post it to the local team.

Ethnographic studies

The final component of our reseach design – the ethnographic studies – allowed two research teams to step outside the survey framework and to become more fully involved in the everyday lives of young people. This was done by a less rigidly structured and more exploratory style of interviewing in Kirkcaldy and by ethnographies of particular everyday social settings in Sheffield.

The distinctive features of the ethnographic approach are 'naturalism' and 'holism' (Hammersley, 1987). The researcher uses participant observation and unstructured but informed interviewing, with an emphasis on disturbing the research setting as little as possible. The focus of investigation is the 'case' in which all the elements (actions and processes) are seen as inseparable. The extraction of variables reflecting regularities in behaviour observed across individuals in the survey gives way in ethnography to the elucidation of a single system of interconnected values, actions and processes treated as a totality. Placed alongside the survey findings the 16–19 Initiative's ethnographic studies provided an additional set of perspectives and levers on understanding youth experience.

In Sheffield five groups were selected for study: two YTS groups, one male (building operatives) and one female (institutional care); two mixed BTEC groups, one mainly female (fashion design) and the other more equally matched (hotel management and catering); and a mixed group of sixth-formers doing A levels. In Kirkcaldy, case studies were based on five individuals who were all interviewed on a number of occasions, together, in some cases, with parents.

Sheffield

The Sheffield research was novel in applying to the study of further education and training, theoretical perspectives from the sociology of education and from youth ethnography (for example, Hargreaves, 1967; Lacey, 1970; Willis, 1977; Aggleton, 1987). Such studies have given prominence to social class, gender, race and the wider social structures in shaping young people's career paths while emphasizing the capacities of young people themselves to negotiate their career paths and identities. Young people are viewed as proactive rather than merely reactive agents within socialisation processes, engaging in various forms of accommodation and resistance.

A distinctive feature of the research strategy was the comparative study of groups of young people on different career trajectories, following principles of theoretical sampling (Glaser and Strauss, 1967). In planning these studies the ethnographers concerned identified a number of factors which were expected to differentiate critically between the experience of different groups of young people, chiefly: the status of their course; the field of employment for which they were training; gender; and social class. Five groups were selected on three of the career trajectories introduced earlier. The groups were located in four further education colleges and a school sixth form. All institutions were, however, in the process of being reorganised into tertiary colleges.

Fieldwork with each group spanned approximately two years, beginning with intensive participant observation over two terms and follow-up visits for a further year. The main research sites were colleges, workplaces and schools, where the ethnographers spent time with young people in a wide variety of situations: in lessons; in off-the-job training sessions; on work placements; during coffee breaks and lunch hours; in pubs during and after college; and on various excursions around the city.

Kirkcaldy

In Kirkcaldy an expanded interview schedule was used in both rounds of interviewing to explore aspects of young people's everyday lives in much greater detail. The interview schedules were semi-structured, organised by topic and with the possibility of some reshuffling in the interview situation to keep a natural flow of conversation. Although the degree of structure did impose a framework on the data collected, the schedules were carefully piloted to ensure that they did relate to young people's own concerns within our selected areas of interest.

Case studies were made of five individuals who were interviewed on between three and six occasions and whose parents were also interviewed whenever possible. The original aim was to move out from individuals to key members of their social network, interviewing them in turn, thus building up a comprehensive albeit egocentric picture of an individual's social world. However, we found that young people were reticent about volunteering their partners and friends for interview, and practical considerations also worked against this expansion of our interview sample. We persisted with persuading young people to allow us to approach their partners, but permission was not granted in every case.

In both rounds of in-depth interviews and in the case-study interviews, the interviewers had a carefully piloted interview guide but were encouraged to adapt the interview to the respondent. Interviewers were equipped to do this by being well briefed on individual biographies before the interview as revealed through respondents' completed questionnaires, and, at the time of the second interview, by having read the transcript of the first interview.

Analysis

The design adopted for the project may be seen as multi-level and multi-perspective in form. It offered a particularly rich variety of analytic possibilities.

The area-based surveys enabled us to assess experience quantitatively and the different economic and cultural conditions to which it related at an aggregate and sub-group level. The longitudinal data collected, through the two follow-ups, enabled us to chart the changes in the lives of individuals and groups over the ages 15–20. All the figures and tables we present charting groups of respondents' movements across the three waves of the survey are based on those who completed questionnaires in all three waves of the survey.

For large samples of the kind we used, quite small differences between percentages and between mean values and correlation coefficients are statistically significant, which cautioned against making too much of this feature of the data. Nevertheless, we needed to be sure that the statistics we used to draw conclusions could not have 'arisen by chance'. As a rough yardstick for subsamples of 200 or more, a difference in percentages of at least 10 and a difference in means of at least 1.0 is needed to achieve statistical significance at the 0.05 level, and for a sample of 200, a correlation must be at least 0.14 (Table A1.3 in Appendix 1).

Data from surveys are, of course, mainly used quantitatively. To elucidate the processes that lay behind the figures they yield, we needed to go to the experience of individuals and groups as revealed in the interviews and the ethnographic studies. Here the analytic techniques focused more on looking for links between patterns of events in a young person's life and past circumstances, with a view to unravelling the contexts and antecedents of personal action. It was then possible to go on to seek commonalities in experience among a number of individuals pointing to the social and cultural values that could be identified with particular peer groups. In the ethnographic work it was possible to observe and interpret group influence and experience as it actually occurred. What is it like to be on a YTS scheme, a BTEC course, or doing A Levels; what does it mean for the individual in sociocultural, economic and political terms? How do you and your friends express your attitudes towards it? What do you gain from it? Do you lose being on it? Blending such information with the statistical data enabled us to uncover an exceptionally detailed tapestry of post-16 experience. The socialisation processes underlying the construction of careers and identities are revealed both in the broad patterns and the rich textures of individual and group life.

Chapter 3   CAREER PATTERNS

Introduction

Throughout the 1980s, as we saw in Chapter 1, young people were at the receiving end of significant policy changes reflecting changes in the national and local economy. After the slump at the beginning of the decade, concentrated in the traditional manufacturing areas of the country, by the end of the 1980s there were signs of an economic up turn, with unemployment falling (Central Statistical Office, 1988). Demographic change was also favouring 16-year-old school leavers. The falling birthrate in the late 1960s produced a diminishing pool of potential job entrants, and employers were once again competing strenuously for those who were available. When we studied them, contrasts in the prospects for young people were somewhat starker. Some at least were poised to enter a decade of opportunity; others were facing exceptionally difficult problems in gaining employment. Most school leavers faced chosing between a variety of training schemes rather than the full-time jobs they had traditionally entered. Their exit routes from education have been extensively charted in the national Youth Cohort Studies (see, for example, Jones *et al.*, 1987; Courtenay, 1988; Gray *et al.*, 1989; Jesson and Gray, 1990). Who you were and where you lived were crucial in determining where you went, as will become clear in this chapter.

In this chapter we address three issues. First, we examine the pattern of early careers after the completion of compulsory schooling. Second, we examine the features of young people's backgrounds and other characteristics, including attitudes, which accompanied different careers. We conclude by considering some lessons for policy that can be learned from the findings and set the likely policy agenda for the 1990s.

Routes and destinations

The fifth year of secondary school in England and the fourth year in Scotland, when pupils are aged 15–16, marks the end of the statutory requirement to attend school. What happens to young people at the end of it? In each wave of the survey, our respondents completed a diary describing what they had been doing in three-month intervals from the time they were in the final compulsory school year. In the first wave for the older cohort this covered a two-year interval; the younger cohort was still at school. By the third and final wave, we had information extending over four years up to the age of 19–20 for the older cohort and for two years up to the age of 17–18 for the younger cohort. For each three-month interval respondents recorded whether they were in full-time education (in a school or college), employed full-time or part-time, on a youth training scheme, unemployed or out of the labour market (for example, with domestic responsibilities). Figures 3.1–3.4 show changes in these statuses over time for the older cohort, in each of the four areas.

Staying on in education

Figure 3.1 shows the proportions of the older cohort staying on in education after the final compulsory year over the ages 16–20. The pattern is one of plateaux and troughs as young people leave the system, mainly in the summer months, and there are clear area differences. In the first post-16 year continued participation in education ranged from over 60% in Kirkcaldy to just over 40% in Sheffield. By the third year, marking the start of higher education, the difference between the Scottish and English areas had largely disappeared, but a gap re-emerged again as more young people in Scotland went on to higher education. The lowest participation level at this point was in Swindon, where our interviews revealed that employers were offering strong incentives for academically qualified young people to enter employment. Half the A-level students in Swindon entered a job at 18, compared with less than a fifth in Liverpool (Evans, 1990). But many of these returned a year later having had a 'year off' from education or because the employment alternative had turned out to be not as appealing has they had originally thought.

Changing economic circumstances over the period 1985–7 also appeared to be affecting participation. Although in Kirkcaldy the proportions of the older and younger cohort staying on were much the same, in England, in line with national trends, there were signs that a higher proportion of the younger cohort was opting to stay on, especially in Sheffield and Liverpool.

More girls stayed on than boys for one year but not in all years, suggesting that labour-market effects were influencing girls' decisions to stay on, with the gap between the sexes smallest in Swindon and largest in Liverpool. Girls often continue with education to undertake the pre-vocational clerical and business studies courses that employers favour, but by the end of the

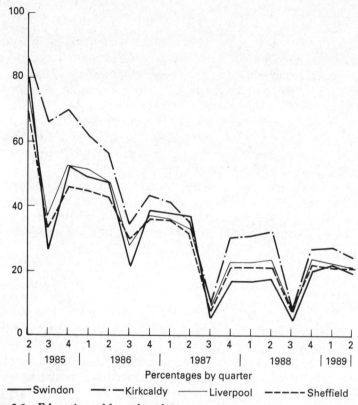

Figure 3.1   Education, older cohort by area

period studied the boys had overtaken them in all areas as entry to higher education took over.

Educational attainment was assessed from scores based on public examination results, GCE and CSE, Scottish Highers and O grades at the time, and the scores were then grouped into four equal ranges (quartiles). Social class was assessed from father's occupation using the Registrar-General's sixfold classification, ranging from professional to unskilled occupations (Appendix 2).

Finally, a feature of post-16 education, especially in Scotland, was the increasing numbers staying on to pursue a non-academic curriculum (that is, not following the Highers route), typically for a year or less. As would be expected, the one-year stayers had better 16-plus qualifications than the leavers. They also tended to come more often from middle-class homes, but there appeared to be no clear effect of school or local labour market on their decisions. As might be expected, for both sexes and cohorts in all areas, participation rates were much higher among those in the top bands of educational achievement than in the lower bands and among those coming from non-manual family backgrounds.

Getting a job

The preferred alternative to staying in education for most young people is getting a job. How successful our respondents were is shown in Figure 3.2. The numbers getting jobs steadily increased across the four years, rising to around 60% by age 20, but throughout there were large area differences. By the end of the first post-16 year just over a quarter of the Swindon sample were in jobs, compared with less than a tenth in other areas. This gap continued at much the same level right through to age 20, at which point another gap opened up. The poorer long-term job prospects of young people in Liverpool were shown by a 10% lower employment rate there than in Sheffield and Kirkcaldy. Comparing extremes, by the end of the teens 20% fewer young people in Liverpool were in employment than in Swindon.

Most young people who got a job soon after leaving school, appeared to be successful in hanging on to some form of employment afterwards. Few returned to education, at least during their teens. Once the positive attractions of income and job prospects had been experienced, studying other than part-time held no appeal. On the other hand, as our interviews revealed, dissatisfaction with first jobs was commonplace, and there was much movement from one job to another, especially in Swindon where employment opportunities were plentiful.

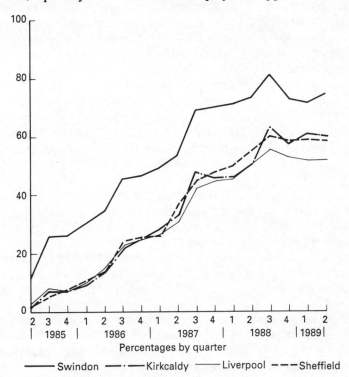

Figure 3.2 Employment, older cohort by area

One boy who had left school at 16 and was a trainee accountant had remained with the firm for four years, and at the time of interview he was a senior with the practice. But two years ago he had decided he wanted to change from a career in accountancy to journalism. So in the evenings he had studied for an A level in English, and in a year's time he planned to apply to polytechnics to do a degree in Politics or English. He believed he would get more out of higher education tham someone going straight in at 18.

As girls en route to secretarial and clerical occupations often stayed on in education for a year, male early employment rates tended to be higher initially. But except in Kirkcaldy, where the girls stayed ahead, the rates had equalised everywhere else by the age of 19. As might be expected, getting a job at 16 was associated with a working-class rather than a middle-class family background. In relation to educational attainment, young people in the middle bands were the ones most likely to have got jobs. Those in the top band were most likely to be staying on at school and those in the bottom band tended to be unemployed or on a training scheme.

Youth training

Those at 16 who were unsuccessful in getting jobs or wanted jobs that were not on offer to 16-year-olds, typically entered the government YTS. As Figure 3.3 shows, in all three English areas the proportions in training peaked at the end of the first school-leaving year. In Kirkcaldy, because people were leaving school later, maximum take-up was delayed by about a year. Again there were striking area differences, with substantially lower levels of take-up in Swindon, never higher than 17%, than in Liverpool and Sheffield, where over a third were involved. By the end of the second year youth training in Swindon had virtually disappeared. Up to a fifth of our respondents were still involved in Liverpool and Kirkcaldy and nearly a sixth in Sheffield. From age 18 'training' was a residual category with less than 5% involved in all areas, and what was left was largely confined to the Community Programme and (adult) Employment Training (ET). In 1988 YTS was changed from a one-year to a two-year training programme and became, in principle, exclusively employer-based. This extended the period of involvement for the younger cohort, but, significantly, the proportions taking part in YTS in both the older and younger cohort across the period of the survey were much the same.

Although youth trainees were to be found in all the four bands of educational attainment, the great majority came from the bottom two. Only a twentieth of the top band had entered YTS, compared with a quarter of the band below and two-fifths from the bottom two bands. In addition, YTS participants were more likely to be drawn from manual social class backgrounds. In Sheffield and Kirkcaldy, males and females took up YTS in equal numbers but in Swindon and Liverpool more males were participating. This balance between the sexes contrasts with the old craft apprenticeships, which YTS was intended to replace, and which were almost exclusively a male preserve. But

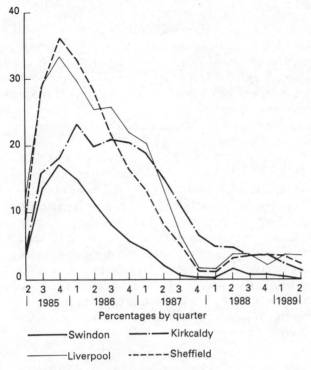

Figure 3.3 Youth training, older cohort by area

within YTS itself, the sexes separated on traditional lines: girls were being trained predominantly for administrative, secretarial and clerical occupations, and boys, covering a wider range of occupations overall, were most frequently heading for skilled and semi-skilled manual occupations.

Although YTS entrance tended to be at the lower end of the educational attainment range, within YTS itself attainment affected the kind of scheme the young person was on. The better the school-level qualifications the greater the chance of entering the preferred employer-led training, with improved prospects of being taken on as an employee at the end of the scheme. Such employer-led schemes were almost indistinguishable from apprenticeship and full-time employment in Swindon; in Liverpool, because of the economic difficulties, they were much more difficult to find. Liverpool employers could be much more selective as to whom they took on for full-time employment and often used YTS as a government-subsidised means of grooming and selecting potential employees. Those left behind, who often came from minority ethnic backgrounds or were socially disadvantaged in various ways, were most frequently to be found in the less popular mode B (community-based) schemes. The one exception was the Information Technology Education Centres (ITECs) which were typically seen as providing worthwhile training and in consequence were difficult to get into even in Swindon.

Unemployment

The continuity between YTS and unemployment can be seen in the jagged pattern of Figure 3.4. The peaks correspond to the troughs in the educational participation rates. After peaking in the middle of the first post-16 year, unemployment rates dropped to half their peak level as jobs or, more typically, training schemes, were entered. Rates then rose throughout the second year and until the middle of the third year, as drop-out or completion of YTS occurred and more young people left the education system, peaking at 25% in Sheffield and Liverpool. From then on the rates roughly halved, so that by the end of the teens in every area except Liverpool less than a tenth were unemployed. Liverpool and Sheffield's problems were manifest across the whole period, with Liverpool having the highest rates over the first two years and Sheffield over the second two years. The striking contrast again was Swindon, where unemployment levels only once exceeded 10% and by the second quarter of 1989 were close to zero. The pattern in Kirkcaldy was slightly different, reflecting the more extended schooling in Scotland, with a larger number of exit points in the summer months of each year. Thus school leavers recorded themselves as unemployed when in many cases they were simply on holiday preparing to seek jobs instead of returning to education in the autumn term. But overall their unemployment rates were lower than in Sheffield and Liverpool.

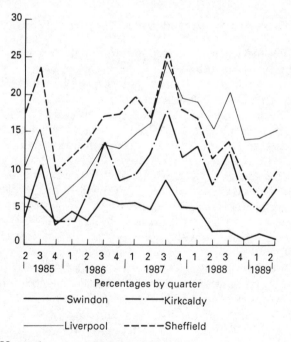

Figure 3.4   Unemployment, older cohort by area

Young people's perceptions of the difficulties in getting a job reflected a realistic appraisal of local opportunities. Two-thirds of both cohorts in Liverpool reported that it was difficult to get jobs locally, compared with half in Sheffield and Kirkcaldy and less than a tenth in Swindon. However, when asked what they expected to be doing in a year's time the majority of school leavers, even in Liverpool, expected to be in a job. Liverpool young people, however, were also more likely than those in other areas to expect to move out of the area at some time to get a job. This intention was expressed by 70% of the older cohort in Liverpool, compared with 60% in Kirkcaldy and about half in Sheffield and Swindon. These results point to a kind of local labour-market pessimism in Liverpool which was not found to the same extent in other areas. Sheffield had also suffered high levels of unemployment, but the strong commitment by the authorities there to 'training', followed by a fairly rapid recovery of the local economy, was perhaps boosting confidence in a way not possible in Liverpool.

Early careers

The data we have considered so far provide snapshots of post-16 occupational statuses for the whole population in each area at particular ages and at particular points in time. To find out what happens in the lives of individuals, we need to trace their progression from one occupational status to another from age 16 to age 19.

By comparing the statuses of the same individuals at one point in time with their positions two years later it was easy to see some distinctive patterns. For example, the great majority of those who had started jobs at 16 were still in a job, though not necessarily the same one, a year later. Because of the value placed by employers on real work experience, once a 'toe-hold' is obtained in the labour market it is relatively easy to hang on to it. For those who continued with education after age 16 there was more of a split, with a substantial minority leaving usually to enter a job. For those in YTS schemes or unemployed there was a further different pattern. The majority of YTS participants went into jobs, though far fewer in Sheffield and Liverpool than in Swindon. Among the unemployed, although the same proportion got jobs as YTS participants in Swindon, in Sheffield, Liverpool and Kirkcaldy they were half as successful. The destination of the majority (59%) of unemployed in Sheffield and Liverpool was further unemployment; in the case of Kirkcaldy half were still unemployed and a quarter went on to YTS.

From the whole picture of individual transition patterns from age 16 to age 18 it was possible to identify initially five main career routes (trajectories).

Type A trajectories
1. An academic (A-level) route through full-time education for at least two post compulsory years (academic) (19% older, 25% younger).

2. Full-time education of a vocational and general nature, but not leading to A-levels (vocational) (20% older, 22% younger).
3. The traditional transition from full-time education to full-time employment (job) (15% older, 13% younger).
4. The 'two-step' transition to employment including a period of more than six months on YTS (YTS–job) (12% older, 11% younger).
5. Experience of YTS and unemployment, but no full-time job for six months or more (no career) (34% older, 29% younger).

In 1988 the economy was improving in all areas. YTS had been extended to a two-year scheme and social security benefits were withdrawn from young people. Although the younger cohort's experience could be mapped into the careers trajectory classification, the new situation prompted a revision. A further refinement reflecting the changes and applying particularly to the younger cohort is shown below:

Type B trajectories
1. An academic route through full-time education for a least two post-compulsory school years (academic) (30% older, 37% younger).
2. Just one year in post-compulsory education after age 16 (other education) (9% older, 12% younger).
3. Through YTS into the labour market (YTS–job) (26% older, 25% younger).
4. Post-compulsory education plus YTS, though not always in that order (job) (5% older, 5% younger).
5. Traditional transition involving neither post-compulsory education nor YTS (traditional) (29% older, 21% younger).

Although by 1988 the proportions remaining in education were the same in both cohorts, those who had left were then predominantly on the traditional (direct entry to jobs) routes or the 'two-step' route via YTS. 'Unemployment' has largely been eliminated as the legislation intended it should be. We use both classifications in the analyses reported in this and later chapters, but principally the former one.

How do the five post-16 career patterns differ by area, gender, age, social class and educational attainment? Table 3.1 shows the percentages of the young people defined by each of these characteristics on each of the trajectories in the first classification above. Area comparisons were consistent with those we considered earlier, with the school-to-job trajectory the most common in Swindon and the YTS/unemployment (no career) trajectory the most common in all the other areas. Gender comparisons revealed the slightly greater take-up of education after age 16 by girls and the smaller number proceeding directly into jobs. More boys were proceeding through YTS or making the traditional transition directly into employment. The younger cohort, too, were taking to post-16 education in greater numbers, which at a time of revival of the demand for youth labour, might suggest that the government's message about the value of vocational education and training was getting through. At the same time, few of our 16–18-year-olds were eligible for educational maintenance grants, in contrast with the YTS allowances and social security benefits for the unemployed that they did have access to. The most plausible explanation is that the nature of local employment was changing and in areas of high unemployment local employers were setting higher standards for job entrance, so that there were extra incentives for staying on. Nevertheless, the difference in education take-up between the older and the younger cohort was still relatively small (8 per cent); and over half the younger cohort were off school registers at the age of 16.

As we might expect, the really big differences between career trajectories occurred for family social class, and even more so for educational attainment. Young people from professional family backgrounds were concentrated in the academic trajectory and those from manual backgrounds, especially partly skilled and unskilled, in the YTS/unemployed trajectory. In between were those exhibiting social mobility upwards or downwards. Over a sixth of those from manual family backgrounds were on the academic route and about a third overall were staying on after age 16. At the other end of the scale in the YTS/unemployed category there were surprisingly high numbers of young people from non-manual family backgrounds; many of these had left the education system but had failed to settle into any permanent kind of work. Parental support might well have been buttressing them against harsh labour-market conditions. For educational attainment the relationships were even more clear-cut. Four-fifths of those in the top attainment bands were on the academic and vocational education routes; over half were pursuing A levels. At the other end of the scale, nearly two-thirds of those in the bottom attainment band had failed to start a career, a figure that rose to three-quarters in Liverpool and Sheffield. Only one-tenth of this group stayed on in education on either the academic or vocational route.

It is for this last group that we see the consequences of lack of employment opportunity for the most disadvantaged. The community-based YTS schemes – involving 40% of Liverpool trainees, compared with 26% of Swindon trainees – had not compensated for their poor school performance by getting the trainees work, but seemed to have performed more of a 'holding' or 'warehousing' function to be followed by unemployment later on. Only in Swindon, where a wide range of peripheral manual work was to be found in a buoyant local economy, were jobs for this group relatively easy to obtain.

Table 3.2 shows the routes taken after age 18 by those in the older cohort, in each trajectory under both the old and new classifications. As we might expect, between 18 and 20 both sets of post-16 career trajectories reverted largely to the traditional post-18 pattern. The two major trajectories remaining were the academic one, in which half the original group were located, with the rest mainly in jobs. It was also interesting to see that more of those who

Table 3.1 Career Routes at age 16–18, by area, gender, cohort, educational qualifications at 16, and social class

	Career Route					
	Academic Education %	Vocational Education %	School to job %	YTS to job %	YTS/unemployed %	n
Area						
Swindon	21	21	29	11	18	901
Sheffield	20	17	9	16	38	947
Liverpool	20	22	11	10	37	833
Kirkcaldy	24	21	8	11	36	1014
Gender						
Male	20	20	17	13	31	1740
Female	23	21	11	11	34	1955
Cohort						
Older	19	20	15	12	34	2177
Younger	25	22	13	11	29	1518
Educational attainment						
Top quartile	56	25	8	3	8	1052
2nd quartile	17	30	16	15	23	901
3rd quartile	4	18	18	19	41	846
Bottom quartile	2	8	16	12	62	882
Social class						
Professional	50	18	9	9	14	188
Intermediate	37	26	11	9	17	618
Skilled non-manual	30	22	13	10	25	358
Skilled manual	16	21	17	13	32	1123
Partly skilled	12	17	18	14	39	521
Unskilled	16	11	14	15	43	196

joined YTS had subsequently become unemployed than those who had gone directly into employment from school. The major route, of course, for all school leavers was the employment one, with up to four-fifths taking this route and the bulk of the rest becoming unemployed. Even among the 16–18 academic route nearly a third went into employment.

The best predictors of the routes taken after age 18 were educational achievement at 16, and area of residence. Previous gender differences, such as the greater proportion of females in education and the smaller proportion in employment, tended to disappear after age 18. Area differences were sustained, with a greater proportion taking the educational route in Kirkcaldy. Swindon had substantially more on the continuous employment route, and a lower proportion on the unemployment path.

Our identification of these post-16 career patterns did not mean that all the young people were very similar in each of them. The interviews revealed much more about the way the trajectory had been entered and the complicated further considerations, pressures and choices that operated within it. Typically, parents had been critically important in the decision to stay on at school. In the academic route three-quarters said their parents had encouraged them to stay on, a figure which dropped below 30% for all three school-leaver trajectories. School leavers generally said that their parents had left the decision up to them, but a fifth said their parents had encouraged them to leave. Trouble at school was acknowledged by 60% of those respondents who had gone straight into jobs or had failed to established a career, compared with only 40% of those staying on or those who had got a job via YTS.

But many of those who had left had clearly thought better of it afterwards. Three-quarters of those in the academic group said they were very satisfied with the decision they had taken, compared with under 60% of those who had got jobs direct from school or via YTS and only 35% of those who had failed to establish themselves in the labour market.

Individual life stories illuminated the picture even further. Thus at one end of the spectrum on the academic route were young people for whom anything other than staying on to take A levels was unthinkable, with or without a particular occupation in mind at the end of it. At the other end, in the YTS and unemployment groups, were young people for whom secondary education had been an increasingly irrelevant and unwanted experience. Reinforced by poor exams results (60% had not taken any exams at all) and a gloomy view of their prospects from teachers, leaving at the earliest possible age to get a job and earn money was the only serious option. In between were young people and their parents realising past expectations and weighing up the pros and cons of the different choices open to them. The realities of changing labour-market opportunities were compelling more to stay on than in the past. More of the younger cohort were having to take post-16 education and training seriously as a preliminary to getting a job. But the overwhelming desire of potential school leavers to get jobs rather than training schemes was ever

Table 3.2 Post-18 careers by career trajectories 16–18 (%)

| | 16–18 trajectories (Type B) | | | | | |
18–20 trajectories	Academic	Other education	YTS–job	YTS/ed	Traditional	Total
Higher education	51	2	2	2	1	21
Other education	15	6	3	2	4	8
Employment	29	85	77	84	80	60
Unemployment	5	8	20	12	16	11

| | 16–18 trajectories (Type A) | | | | | |
18–20 trajectories	Academic	Vocational	Job	YTS–job	YTS/unemployment	Total
Higher education	56	11	0	0	2	18
Other education	8	5	0	0	3	7
Employment	32	69	88	88	59	60
Unemployment	4	15	12	10	36	15

present. For most of them the premier academic route was so removed from their experience as to be relatively meaningless. If they decided to stay on, it was to give themselves that 'little bit extra' to offer potential employers in what was still in some places a pretty desperate competition for jobs.

Another variation which we noted earlier was the group of A-level candidates whose studies were primarily functional and job-related rather than motivated by the intrinsic satisfaction of extended education with the promise of a professional career. Subjected to the blandishments of employers in the expanding labour market of Swindon, many decided to opt at 18 for money and immediate job prospects instead. The significant feature of their position, however, was the further choices that were open to them. The high-flyer A-level label had good currency with employers, regardless of the subjects taken. This gave those who had acquired it opportunities to change jobs and sample the labour market. They could also choose to return to education later to do a degree at a university or polytechnic, and many did. Disillusioned by the limitation of the jobs they had been offered or merely satisfied that they had had a year off to experience employment, many realised that their best prospects still lay with higher education. By the third wave of the study (1989) the gap between the proportions of the older cohort in higher education in Liverpool and Swindon was much reduced. We encountered a number of young people who had entered jobs with banks and building societies who planned such a return. In some cases a degree course was part of the package that employers had offered them.

Those who had entered training schemes and had then got jobs or had drifted in and out of schemes and the employment queue demonstrated the inseparability of training as a saleable asset from the state of the local labour market. Two-fifth of trainees were retained by employers in all areas. But for those who were not retained, job prospects were heavily dependent on where the training had been done. In Liverpool, Sheffield and Kirkcaldy nearly half the trainees became unemployed after leaving their schemes; in Swindon only one-tenth.

It was clear that the best prospects of employment came with schemes run by local employers. But colleges and ITECs came off best in equipping young people with vocational qualifications. The Training Workshops and Community Project Schemes came off worst on all counts. They had poorer-quality intakes, who were least likely to gain further qualifications, and who were less successful in subsequently getting jobs. They were concentrated in the high-unemployment areas. The problem with them was that the young people on them were often being trained in skills that were not in great demand.

One young woman we interviewed in 1987 was typical of many. She had just finished a YTS working with animals, mainly doing kennel work. She had enjoyed her time on the scheme, but simply could not find work afterwards, being unemployed for two months, before doing domestic work for four months. At the follow-up interview she was working in a home for the elderly, but this was temporary and would soon end. Her present feelings were of great insecurity about the future; she would be happy to find a permanent job and a 'nice boyfriend'.

It is clear that YTS was benefiting those young people who succeeded in getting on schemes where the retention rate was high. Furthermore, their chances of being kept on as employees were greatly enhanced if they succeeded in gaining further qualifications. But YTS had become a highly stratified provision (see, for example, Coles, 1988), and in seeking to understand how it affected young people's careers we needed to see how schemes varied in terms of quality of training, characteristics of trainees, recruitment practices, and influence on future careers.

In the best kind of schemes, described by Raffe (1987) as 'sponsorship', something akin to a traditional apprenticeship was on offer, but with the added advantage for girls that they were not excluded. Such schemes were known about through local grapevines and the employers who were responsible for them could afford to be selective in recruiting. Once on such a scheme the young person was certain to continue in full-time employment. We found less evidence for what Raffe has called 'credentialling', where a scheme produces qualifications, but the trainees then have to compete again for work with the firm at the end of it. More common was the 'contest' scheme where far more trainees were taken on than the employer needed and then, on the basis of their performance in the job, some would be retained. Such schemes extended the 'warehousing' function of YTS, that is, keeping people off the dole queue (which they were free to join in 1987 and 1988). As such writers as Lee *et al.* (1990) and Jarvis and Prais (1988) have shown, many schemes in this sector imparted only very low-level skills and, if employer-led, were often so job-specific that they had little currency in the external labour market. Community-based schemes, which were common for our older cohort, were often entered by young people with poor educational attainment often from minority ethnic backgrounds. They gave little access to firms' internal labour markets and in areas of high unemployment rarely led to jobs. Trainees were basically in a waiting room having to join an extended job queue. They could lose their place in the queue through poor attendance, work records or references, but it was more difficult for them to enhance their past prospects through extra effort on the scheme.

At the beginning of our surveys, unemployment was a serious option for young people and they could claim social security benefit. It was typically a fairly brief episode prior to returning to education, entering YTS or obtaining a job. Sometimes it was experienced as part of a chequered early career, with unemployment spells interpersed with YTS and unskilled jobs. A small heavily disadvantaged minority experienced more prolonged unemployment. Such cases were encountered particularly in the Liverpool and Sheffield samples. This is how one boy in Sheffield saw them:

I have just got a job playing football, but most of my mates will leave school the same time as me and will go straight onto the dole because of the lack of jobs. They see nothing left in Sheffield and spend most of their time sleeping, drinking and fighting. Surely there must be more to life for my mates. In the day they wander about town shoplifting because they can't afford to buy things. At night they fight with rival gangs to pass the time. I think I have been lucky to escape this.

Levels of satisfaction with their situation were substantially lower among such unemployed young people than in any other group, and those we encountered in it, seemed to have got there more through a vicious downward spiral than through personal choice. Typical was a young man who was unemployed in 1988 having left school at the earliest opportunity three years earlier. His mother had originally pushed him towards YTS and arranged the initial interview for a place on an electrical engineering scheme. He had started this, but found the training very basic and too easy, leaving after seven weeks. Since then he had been more or less permanently unemployed, though at the time of interview he had embarked part-time on a City and Guilds plumbing course, hoping eventually to become self-employed.

The difficulty many of these young people face is that prospective employers are offered an ever-lower level of attributes of interest to them. In the British labour market, these attributes include school-based qualifications and work experience; a young person with neither is seen as too much of a risk to be taken on.

In many other countries, and especially in North America, unemployment is typically replaced by part-time work and sometimes part-time study over an extended period (Ashton and Lowe, 1990). Though common among many adult females in Britain, such part-time work is very rare for young people. In 1984, 90% of part-time workers were over 21 (Dale, 1989), and we found very few in our sample. Though part-time jobs in shops or delivering newspapers during the school years are common – 50% of our younger cohort had had a part-time job at some time in the past – there is little scope for this kind of work after full-time school is over except alongside education as done by students. Evidence from employers' surveys suggests that, rather than taking on 16–17-year-olds for part-time jobs, companies had a preference for students or married women (Roberts *et al.*, 1987). In any event, as Dale (1989) points out, for the small number who do get part-time jobs after leaving school the indications are that it actually depresses their future employment prospects. Usually it was treated as a complement to unemployment rather than to full-time work and counted against young people in trying to establish a career later on.

Attitudes and values

It will be clear from what has been said so far that career routes have origins much deeper in the structures of society than in the employment opportunities on offer in a particular locality or in the credentials young people acquire or fail to acquire from the education system. They also express quite different sets of values. What it is to become an adult and what kind of adult one wants to become is the manifestation of a socialisation process beginning at birth and finding a particular form at the time of puberty, when the shaping of adult identity gathers pace. From then on the pressures from family, on the one hand, and the peer group, on the other, reinforce each other in shaping the path to adulthood. We examine the change in these dynamics across the late teens in a later chapter. Here we focus on the values that accompanied particular career decisions.

The degree to which a person wants to be in paid employment reflects commitment to the 'Protestant work ethic' (Weber, 1904; Furnham, 1984), seen in Western society as an important part of adult identity. 'Employment commitment' has proved useful in earlier studies of the psychological effects of unemployment (Jackson *et al.*, 1983); adverse effects are most evident when commitment to work is strong. It also helps explain how young people become 'discouraged workers' (Raffe and Willms, 1989), opting for education rather than the labour market when jobs are scarce. Concern has been expressed in recent years about the erosion of the work ethic because young people have become increasingly attached, so it is said, to dependency. There was little sign of this in our sample, but an indication perhaps of a more balanced view about employment and its alternatives than might have been found twenty years ago. For example, in 1987 only a quarter of our respondents disagreed that 'having almost any job is better than being unemployed'. Majorities also agreed that you do not have to have a job to be a full member of society and that you can get satisfaction out of life without a job. The sample divided equally on the issue of whether people should hang on to jobs when they have them even when they do not like them.

What is the significance of youth training in early careers? For young people its main if not only value lies in the progression to a proper job (Banks and Davies, 1991). The difficulties many young people had in getting jobs after YTS had created a kind of 'folk lore' about its 'slave labour' qualities. Young people had a short-term instrumental orientation to training, typically seeing it as a poor substitute for work. They often encountered a degree of exploitation by employers: insufficient pay and no guarantee of employment at the end of the training. Among our respondents opinions were evenly divided. Just under half agreed that 'youth training schemes are just slave labour' and just over half thought that it is better to get some kind of training than to go straight into a paid job. Despite all the Thatcher government efforts to establish a universal 'training culture' on Continental lines, there were few signs from these replies that most school leavers had taken it on.

Much of the government initiative in the training field and in school curriculum reform has concentrated on heightening interest in new technology and encouraging training in it (Breakwell *et al.*, 1988; Grant, 1987). Here more success was evident, with technological training and the need to learn about computers being generally favoured. A majority also said they would like a job involving new technology (though a fifth would not). We may conclude that awareness of new forms of business and the means of production had permeated quite widely, but it had not yet had the affect of shifting basic positions about work and the ways of entering it. Pay and prospects of the kind associated with a good 'youth job' still appealed much more to a large proportion than vocational preparation and youth training.

A final aspect of work values concerns conceptions about the 'economic locus of control' (Banks, 1988). Using a set of questions about the causes of success in getting a job, of career success and of poverty, we were able to distinguish those young people with internal attributions from those with external ones. The majority rejected the view that getting on in work depended on other people or was just a matter of chance, and believed that those people who did succeed generally deserved it. There was more ambivalence about the causes of poverty. Although few thought that people who were poor had themselves to blame, the majority also rejected the idea that bad luck causes people to be poor and that getting a job is just a matter of chance. They were also equally divided over whether 'the system' could be blamed for people's poverty.

By combining the items relating to these topics, four scales representing more deeply felt orientations were constructed: 'employment commitment', 'support for training', 'support for new technology' and 'belief in an internal economic locus of control' (Appendix 2). It was notable that employment commitment was stronger in the older than in the younger cohort and higher in Kirkcaldy than in any of the English areas (Banks, 1988).

Figure 3.5 plots the average scores of the older cohort on each of our five original career trajectories. It is notable that those closest to the labour market expressed the strongest commitment to employment, with those in jobs having the highest scores. The least committed young people were those in the academic group and to a lesser extent the vocational group. The interesting point about these differences is that they began to emerge while the respondents were still at school. We asked those in the last year at school what they intended to do after 16; those who planned to remain in education a year later had lower employment commitment, a difference which increased over two years. Thus we observed a form of anticipatory socialisation taking place. Employment attitudes prior to age 16 were a significant predictor of early career area differences and also became more marked across time; this was not surprising in view of the huge variations in the returns on employment from one area to the next. By the end of the survey in 1989, the average employed 19–20-year-old male in Swindon was earning £105.00 per week, compared to an equivalent figure of £66.50 in Sheffield, £56.90 in Kirkcaldy and £53.40 in Liverpool.

In relation to support for training, the younger cohort had a more positive attitude on average than the older group, suggesting that YTS was becoming

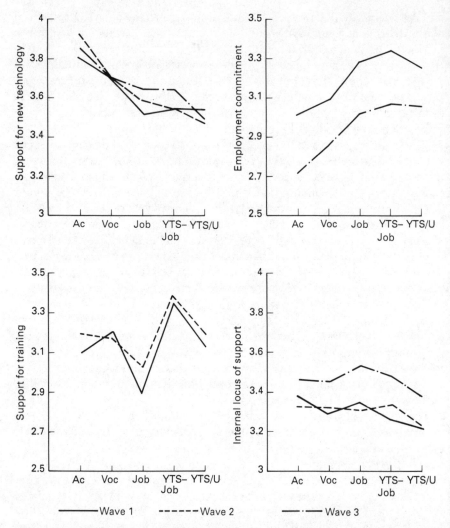

Figure 3.5 Work attitudes, mean scores by career trajectory by wave

more widely accepted. Overall attitudes to training were at much the same level in all career trajectory groups except in the group that had succeeded in getting a job after YTS, where attitudes were very much more positive. It was particularly notable that the group who had experienced mainly unemployment and training were little more supportive of it than any of the others. This picture merely reinforces the point that the value of training for young people lies in its progression to a proper job (Banks and Davies, 1991). If no job materialises then inevitably the evaluation of training will be negative. Motivation to train currently runs on motivation to work, whereas education can be seen as being an end in itself. As Raffe and Smith (1987) put it, 'education for education's sake is a reasonable aim, but YTS is presented to young people as a training scheme and training for training's sake is a contradiction in terms'.

Support for new technology showed another interesting pattern. The association of staying on in education and an increasing interest in and motivation to work with new technology was apparent, with the highest scores among those who had stayed on. Those least interested in new technology were in the school-to-job group and the no-career group. The significance given to new technology in effective YTS schemes was shown by the substantially more positive attitude to it among those who had got a job via YTS. There were no cohort differences for this scale.

Finally the scores for belief in an interval economic locus of control confirmed earlier findings of the association between 'internality' and success. Those who were the least fatalistic and believed that people could exercise control over their lives, were to be found in the group staying on in education and, interestingly, those who had got a job directly after leaving school. More fatalistic attitudes were evident in the two YTS groups, especially the YTS/unemployment group where no permanent work had followed the training.

These relationships remained reasonably constant over three waves of the survey, though generally the difference between the career trajectory groups grew smaller as the respondents grew older. As we shall see in Chapter 7, their association with the range of other social and political attitude dimensions points to their origins in a deeper set of values. Poor educational attainment, strong work commitment, dislike of new technology and training are all interrelated. Their manifestation at 16, and the persistence of the relationships with career trajectory beyond it, suggests that much of whatever it is that prompts young people to embark on particular career routes at age 16 – whether to stay on in education or to leave – is laid down earlier in life in the family and in the peer group.

Some policy issues

Area differences

Although educational participation after age 16 was not that dissimilar across the English areas, it was noticeable how some 18-year-olds with good qualifications in Swindon entered the labour market for a year or so, only to become disenchanted and return to higher education. The relatively plentiful job opportunities in Swindon allowed this to happen, with employers offering attractive incentives to recruit young people. Age for age, however, overall educational participation increased over the two years of the study, in all areas.

The buoyant economic conditions in Swindon were most marked, however, in the creation of a huge cadre of young workers. Thus, very soon after the summer of the school-leaving year a quarter of the Swindon sample were in employment, compared to 6–8% in other areas, and this difference persisted through to the age of 20. Correspondingly, participation in youth training was lowest in Swindon, half the level of the other areas. Swindon employers found it unnecessary to provide YTS places in a highly competitive labour market, preferring to recruit direct into real jobs. In a sense their employment policies had not really altered since the 1970s. The 'training culture' had passed them by.

In contrast, Kirkcaldy was a self-contained but by no means homogeneous labour market, incorporating the new town of Glenrothes and Kirkcaldy itself, together with a number of smaller towns and outlying villages. There was a mixture of declining industries and growing new-technology companies, with the net result that labour-market opportunities varied considerably in the area. Scottish traditions in education also contrasted with those of England. There was a higher participation rate, especially among 16–17-year-olds, with many of the Kirkcaldy sample pursuing non-academic courses through the 16+ Action Plan. By the end of the teens the differences, although still present, were much reduced. More were staying on in higher education.

Except for the delayed start in entry to training or to the labour market in Kirkcaldy, employment and training there were similar to employment and training in Sheffield and Liverpool. Unemployment among young people reflected the local level for adults and in Kirkcaldy was somewhat lower than in Liverpool and Sheffield, but higher than in Swindon.

Both Sheffield and Liverpool had recently suffered particularly vicious consequences of the early 1980s recession. Although, historically, their economies had developed along quite different lines, in the late 1980s, from the perspectives of young people the two cities looked more similar than any of the other areas. Particularly crucial, of course, were the high unemployment levels during the 1980s, which had blighted the career opportunities of a whole generation in both cities. Rates of participation in education were similar, and on the increase in the younger cohort, while youth training was relatively well developed in Sheffield, a factor contributing to the higher level of participation and the creation of more positive attitudes to training as a personal investment. It is clear that labour-market effects are dominant in shaping opportunities but can be moderated substantially by two types of influence: local policies towards post-16 education and the training and the national system of provision and qualifications.

This raises questions for policy-makers locally, especially in the new TECs which we consider later, but also nationally. Not only does the reform of the whole system of education and training after age 16 need to be considered, but also ways of changing values, especially among employers. While jobs without training are sought by substantial numbers of young people at the earliest possible age and while employers in expanding labour markets are keen to offer them, there is little hope of bringing about the changes that a modern economy demands.

Does gender make any difference?

The surprising finding was that differences were not particularly marked, and tended to be in the traditional directions. Girls tended to stay on in education in greater numbers to pursue secretarial and clerical qualifications, especially in the immediate post-compulsory year. Boys, on the other hand, were initially keener to get out to work, usually in manual jobs, as soon as possible. The girls were subsequently overtaken by boys going on to higher education. It was also noticeable that in the English areas more females than males were in employment by the age of 19.

Gender differences in YTS participation rates were not consistent across the four areas, but in Swindon and Liverpool males were slightly more likely to take the YTS route into the labour market. The employing and training sectors also reflected the traditional gender divisions in occupational aspirations and opportunities, with girls more inclined towards a narrow range of jobs in the office and service sector, and the boys tending to enter a more diverse range of jobs in the production and skilled craft and service sectors. The policy issue here is how to realise past commitments to opening up more opportunities for girls in a wider range of occupations. Expectations are set early, which means that a major part of the task has to take place in education. But employers' attitudes also need to change.

Educational achievement, career trajectories and social class origins

While social class remained a powerful global force, its immediate impact on the distribution of career opportunities operated largely through its link with educational achievement. Career trajectories, which overlay class origins with educational attainment, were a more significant way to stratify young people. Academic qualifications bestowed career benefits, and the introduction of YTS did not have a very marked effect on redistributing labour-market opportunities. Thus, the traditional predictors of success in the labour market – locality, class, gender, education values – were still important.

At the same time, young people appeared to show a high degree of optimism in their expectations, but had realistic perceptions of local opportunities. Thus far more young people in Liverpool than in Swindon thought that job prospects were poor and more planned to move at some time to seek work. The difficulty for many who want to seek opportunities elsewhere is gaining good information about the jobs and training that are available, and, if they do move, finding the necessary social support and housing that successful relocation requires.

Staying on in education, especially on the premier A-level route, remains fundamentally a selective process with markers of likely success and failure laid down fairly early on. This is more of a problem in England than Scotland where a broader post-16 curriculum is on offer and more go on to higher education. There is much for English educational policy to learn from this.

The delivery of YTS

By the end of the 1980s YTS was at something of a transition point. The responsibility for organising and delivering youth training at the local level was in the process of being invested in the new Training and Enterprise Councils (TECs). Between 80 and 100 TECs were to be created over a four-year period, each based in a distinct locality (Department of Employment, 1988). TEC boards are dominated by local businessmen, with the clear intention of enabling training to be more employer-driven than in the recent past. The TECs were designed to fulfil a number of key roles, underpinned by five principles. First, national training and enterprise programmes needed to be tailored to the needs of local labour markets, hence TECs were to be locally based systems. Second, TECs should be central to an employer-led partnership. Third, there was a need in some areas for a targeted approach towards community revitalisation as well as the co-ordination of policies and programmes. Fourth, there should be an emphasis on performance, with the aim of attaining better value for money, greater efficiency and a high return on investment. Finally, the intention was to create an enterprise culture.

TECs have been given responsibility for delivering training programmes for the unemployed and for supporting local training as best fits an assessment of local needs. The next move will inevitably be away from educational venues, towards a more entrepreneurial, near-market style of employer-led schemes. The TECs will subcontract training to training providers, and responsibility for standards of achievement will be linked to National Council for Vocational Qualifications (NCVQ) levels. Among their aims is to help ensure that young people acquire the skills the local economy needs, and to do this by youth training programmes. One persistent theme of the 16–19 Initiative is the primacy of local labour-market opportunities in determining the early careers of young people. Thus there is a degree of synergy between our research findings and recent policy changes. But more importantly, the approach taken in the 16–19 Initiative to analysing careers could profitably be applied to the planning and evaluation process necessary for TECs to achieve their objectives.

In addition to seeing TECs as the regulators of the local training market, the CBI (1989) has recommended that from the age of 14 individuals should possess their own careership profile, which 'records achievement and identifies development needs'. Related to this, the idea of training credits was introduced in October 1990, allowing each school leaver the freedom to 'spend' a voucher for a given amount of training. Whether this will materially affect the labour-market opportunities of young people remains to be seen. It may be something of a test-bed for similar applications in related educational fields.

Related to the establishment of TECs are the changes introduced and to be introduced by the NCVQ. Set up in 1986, the NCVQ aims to reform the system of vocational qualifications that will cover all categories of employment and will be in place in 1991. Reform is undoubtedly overdue. Currently there are no readily available statistics on the vocational qualifications of the workforce, on the number of qualifications awarded annually, or on the costs of the system. The new framework includes securing standards of occupational competence that are assessed and accredited by approved bodies. The NCVQ task is clearly a complex one, and it is not without its critics (see, for example, Green, 1986). While some degree of success at the lower levels (those qualifications achieved by YTS trainees) can be expected, it remains to be seen whether comprehensive coverage of all occupations can be achieved.

Higher education

The consequences of underinvestment in educational opportunities and restricting access to higher education are very clear. It can be argued that there is a link between national economic prosperity and spending on higher education, research and development. One simple measure is the number of scientists and engineers engaged in research and development per 10,000 working people. During the 1980s the USA and Japan had over 60, West Germany over 50, France over 40, and all were on the increase. The UK is alone in having under 30, a figure which is declining. The government's target of doubling student numbers by the year 2000 looks unrealistic given the current annual funding increases of 2–3%. Contrast this with the situation in France, where the higher education system received an extra £1.7 billion between 1990 and 1991 for university development and renovation. The new expenditure is designed to cope with an increase of 400,000 in student numbers by 1995.

The UK is one of the few European nations with a labour market that includes large numbers of unskilled 17-year-olds, the reverse side of the coin of low post-16 educational participation. France has set a target of 80% gaining the *baccalauréat*, the university entrance qualification, by the year 2000. Our more limited aim of 50% (CBI, 1989) needs to be reappraised if we are to keep up.

Apart from this, the relatively low levels of funding for higher education also point to the influence of structural factors, and the associated values and expectations of different groups in society. Thus not only does access to higher education need to be opened up, but also the attitudes of the young need changing so that investment in further training and education is seen as a positively desirable goal by larger numbers than at present. The position is slowly improving, but, as our research has demonstrated, the desire to enter the labour market at the earliest opportunity is still very strong among the youth population, and employers reinforce it with the desire to recruit young school leavers and train them on the job. What is needed are greater incentives to stay on in education after age 16, incentives that are short-term and financial, as well as long-term in holding out the prospect of more rewarding careers.

Conclusion

This chapter adds up to a raft of issues which policy-makers will need increasingly to address throughout the 1990s. As the nature of employment continues to change at gathering speed, there will be a growing need for different kinds of education and vocational preparation to underpin it. We need to consider whether the majority of those in our school leaver trajectories were being adequately prepared for the labour market of the future, and whether those staying on and ploughing the traditional furrows were being equipped to meet the demands of a modern economy. As many commentators have argued, there is a pressing need for a shift in the distribution of young people across the trajectories – not only towards more of them staying on after age 16, but also towards substantially increasing the numbers continuing after 18.

But staying on for the sake of staying on may be little better than leaving. For some it certainly bestows no financial benefits. What also matters is the content of post-16 educational experience. Ways need to be found not only of making it more relevant to society's needs but also – vitally important – of making it what young leavers themselves would like to do.

Chapter 4 HOME LIFE, SOCIABILITY AND LEISURE

Introduction

In this chapter we discuss the domestic and leisure aspects of young people's lives. This would be impossible without talking about differences between boys and girls, young men and young women. Young women are on average several years ahead of young men in making key life-cycle transitions. Moreover, throughout the teenage years, young men and young women have somewhat different leisure patterns. And additionally, girls are typically more connected with their family household than boys. The assumption that a 'domestic career' is for girls a higher priority than an occupational career, with the converse being true for boys, has been re-examined and reassessed in recent work (Pollert, 1981; Griffin, 1985; Wallace, 1987). But clearly it remains important to consider the relationship between 'domestic career' and different educational and occupational paths for boys and girls, and this is an issue to which we will return.

First, consideration is given to home life and relations with parents; then the focus shifts to leisure time spent outside the home and the nature of social relationships. We then move to dating relationships and partnerships leading to key life events including leaving home, marriage and having children. In a particular sequence these life events make up a conventional 'domestic career' – finding a partner, setting up home and bringing up children. Though these last activities may be expected to be rare in a sample of people under the age of 20, where such accelerated domestic careers do occur they are of special interest and the events preceeding them are well represented in our sample.

A recurring theme in the analysis are the disparities in opportunities and resources available to young men and women and how these relate to social backgrounds. It has been suggested that gender and social class interact to produce a hierarchy of advantage and disadvantage for young people (see, for example, Allen, 1979; Edgel, 1980; Deem, 1986). Middle-class males have the best access to material resources, domestic support and extensive social networks; their lives can be considered 'leisure-rich' (Roberts, 1984; Roberts *et al.*, 1990). At the other end of the scale, working-class girls often have the most impoverished personal lives, with poor access to money and material resources, more restricted leisure activity and the expectation that they will provide domestic services for the family in a way that boys do not. These differences interact with employment routes and aspirations. They direct working-class girls towards jobs which in various ways serve the domestic career. Early marriage and having a family is typically expected, as are part-time or full-time work soon afterwards in order to support the family income. Unemployment accelerates the process because, in the absence of work, girls are expected to fulfil a domestic role in the home or to move out to establish a domestic life of their own (see, for example, Griffin, 1985).

To investigate the processes involved, we use our survey data to highlight broad transition patterns. In addition, to illuminate their complexity and meaning in the lives of individuals, we draw extensively in this chapter on our interview data collected in Scotland, where domestic careers were a special focus of the initiative. Nine young people have been selected as case studies.

Alistair and Patsy were following an academic career trajectory. Morag, a student nurse, was following a vocational trajectory into nursing. Gordon, Keith and Donna made the traditional transitions straight from school to work at 16 and had managed to remain in employment. Julie obtained a clerical job via a YTS scheme and Valerie and Robert had been on YTS or unemployed between 16 and 18. Though a typical group in many respects, six of them who had left home were selected as exhibiting accelerated domestic careers. Patsy and Alistair were university students and Morag was a student nurse living at home. Keith, Robert and Valerie were living with partners away from their parents. Donna, though still at home, was also in advance of the majority of her age group: she was the unmarried mother of a small child.

Living at home

The great majority of our sample, even at the end of the teens, were still living in their parents' homes. Nevertheless, changes in their home lives were occurring throughout the whole period. Most were taking responsibility for their upkeep by paying board and some, usually girls, were increasingly doing housework and helping the family in other ways. In parallel, there were changes in when and how time was spent with the family and in the use made of the home for leisure.

With the exception of those still in education, almost all the young people paid towards their keep at home, usually between £10 and £15 per week. Boys tended to pay more than girls, reflecting their higher earnings. Although the income of young people differed considerably among our four areas, board payments were much the same in all of them. Young people in Swindon, for example, had more money to spend on their leisure than young people in other areas or to save, which is what most of them did. Payments were higher in families where the father was unemployed – a fifth of the households in Liverpool and a tenth of those in Sheffield (cf. Jones, 1991a; 1991b). Hence, those young people living in households which were already underresourced were also having their disposable income reduced. A number of households of this kind were encountered where the young person was the main breadwinner.

Taking more responsibility was accompanied by other changes in the direction of independence within the family. These included being treated more as an adult by the parents, having greater freedom to come and go, and being less home-based in terms of leisure activities, especially in the case of boys. In some homes spending time with the family was largely reduced to eating meals while watching TV, but in others, as our interviews revealed, the quality of relationships was enhanced.

Family leisure and resources

Some family households provided 'richer' leisure environments than others, which was partly a function of material resources. For example, some homes had video recorders and compact disc players. Richness was also evident in terms of pianos, books, encyclopaedias, records, visits to the opera, what Bourdieu describes as 'cultural capital'. Certain tastes, hobbies and sports were routinely encouraged in some homes and never mentioned in others.

Access to certain family resources varied by class and by gender. For example, in semi-skilled and unskilled families access to a car and a video recorder was more common for young men than for young women. Overall, though, the anticipated differences between males and females were not always born out by the data. Although more boys than girls had access to motorbikes, bicyles and cars, more girls reported having space to entertain their friends. There were no differences in access to telephones and radio cassette players nor in having a room of their own. Ownership of bank accounts, credit cards and other financial aids was also equally common for both sexes.

Family closeness

In 1987 we asked young people to tell us to what extent they agreed with the statements 'If you live with your parents they can tell you what to do' and 'People should realise that their greatest loyalty is to their family'. At 15–16 and 17–18 the majority agreed with both statements. However, willingness to be ruled by parents diminished with age, although commitment to the family apparently did not. Only 53% of the older cohort agreed with the former statement, compared to over 70% of the younger age group. In 1989 we asked whether respondents agreed with the statement 'I feel my parents treat me like a child when I am at home'. The majority disagreed with this statement, indicating some satisfaction with how they were treated by their parents, but minorities – slightly more girls than boys and more of the younger than the older age group – did agree. At all ages more girls reported more often spending time with parents and siblings than boys. This is despite the fact that girls tended to leave home at earlier ages and were involved at earlier ages in dating relationships. Girls were more often able to talk to their parents and to feel that their parents were in touch with their lives than were boys. Among both boys and girls it was mothers more often than fathers who were identified as somebody with whom they could talk.

Domestic work

As we have noted while living 'at home', girls put more work into their family households and took more responsibility for looking after themselves, as shown in Table 4.1. Their contribution increased with age. While boys and girls contributed financially to the household by paying 'board' or 'digs' money, about twice as many girls made a regular contribution to cooking and cleaning. The only chore done more frequently by boys was the less frequent task of household repairs. A substantial minority of girls – about 30% – and about half of boys did very little. Not surprisingly, both boys and girls tended to do more if both their parents were in employment. To quote Julie: 'Before my mum was working full-time I did not have to do anything because my mum usually done it. I would do the dishes at tea time.' Since her mother had got a job she did more tidying up and shopping and some washing, but her mother still did the bulk of the cooking. She indicated that her sister did about the same amount of work as herself, while her younger brother, who was 14 at the time of the second interview, did nothing in the house. Patsy cooked for the family and did cleaning and tidying when she was at home from university in the holidays. The picture for boys was very different. Gordon's mother made all beds and did all cleaning and cooking. 'The only thing I have to do in my room is keep my clothes tidy. My mum does all the washing and cleaning.' His mother always did all the dishes. He only cooked when she was not there and never cooked for others, just himself.

Class differences interact with gender differences. There was both a class gradient in how much boys did, with more working-class boys doing less, and in how much girls did, with more working-class girls doing more.

These class and gender differences occurred despite the fact that girls from all class backgrounds generally believed that jobs around the house should be shared equally. Indeed, girls typically had more egalitarian views than boys on a variety of questions concerning the distribution of opportunities and division of labour between men and women, especially over looking after children, though the majority of boys agreed with them. A minority of boys continued to regard housework and, especially looking after children as 'women's work' and some who did not take this view still seemed to avoid translating their more egalitarian beliefs into practice. Those who were doing the most also held the most egalitarian views.

Table 4.1 Percentage doing household tasks by age and sex, 1988

| | 16–17 | | 18–19 | |
	F	M	F	M
Cleaning own room	94	84	94	79
Other cleaning	52	29	59	30
Shopping	28	18	41	24
Making meals for others	40	21	50	27
Household repairs	9	41	15	45
Paying bills	4	6	18	18
Washing up	73	55	77	52

Young women appeared to have less choice. Most were involved in housework whatever their opinions. The longer-term benefits for them were greater knowledge of household management and a realistic assessment of their ability to look after themselves and others. The costs were that their leisure time was differentially curtailed and that they were prepared for subsequent inequalities in the division of labour between adult men and women.

Leisure life

Complementing the changing nature of home life and relations with parents was the changing nature of leisure outside the home. The really dramatic shifts in interest usually occur around puberty, well before the age range of our study. Nevertheless, changes continued as group social activities gave way to partnerships, with again quite marked differences between the sexes. Table 4.2 selects contrasting leisure activities from the large number we asked about, including smoking and drinking. Table 4.3 shows the companions our respondents spent most of their free time with at different ages. Church attendance, very much a minority activity, fell to near zero by the end of the teens for boys, but maintained a level of 15% for girls. Youth club attendance declined similarly, but this time more among girls than among boys. Although a third overall were participating at 15–16, less than one tenth were still doing so at 19–20. For sports there were much larger gender differences, with boys either participating in or watching sport at twice the level of girls. Even so, by the age of 19, two-fifths of girls said they were doing some kind of sport.

Table 4.2   Leisure activities and age (%)

Leisure activity*	1987 15–16 F	M	1988 16–17 F	M	1989 17–18 F	M	1987 17–18 F	M	1988 18–19 F	M	1989 19–20 F	M
Attending Church	20	15	17	11	19	11	17	11	15	9	15	7
Attending youth club	35	37	15	24	16	19	14	20	9	15	5	12
Doing sport	25	43	51	79	43	68	22	37	46	73	43	65
Watching sport	49	70	25	52	11	34	41	65	20	46	10	36
Going to pubs	25	30	60	61	79	82	80	78	85	87	82	89
Going to dances/discos	52	32	57	45	69	63	66	57	65	62	66	64
Drinking alcohol	3	5	9	13	14	23	16	25	17	31	19	37
Smoking	20	15	22	18	22	17	27	26	26	23	25	22

*Once or more a month, except 'drinking alcohol' (three times or more a week) and 'smoking' (every day)

Table 4.3   Type of leisure companion (%)

Persons with whom time is 'often' spent	1988 16–17 F	M	1989 17–18 F	M	1988 18–19 F	M	1989 18–19 F	M
Parents	53	40	45	28	56	34	48	31
Siblings	38	29	33	21	44	29	38	25
Partner	66	51	68	57	74	58	75	66
Close friend	73	66	66	61	70	64	65	61
Mixed group	50	51	46	45	45	50	44	43
Single-sex group	48	61	44	56	42	56	41	54
Alone	27	28	27	30	27	24	26	24

For dances and discos and pubs, the picture changed again. Substantially more girls than boys at the younger ages were going to them, but by the end of the teens the boys had caught up. Both boys and girls were frequenting pubs at all ages to much the same extent, with the proportion going once a month rising from a quarter at age 15–16 to four-fifths by the age of 19. But more boys were drinking alcohol between three and seven times a week at all ages and especially in the higher age groups: by age 19 over a third of of boys and a fifth of girls reported drinking at this level. Smoking was equally common among both sexes, and barely changed with age. About a quarter reported smoking every day.

Some of the change in young people's leisure reflects increased income, and variation reflects differences in spending power. There was a significant difference in the income and spending power of 15–16-year-olds and those over 16 who had left school and were receiving an independent income in the form of a training allowance, social security or a full-time wage. Moreover, these independent incomes were also divergent, with young people in well paid jobs leaving behind those on benefit and training allowances.

By the age of 16–17 the majority of young people had a bank account and just over half were saving money each week. By age 18-19 over half had a cheque book. Only a minority of young people had credit cards, but many had taken on credit by buying items through catalogues. This type of credit was more common among girls than boys. Half the girls and a third of the boys had bought items this way at age 18–19. Not surprisingly, those who earned more were more likely to save and more able to spend money on commercial entertainments like discos and the cinema. Spending diaries completed by 55 respondents indicated that young men generally spent more on entertainment than young women. This was a reflection partly of higher earnings but also of conventions with regard to boys paying for girlfriends as well as of the greater use made by young men of public leisure facilities.

Girls' earlier attendance at discos reflects the fact that they were 'going out with' the opposite sex and seeking partners at an earlier age than boys. By the age of 19, boys had caught up with girls, indeed had overtaken the girls in some cases – especially those from non-manual backgrounds and those in higher education. But boys maintained more interests pursued through organisations and/or public facilities. More young men, and particularly young men from middle-class backgrounds, had maintained an interest in sport or some other hobby or club activity. Girls, and many working-class boys, may have been doing other things informally and in unstructured settings, but, as Roberts *et al.* (1990) conclude, 'the women [and many working-class men] were missing out on the experience of being active in voluntary associations ... acquiring the skills needed to be active and assertive participants, and even influential members of such groups'.

What young people did in their leisure time was also related to their career trajectory. Those on the academic and vocational trajectories were behind the others initially in going to pubs and discos, but had caught up with them by the age of 18. Not surprisingly, it was those young men and women with a history of unemployment that had lower rates of participation in many of the activities we investigated. They were less likely to go to cinemas, parties, dances or discos, play sport, visit pubs and to drink alcohol several times a week. But they were more likely to smoke, reflecting presumably the greater strain and boredom with their situation. The unemployed, and particularly unemployed women, appeared to have been suffering from the most acute 'leisure poverty' while students and employed men were the most 'leisure-rich'. Area differences in leisure 'richness' and 'poverty' reflected the different labour-market opportunities. Hence Liverpool had the highest concentration of young people suffering from leisure poverty. Swindon stood out, in contrast, as an area of relatively high employment and high wages for young people, and therefore one in which young people were relatively 'rich' in their consumption of commercial leisure. On the other hand, many complained about the lack of facilities for young people there, as they did in Kirkcaldy. The big cities of Liverpool and Sheffield had in one sense more to offer young people in terms of a vibrant leisure culture which could accentuate the problems of the unemployed.

During the years between ages 16 and 20, the significance of parents and the ambience of their family household inevitably wane in young people's lives. Neither young men nor young women shared much leisure time with their families, whether or not more time was spent 'at home' than 'going out'. Both sexes reported spending more time with friends or partners than with parents and siblings. Most had stopped going on 'family holidays' and on family visits to other relatives. Against this general trend, there were some households with exceptionally high rates of joint activity. There were a few sporting families. Gordon, for example, continued to play golf and snooker with his father on a weekly basis. And a few religious families such as Valerie's spent at least Sunday together in worship.

On the whole, however, when they were at home, most young people spent their time either in their own rooms or watching TV rather than interacting with 'the family'. Home was seen typically as a convenient base, a place for recuperation from which to go out for recreation, and it appeared a cheap and an easy place to be.

This is not to say that 'home' was not important in their lives. Although the majority agreed that 'it's better to get a place of your own if you've got the money', many were painfully aware that they did not have the financial resources to leave home. Also, some felt they did not have the practical skills and emotional resources to live elsewhere. About a quarter of those aged 17–18 agreed that 'having a place of your own is too much worry', sentiments shared by only 20% of young women and 17% of young men aged 19–20.

Parents seemed to be relatively insignificant figures in terms of advice and discussion about everyday personal decisions. We asked young people a series of questions about who influenced them most in making certain types of decisions: what to wear, with whom they spent their time, what to do with their spare time, what job or career to choose, how to have their hair styled, whether to use contraceptives, and what to spend their money on. They had a choice of answers: parents/step-parents, friends of your own age, partner/girl or boyfriend/wife or husband. For each decision, with the exception of choice of job or career and what to spend their money on, no more than 12% said 'parents'. Girls were slightly more likely to say 'parents' than boys, and the 17–18 age group were more likely to than the 19–20 age group. Arguably the decision concerning job or career is the only one listed which could seriously shape life chances. Decisions in the province of personal life were made more with the help of friends or partners.

In contrast to the general picture of attenuating relationships between parents and children, some young people told us of how their relationship had deepened and become a more significant intellectual and emotional resource. This was more typical of young people from middle-class backgrounds who had already left home. As Patsy, a university student, put it:

> having been away, I find it much easier to go home and talk to my parents and sort of have conversations with them rather than just be in their company. And I think I talk to them a lot more.

Friendship and courtship

Between the ages of 16 and 20 social relationships inevitably change. The general trend suggested was for young people to move from same-sex groups and same-sex 'best friend' relationships to 'going out with' someone. While for the majority 'going out' involved someone of the opposite sex, this was not the case for all. While our data describe the general pattern, the homosexual minority cannot be distinguished. Our approach in framing questions on sexuality was neither to assume heterosexuality nor to seek a declaration of heterosexuality or homosexuality. Although this approach has the merit of being non-threatening to the respondent, it does mean that the minority are lost in the general picture.

Change in who was and who was not a friend often occurred at the time of leaving school. The likelihood of losing touch with school friends was exacerbated for some young people in Kirkcaldy by the fact that secondary school pupils were often drawn from a number of small towns. Because school friends were not always local, there was no natural basis for contact after leaving school. Loss of contact with school friends could also be exacerbated by geographic and social mobility, particularly in Swindon because its buoyant labour market facilitated such mobility. Entry into certain occupations which required intense occupational socialisation also separated young people from former friends. Morag, the student nurse from Fife, was still seeing some of her friends from school days at the time of her second interview. She met them to play badminton or sometimes with her nursing friends for a drink. But she commented that they 'are not the same ... They don't know much about what I'm doing. I never know what they're all doing ... We're not as close as we used to be.'

A marked gender difference among young people in most Western societies is the earlier involvement of girls in dating and courtship. Hendry (1983) has suggested that this involves a narrowing, if not an impoverishment, of girls' sociability and leisure. The conventions of men 'taking out' women are not dead and generally men 'take out' women who are slightly younger than themselves. While formal barriers to legal and financial equality have now been removed, men still tend to be better off than women. Young men's advantages in the labour market translate into more money in their pockets. At age 17 our male respondents were on average £4 a week better off than the females. Conventions concerning sexual conduct which place greater value on faithfulness, chastity and 'good reputation' for women also emphasise the double standards for men and women and a degree of male dominance in the relationship.

Girls' earlier participation in dating should not be confused with readiness to become involved with sexual relationships. Because there were obvious difficulties with asking questions about sexual activity in a postal questionnaire sent to young people's homes, no attempt was made to do so. However, we did include a number of attitude items concerned with sexual behaviour in our questionnaires. These reinforced the conclusion of earlier studies (Wilson, 1978; Farrel, 1979; Lees, 1986) that young women are much less comfortable with the idea of casual sex than young men. Response to questionnaire items also suggested that young women were taking the dangers of AIDS more seriously than young men (although, interestingly and worryingly, concern about AIDS appeared to be diminishing over time in both sexes). Differences between young men and young women were not as simple as young women being generally more conservative in sexual matters than young men. More young women than young men agreed with the statement 'There is nothing wrong with homosexual relationships'.

By the age of 16 significant proportions of boys as well as girls, from all backgrounds, had a girlfriend or boyfriend. While marriage and cohabiting and to a lesser extent being engaged were minority statuses between 16 and 20, having a boyfriend or girlfriend was common by the older ages. Three-quarters of the girls aged 18 and over said they often spent their spare time with a partner. Having a boyfriend or girlfriend was not necessarily a fixed status, once achieved, but rather something that young people moved into and out of. However, even in the younger age group a majority of girls consistently maintained that they often spent time with a partner.

We saw earlier how other relationships were giving ground to those with partners: spending time with family and friends declined as did, to a much lesser extent, spending time with a close friend or in a group. These changes happened earlier for girls, but more of them also continued to spend time with their family and close friends, while more boys continued to spend time with a same sex group.

Julie's way of partitioning her time was typical. In the last week before the interview, she had spent Friday and Saturday night with her boyfriend. She went on a walk with her boyfriend during the day on Sunday and spent Sunday night at home. She spent Monday evening with her boyfriend. Of the remaining weekday nights, one was spent at home, one out with a group of five other young women, and one round at a female friend's house. A lot of her predominantly female friends were engaged, and some were married and some had children. Two years later she had been engaged for ten months, but still spent a lot of time with her best friend and other women friends.

Gordon's social life contrasted markedly with that of Julie. In the week prior to the first interview, he was in a pub with his mates five nights out of seven. He described himself as having had lots of girlfriends, none for more than about four weeks, occasionally with sexual relationships. Two years later he still saw his best male friend more than anyone else – about four nights a week – usually with others in a public setting. He had made new friends at work but they did not live locally so they met up at weekends in discos in Kirkcaldy. He did not have a girlfriend and commented: 'Too close to Christmas!', meaning he did not want to spend money on 'taking a girl out'.

Keith displayed another pattern. When first interviewed he was very involved in sport and went to a fitness room twice a week, where he met his friends. He had joined the Territorial Army (TA) as soon as he was old enough, went to meetings once a week and away with them regularly at weekends. He did not have a girlfriend and talked about not wanting to be married or tied down until 21–23. At the second interview he was still in the TA, but was then living with a girlfriend and the father of her child.

Although in general the pattern of relationships did not vary significantly with occupational or educational route, there were two groups who did stand out: those who had stayed in education and unemployed young men. Not surprisingly, those still in education were tending to spend time with groups of friends. They were also slower to make the shift from close friend to partner.

When Patsy had gone to university she said of her former best friend in her home town that she is

> quite happy just to stay where she is and she's been going out with some boy for quite a while and I think she's going to get engaged and she will just settle down. And I can't see myself at all in that position. It's a different situation.

Two years later she had just finished a relationship with a student boyfriend that had lasted just over a year.

> I just felt I'm going away for a year coming up and I don't want to feel that I can't go, or just basically I'm not ready for the sort of commitment that he was looking for. And as far as I'm concerned that's not a lot of use, if we sort of continued seeing each other and he was constantly looking for a lot more than I was.

Contact with friends in Fife was much reduced and 'keeping in touch' was maintained through exchanges of information through her university friends about people they knew at school.

However, while girls in academic trajectories were less likely to report often spending time with a partner than girls who were employed, more did so than boys. While staying in education did not disturb differences between boys and girls in this respect, unemployment appeared to exacerbate them. Girls with a history of unemployment were almost as likely as employed girls to spend a lot of time with a partner, and, indeed, more likely to do so than girls who stayed on in education. Boys with a history of unemployment, on the other hand, were significantly less likely to spend time with a partner than boys who had experienced stable employment. Because of the conventions of boys 'taking out' girls, boys without jobs were more inhibited than girls from dating. Many could drift into what Wallace (1987) describes as a kind of 'perpetual adolescence' with much emphasis on bravado and risk-taking, but little real social contact with the opposite sex.

Another aspect of friendships revealed the same pattern. In 1988 and 1989 the young people were asked to name 'the four friends you see most often' and to tell us whether they were male or female and to answer some other questions about them. At age 16–17 almost half the boys named four male friends and almost a third named one female and three male friends. At age 18–19 the number who named only boys had shrunk to 38% and those naming one girl had increased slightly so that most boys were divided fairly equally among these two options. Among the girls, the most common option was never four friends of the same sex but rather one boy and three girls. By age 19, 26% of girls were naming four girls as the friends they saw most often and 47% one boy and three girls.

It has been suggested that as girls start dating, their friendships with other girls are more likely to break down than boys' same-sex friendships. Female friendships are more difficult to drop into and out of, being less often constructed around an institutional setting such as a pub or club and typically more intense in time and emotional energy (Griffin, 1985).

Although there is little evidence of this from our survey data (cf. Griffiths, 1988; Roberts *et al.*, 1990), the interviews showed that some young women who spent virtually every evening with their boyfriends did so at the expense of friendships: 'I've drifted away from all my pals, ken when I'm out with my boyfriend.' Morag's boyfriend had explicitly objected to her going out 'with the girls', especially to pubs and discos where she might meet other men. She had just broken off her engagement, and when asked 'Do you want to actually get back with him?' she said:

> Sometimes. I enjoy my freedom as well. I enjoy doing what I want, when I want, with whom I want. I like to decide half an hour before I go out – let's go to [a disco] or somewhere. I could not do that before.

Young women who were unemployed or out of the labour market normally saw female friends during the day and spent a great deal of time with their boyfriend in the evening.

Valerie was unusual because she had been going out with the same boyfriend from the age of 14 and had married at 17. Her social life had been largely shaped by her boyfriend's social world. The young women with whom she remained friends were girlfriends of her husband's male friends. She and her husband did not go out very often because of lack of money but when they did it was usually with her husband's brother and sister-in-law or her husband's best male friend and his girlfriend. When her husband went out with his friend she 'sat in with' his friend's girlfriend.

Some young men commented that having a girlfriend had affected their relationships with their male friends. Robert, a brickie's labourer, commented: 'Before I met my girl, I used to go out every night. I used to be with them [mates since schooldays] all the time. But it's just two or three nights a week I see them now.' The effect that Robert refers to is qualitatively and quantitatively different from the putative effect of a boyfriend on female friends. His mates are not marginalised in his social life. The 'now' referred to is our second interview with him when he was about 20 and living with his fiancée. His mates often dropped by his house and he went out with them on a Friday night. He and his fiancée did not go out much. Mates and his fiancée were kept separate outside the house. 'I never go out with my friends when I'm with her, when she's there like. They're a bit rowdy when they get going.'

Robert's experience contrasts with that of a university student with a working-class background. Alistair had a steady girlfriend but, like Robert, had not lost contact with his mates. Indeed, he had managed to maintain something of the for-men-only contact Robert had with his mates as well as an entire other social life which was less exclusively male. The former were part of his 'home' life, whereas the latter were part of his university life. His social scene was diverse, and arguably richer than Robert's, as a consequence. And, unlike Robert, his girlfriend was assimilated into socialising with some of his male friends.

When Alistair was away at university he spent a lot of his free time with his girlfriend. At the first interview he described his routine as follows:

> I go out at seven in the morning and don't get home till about half five or so and then I'll sit in till about seven o'clock and go down and see the girlfriend and go out for a couple of drinks or something and come back ... I usually see her four nights a week and the other night I just sit and study.

Also his friends at university were not exclusively male. He kept in touch with his cousin and a mate from his home town and always went out with them when he was 'home'. At the first interview he described his routine for a weekend 'at home':

> Friday, get home about half seven then I'll go out about half nine or ten o'clock with my cousin and my mate, we go along to the local disco and then the usual Saturday just sitting in the house until about three [p.m.]

and then [his mate] will come down and we'll go to Kirkcaldy or something.

On comparing people he knew at university versus those 'at home', he said:

It's a different sort of friendship like. Up there there's that much folk, and I go around mainly with a couple of folk. When I come back here ['home'] I think it's close, you know, a closer friendship 'cos I've known them longer. It's quite good I know a lot of folk up [at university]. ... Friends come and go but you always find that you keep your closest friends.

The survey data support the argument that female and male friendships are different in kind. For each of the four friends named, we asked our respondents whether they were able to talk to this person about a serious worry or personal problem. In 1988, 60% of girls were able to talk to two or more friends, compared with only 40% of boys. Twenty-nine per cent of girls and 42% of boys were not able to talk to any of their named friends in this way. There was also some variation with age, with it apparently becoming easier for both men and women to talk about these things as they grew older. Furlong *et al.* (1989) have suggested that female same-sex friendships tend to be 'dyadic' while male same-sex friendships tend to involve larger groups. However, the interview data suggest that young men often masked dyadic relationships by their use of public settings. Our data also suggest that what boys do and talk about with their mates is qualitatively different.

The evidence we have of male and female social networks led us, like Furlong *et al.* (1989), to be cautious in declaring that girls' social networks are not as rich as those of boys. When asked to keep diaries of whom they saw it was clear that girls' social contacts were restricted by their more limited use of public space than boys, and the greater contact they maintained with their female friends could be seen as further evidence of this. At the same time, their relationships with same-sex friends and with parents, particularly mothers, was apparently more likely to provide them with emotional support.

Key personal events

Certain personal life-cycle events can involve reorganisation in all aspects of personal life. As we noted earlier, these events are generally regarded, like entering the labour market, as significant steps, if not *the* steps, to adulthood. In a particular sequence these life-cycle events make up a conventional personal life or domestic 'career' – finding a partner, setting up home and bringing up children. Most young people aim to make these transitions at some stage, but the timing and sequencing vary in desire and practice.

For the majority of the young people who were the subjects of our enquiry some of these life events were likely to be happening after it was over. In 1988 the median age of first marriage, for example, was 25.9 for men and 23.6 for women, some three to six years off for the majority of our oldest respondents at the time of the last survey (Roll, 1990). Larger numbers have left home by age 20, but again the majority have not. For example, the median age of first leaving home according to National Child Development Study data for the period up to 1981 is 21.9 for men and 20.0 for women (Jones, 1986). Nevertheless, these transitions were within the scope of our study in two important respects. First, a minority did make several of these 'moves' before the age of 20 and they are a subgroup worthy of consideration. But perhaps more importantly, as it brings the majority into focus, each life-cycle event has a prior history worthy of investigation. For example, marriage is preceded by courtship and often formal engagement. Also the values and ideas which inform these moves and which create expectations of these events are part of their prior history. We can at least partially document these histories for the 16–20 age group.

A study which follows a group of young people over time inevitably underestimates the proportion who leave home because, despite efforts to retain them, those who have left are disproportionately lost to the sample with each successive year. The differences revealed by the survey in the rate of leaving home between groups – girls and boys, those in higher education and those not – are real differences supported by other work, but in all cases the levels of leaving home have to be read as underestimates. At the beginning of our study in 1987 the overwhelming majority of young people reported themselves as living 'at home'. As Figure 4.1 shows, one-tenth of both sexes in the younger cohort described themselves as having left their parents' home in 1987 when they were aged 15–16. In each subsequent year more young people described themselves as having left home and a difference opened up between boys and girls, so that, among the older cohort aged 19–20 in 1989, 34% of girls and 26% of boys had left home. However, many moves were to relatives and, at least initially, were often of short duration, with a return home in between.

The proportion of young people leaving home also varied by gender, social class, area and career trajectory. Significantly, more young people whose fathers' occupation was professional or managerial had left home. This is largely because of the high participation of young people from this background in higher education, although a greater percentage of girls left home than boys in this as in every other social class grouping. Young women's propensity to leave home earlier than men is partly explained by the larger minority who moved into early cohabiting and marriage arrangements. However, it seems that more girls were willing to try living away from home than boys when neither of these factors were involved.

As we have seen, girls were generally more experienced at cooking and cleaning for themselves than boys and in this sense they were better equipped to leave home. Interviews and spending diaries suggested that young people

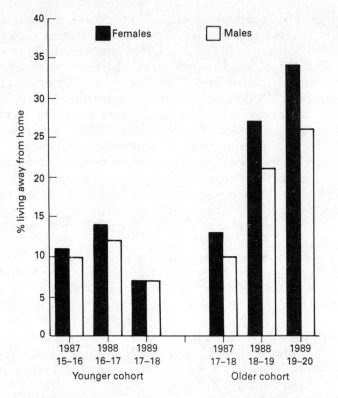

Figure 4.1   Living away from home, percentages by cohort, by age, by sex

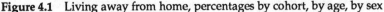

in their own tenancies often relied on café and take-away meals. Young men were less likely to have cooking skills than young women, with consequently higher living costs. Gordon illustrated the difficulties young men had. He left home for a flat with his mates because he was fed up with sharing a room with his brother, whose girlfriend was always there. But the flat only lasted three weeks.

> And it came to the weekends, with being used to having enough money to go Friday, Saturday and Sunday and do what I want, I was a bit skint and that. And one of them decided he was skint as well so he moved back to his mum's so that left two of us, so we just moved back.

Looking at the age and incidence of leaving home from the point of view of the young people's occupational career trajectories, it was those who went on to higher education who were distinctive. By age 19–20 only a quarter of those young people who had stayed on in education were living in their parents' house, with no difference between males and females. This compared with nearly three-quarters of females and four-fifths of males with a history of unemployment. Variations in local housing, education and employment options were also affecting whether or not young people left home. As Table

4.4 shows, of the four study areas, the highest proportions of young women had left home in Swindon and Kirkcaldy, two-fifths of young women aged 19–20 in 1989. This contrasts with a quarter of young women in Liverpool and a third of young women who had left home in Sheffield.

Table 4.4 Percentage of older cohort living away from home

| | 1987 17–18 | | 1988 18–19 | | 1989 19–20 | |
	F	M	F	M	F	M
Swindon	17	32	29	23	42	38
Sheffield	16	7	29	17	33	22
Liverpool	7	10	22	18	24	24
Kirkcaldy	14	11	30	24	41	39

Many young people left home for a period and then returned (Jones, 1986). A third of the younger cohort and just under half of the older cohort who were not living with their parents in 1988 were back in the parental home in 1989. Of the various types of living-away situation, the majority of the small number of 16–17-year-olds who had their own house or flat in 1988 were back 'home' by 1989. Among both the 16–17 and the 19–20 age groups it was the small number living with a relative who were most likely to be back 'home'. The home of a relative appeared to be a temporary 'home from home' for a small minority of young people across the range of different educational and occupational routes. By 1989 more girls had left home at least once than boys. In Liverpool boys often left the area temporarily to seek work. In Swindon, by contrast, 43% of our older-cohort girls had left home at some point. These differences can be attributed to variations in available employment and housing. Liverpool's depressed labour market prompted many young men to leave to seek labouring work in the South of England and then return, a move which was not generally open to unqualified young women. In Swindon, however, there was an above average availability of jobs for both sexes. In this area it was financially possible for more young men and women to try living away from home and more were prepared to do so.

Ambivalence about being away from home, particularly among the younger cohort, was evident. Over a third of them and about a quarter of the older cohort who were living away from home in 1989 agreed with the statement that 'People are better off living with their parents'. This, of course, does not mean that those living away from home would necessarily have preferred to be back in the parental home. Rather it suggests difficulty in managing financially and awareness of a fall in the standard of living. Also those who were living at home did not necessarily feel this was the ideal arrangement. The majority of them agreed with the statement 'It's better to get a place of your own if you've got the money'. The main reasons young people gave for wanting a place of their own were to do with independence. One aspect of this is freedom from questions about 'with whom, where and when they are going'. While most young people living with their parents in their late teens had a key to the house and freedom to come and go, our impression was that girls were more closely monitored than boys. Certainly this was a factor for Morag in her decision to move into nurses' accommodation in preference to staying at home.

When asked at what age they would want to get married, for the three-quarters who had a view the modal preferred age was 24. But girls set an age nearly two years younger than males, 23 compared with 25. The preferred age of marriage varied with career trajectory: far fewer young people in full-time education after age 16 could envisage marriage by 24 than was the case for young people who had left. Of course, what young people wanted or expected did not necessarily coincide with what was actually going to happen. While setting up home, marrying or having children are generally regarded as transitions following employment, unemployed young women particularly often drift into making them earlier (Wallace, 1987; Hutson and Jenkins, 1989). And while young people from different backgrounds had similar views about the ideal age for marriage, those with fathers who had manual occupations were in practice likely to marry earlier.

In 1987, only 12 young women and seven young men were married and 36 young women and 13 young men had children. In the case of the older group of young women aged 17–18, those who were married and who had children constituted 1% and 3% of the sample, respectively. By 1989, at age 19–20, 6% of young women and 5% of young men were married and the same percentages had children; although the two groups only partially overlapped, only 5% said they did not want any children. A growing minority described themselves as engaged: 5% of females aged 16–17, and 20% aged 19–20. The equivalent figures for males were 2% and 10%. Age of engagement was also related to social class. For example, by age 19, only 8% of young women whose fathers were in professional and managerial occupations were engaged, compared with 29% of those whose fathers were in semi-skilled and unskilled work.

But again these statuses were not constant, once achieved, but often changed. Figure 4.2 relates the statuses of the older group of young women in 1988 to their statuses in 1989. It shows that 67% of those engaged in 1988 were still engaged in 1989, with more of the remainder becoming single than married. Engagements were less likely to persist or to result in marriage during these years for young men. Figure 4.2 also shows that the small number of married young women was more than matched by a number who described themselves as 'cohabiting'. This is smaller than for national figures and is probably an underestimate based on misunderstanding of what the word meant. When asked to describe who was living in their household, several times

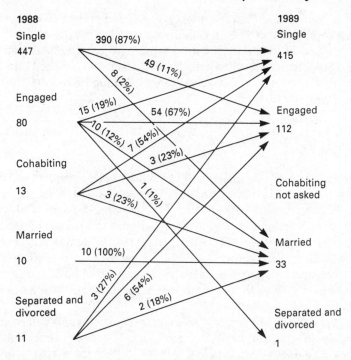

Figure 4.2 Marital status changes over one year, women aged 18–19 in 1988 and 19–20 in 1989

as many girls listed a boyfriend as living with them as declared themselves as cohabiting. The idea of cohabiting as a preliminary to marriage was well established, as our interview material demonstrated.

Like many young people, Patsy talked of the advantage of thoroughly getting to know a potential marriage partner before taking the step of marriage. However, she also commented: 'I don't think it is absolutely necessary to live with somebody to know them all that well.' With her recent boyfriend, her flat had become the base for their sexual relationship since he was still living with his parents. She also knew that her parents would have been upset if he had moved in with her.

Morag, the student nurse, commented: 'I wouldn't marry someone without living with them. You really don't know what they're like until – I mean there might be something that really annoys you about them.' Her sister was already living with her boyfriend and had been for four years, so she knew her parents would accept it. She also cited the example of a friend who had moved in with her boyfriend despite her parents being devout Catholics.

Robert was already living with his girlfriend. He believed that it was important to try living together before marriage, arguing that he did not want to get married and then find that he was facing divorce like his parents. He was also worried about being tied down. 'It will tie me down, because I'm used to doing what I want. Ken what a lassie's like, saying "Are you going out again?" and that.' But when asked if living together had tied him down, he agreed that it had and said that he thought that marriage might not make any difference.

Accelerated careers?

The minority of young people who had already made a number of key life-cycle transitions could be described as having accelerated 'domestic careers'. Early motherhood and fatherhood are often unplanned events. Only a small minority of young people choose to marry young and to have children early. The long-term consequences of such early transitions are not clear, but in the short term looking after a baby in particular can have a profound effect on other aspects of personal life. Unless social networks can accommodate or assist with child care this may be a time of withdrawal from social contact and leisure activities.

Donna was one of our respondents who became a parent before she was 20. She had a job as a machinist in a local factory but her family household was affected by unemployment. Her father had been made redundant from a local pit and one of her two brothers was also unemployed. Her mother had looked after the home full-time throughout her childhood. At first interview she said she spent all her time with her 'pal', a female friend. By the second interview she had a baby and spent her spare time with her boyfriend. Surprisingly little else has changed. This was partly because her life never seemed to have been 'leisure-rich' either in the number, quality and variety of relationships, or in terms of a range of activities, partly also because her mother was able and willing to look after her baby when she wanted to go out.

When asked if she spent much time at home during the first interview she said 'Not really, I just usually get my dinner and watch *Neighbours*, get changed and then just go out to my pal's.' Most nights during the week were spent round at her pal's house or with her pal at home often 'just watching telly'. She had a TV in her own bedroom. She also visited one of her brothers who lived nearby. He was unemployed and separated from his wife, and she would sometimes go in the evening 'to see how he was getting on' and for a chat. At the weekend her pal and she would sometimes go to the pictures and they always went to the local social club for a drink. Her brothers also drank there.

At the second interview, when asked who she spent the most time with, she said 'The baby'. Asked whether she socialised at all, she said: 'Aye. I go out at weekends. I go out on a Saturday [usually to the social club] with my boyfriend.' On further questioning, she talked about going out with two other women friends from work and with whom she was at school, although her previous best pal was no longer mentioned. The activities she took part in with women friends were the same as before she had the baby: 'Just go round to their houses or they come here.' Her only male friend was the boyfriend of one of her two women friends. She also saw her boyfriend virtually every day. He worked during the day and dropped by at some point in the evening. On Sunday they often took the child together to his house and during a weekday she sometimes walked there with the baby and chatted to his mother for something to do. She and her boyfriend were talking about marriage and, unlike the majority of respondents, Donna was much keener on marriage than cohabiting.

Keith and his girlfriend already had a child before they started to plan their marriage. He and his girlfriend had found the transition from going out with each other to living together and looking after a baby a difficult one. In particular, there had been conflict between them over the division of labour in the house.

> Well the first two or three months we fell out quite a lot, like because she's the same age as me, she's twenty she's the same as me, she's always had everything done for her by her mum and dad. She's always had her meals set down to her. And that's what I was expecting when I came home from work every night. But her with [the baby] she was that tired she could not be bothered making a dinner and all this. But she's settled down now obviously. Because I think it is a big jump, moving into a new house to start with because you're not used to getting up and putting the washing on, doing the dishes, putting the dinner on, all that sort of thing.

Keith thought there was no difference between being married and living together, 'just a piece of paper'.

Valerie had chosen to marry when she was 17, having gone out with her boyfriend, who was then 21, since she was 14, and been engaged since she was 15. The timing of their marriage was partly to do with the system of allocating housing. She explained that her fiancé

> had actually put us down as an engaged couple to the housing place, and the woman said if we gave a date for our wedding she would be able to put us on the seven-month waiting list for a house. So he just talked it over with me and we thought the sooner we got married we would be able to get a house quicker.

She and her husband planned their first pregnancy and she was pregnant at the second interview, at age 20.

Valerie's work history fits with the view that early marriage and parenthood are more attractive when occupational opportunities are very limited. She left school without any qualifications and, after a few months' unemployment, went on YTS, which gave her a diploma in typing. On the back of her first questionnaire she complained bitterly that despite this diploma she could not get an office job. She eventually settled for a part-time cleaning job and then managed to get a part-time job in a shop. However, work was still important in her life, partly because her social life was limited and she and her unemployed husband had very little money to spend on 'going out'. She was on maternity leave at the second interview but was already missing the contact with other people that she had through work.

Donna, Valerie, Keith and Robert had all made two or more key transitions by the age of 19 – leaving home, making a future commitment to a partner, establishing a new home with a partner, marriage, having a child. All were from working-class backgrounds and three – Donna, Valerie and Robert – had left school with few or no qualifications and had poor job prospects. Although this was the case for both young women, they were not anticipating escaping from work through having children. Donna's work history was on the face of it much 'healthier' than Valerie's but her prospects were perhaps more limited. By her own assessment there was no hope of any form of promotion. Her work task, sewing straight seams down the sides of garments, held no challenge and the only variety she could hope for was occasional work sewing on collars, a job she had already done to the point of its also having become routine. Parenthood may be a happy accident in this context. Because of the back-up of her mother, Donna's life was enhanced by having a baby rather than radically transformed.

For some young people lack of success in education and the uncertain satisfactions of employment are accompanied by a narrow, if not impoverished, personal life. Donna, Keith and Robert never had a period of their teenage years in which their social life centred on mixed-sex groups. For each of them a partner added another dimension to a previously single-sex social life which continued in parallel unaffected by the new relationship. The form of their same-sex social life assumed heterosexuality and in the case of the men celebrated masculinity. Keith and Robert continued to go 'out with the boys', legitimated in Keith's case by his membership of the Territorial Army. Donna continued going round to see women friends but in their homes, never in a setting which might be deemed inappropriate for women who already had boyfriends.

Conclusions

At one extreme a young person's home life can open up opportunities for expanding leisure activities and widening social networks, while at the other it can narrow these horizons through increased demands for devotion to household duties. Different career trajectories clearly also bring different resources and opportunities for social contact and leisure. Leaving school was most likely to result in schoolfriends losing contact when they were scattered geographically and without any basis for regular contact. Different post-school destinations brought very different opportunities for making new friends. Those who remained in education maintained daily contact with others of their own age. Some young people found themselves working in settings where there were no others of their own age. Those who had come from coeducational schools often found themselves entering a sex-segregated world of work or training. Participation by the unemployed in many sorts of social activity was limited because of their low income. Hence area variation in the distribution of the career trajectories followed between 16–18 and 19–20, affected patterns of social participation and leisure.

Were certain patterns of change in personal life typical of 16–20-year-olds? Leisure settings changed from youth clubs to discos; friends and partners were becoming more central figures in personal decisions than parents and family. The young people who spoke most about enjoying time with their parents were those who had been able to leave home without any substantial obstacles. The pub became the main site of social life outside the home and the TV remained the main source of entertainment within the home. The survey material suggested a general transition in patterns of sociability, with girls a couple of years ahead of boys, from same-sex friendship, through mixed-sex groups, to a social life organised around a partner and ultimately marriage. The interview material offered a more complicated picture. At any one time even those with very restricted social networks had more than one social scene, their friends or friend, their partner and their families.

The common pattern, for both young men and women, was to retain a 'best friend' relationship and/or regular occasions for going out with a group of same-sex friends despite going out with a partner. But the form this took varied between classes and career trajectories and displayed different degrees of leisure richness. Many of those following predominantly working-class career trajectories inhabited a sex-segregated social world: for young men the main sites for meeting 'the lads' were public places, the pub and club; while young women met more frequently in each other's homes. These meeting patterns were attenuated but not disrupted by having a partner. The partner relationship was kept separate. In contrast, the more middle-class and academic career trajectory approach was both to integrate the partner relationship into ongoing social life and to retain some independent relationships. This was possible because of the wider range of prior social relationships, including opposite-sex friendships and mixed-sex groups.

There were also various intermediate positions depending on the types of social world being potentially brought together at the beginning of a relationship with a partner.

While it can be argued that the number and range of contacts people have and the variety of activities in which they participate make them more or less 'leisure-rich', ultimately this is a value judgement. But in terms of number and range of contacts and activities, a class hierarchy was apparent both in terms of material and personal resources in the family home and in terms of the wider range of social opportunities associated with middle-class career trajectories. Gender differences were harder to summarise. Differences were not as marked in the use of public facilities and in access to home resources as we might have expected. But girls were on average worse off financially than boys. Unemployed young people of both sexes were those whose leisure was most impoverished.

It has been argued that the need to 'find' a boyfriend focuses young women on a restricted range of activities and blinds them to others (Hendry, 1976; 1983; 1989). Our conclusion is that having a boyfriend disrupts the social life of some girls and not others. Although going out 'with the girls' might no longer be legitimate in the boyfriend's eyes, social relationships with other women involving going round to friends' houses to chat or watch television remained unaffected. As Griffin (1985) observed, those girls who did not have boyfriends were particularly disadvantaged if their friends who did stopped going with them to discos and pubs. The legitimacy for boys of going 'out with the lads' was not contested in the same way but rather the number of nights involved. Many young people came to arrangements whereby it was possible to preserve something of their prior sex-segregated social world. Our evidence suggested that young women more often took their boyfriends' friends as their friends, than vice versa.

The assumption that a 'domestic career' is for girls a higher priority than an occupational career, with the converse being true for boys, is not borne out by our data. What most young people wanted and hoped for was a job which provided an income and some intrinsic satisfaction. At the point of leaving school young women invested paid employment with as much significance and hope for their future as young men did. The young working-class women we interviewed who were already married, and those who were mothers, had not 'chosen' this route simply to escape from the realities of limited job opportunities (see also Penhale, 1989) and the grind of the unskilled work that was available. (For some young people parenthood was more accident than choice.) Even poorly paid and boring jobs were valued as sources of contact with other people in an alternative social setting to the home.

But, at the same time, for those in unskilled jobs, personal and domestic commitments were not a threat to work commitments as they were for some young women with better career prospects. Hence, there were fewer disincentives in comparison; and having children early might even have advantages later on. As Wallace's (1987) work also demonstrated, young people will not wait for ever when it seems that no improvement in their financial situation is likely. At this point having a baby was seen as bringing additional pleasure to a situation which could hardly grow worse financially.

Nothing in the data suggests that accelerated careers will become more common; in fact, Continental trends towards extended education for more young people suggest the reverse. However, it is clear that once young people have settled on a partner, they usually want to live with that partner. Moreover, by the age of 19 most of our young people preferred to live in their own homes rather than in the parental home. Housing policies and income-support policies are full of contradictions, as Cusack and Roll (1985) have shown. Some assume dependency until the age of 25; others do not. If they continue to fail to take account of young people's desire to live independently of their parents with or without a partner an additional strain will undoubtedly be placed on families (Allatt, 1988; Allatt and Yeandle, 1991). When young people were able to leave home 'naturally' to go to college or university, they talked of a deepening in their relationship with their parents. This benefit could have extended to more young people if suitable affordable housing and the kind of income support that students receive had been available.

Chapter 5 LABOURER, CARER, DESIGNER, CHEF ... : THE MAKING AND SHAPING OF SOME CAREERS AND IDENTITIES

Introduction

In the natural context of everyday life the separate elements of the transition to adulthood in the areas of occupation, social life, family and politics become deeply interwoven. The previous chapters have looked at transition in the area of employment and personal life. In this chapter, drawing on the ethnographic research, we focus on the meaning of these experiences and portray something of young people's lives in the round.

The overall approach to the ethnographic work has been outlined in the introduction to this volume. Here we summarise some of the findings from the Sheffield studies (Bates, 1990; 1991a; 1991b; Quicke, 1990; 1991; Riseborough, 1992a; 1992b), based on young people moving through education and training. These ethnographies explored social processes influencing young people's career paths; the ways in which they experienced these; and the implications for the development of identity. Social class, gender, family background, structures and processes within post-16 education and training and the role of different occupational cultures were central themes in the analysis. All of these were expected to be central factors affecting processes of economic and political socialisation and the development of vocational identity. The ethnographies covered five contrasting groups of young people strategically chosen to allow us to explore these various influences on socialization. The groups ultimately chosen were defined by the occupational career trajectories they were on: a female YTS group training for employment in institutional care; a male

YTS group training for work in the construction industry; a group on a BTEC National Diploma course in fashion design; a group on a BTEC National Diploma course in hotel management and catering; and a group of sixth-formers heading for university.

In exploring the relationships involved between micro-level processes of socialisation and broader social structures, the research has drawn particularly on theories of social reproduction which have richly illuminated other studies of youth transitions (such as Willis, 1977; Griffin, 1985; Aggleton, 1987; Wallace, 1987; Hutson and Jenkins, 1989) and of vocational training (Bates *et al.*, 1984; Cockburn, 1987; Gleeson, 1989; Hollands, 1990; Lee *et al.*, 1990). However, while giving prominence to social class, gender and wider social structures in shaping young people's career paths, the Sheffield studies also sought to capture the creative responses of young people themselves in negotiating their transitions (see also Bates, forthcoming).

The following account provides a series of cameos of the five groups who were the subject of the research. They illuminate some of the complex dynamics of the processes involved in socialisation at this stage of life. The studies also highlight the striking contrasts which emerge between the lives of different groups of young people as their career paths increasingly diverge. Each account covers broadly three areas: family background and education; the experience and perspectives of young people on each course; and emerging vocational identities and explanations of these in terms of socialisation.

YTS

As we saw in Chapter 3, the new form of transition to employment that emerged in the mid-1980s was YTS. Originally developed through the Youth Opportunities Programme as a response to youth unemployment, it later took on the mantle of supplying young people with the skills that it was said modern employment demanded. For young people, however, the ambiguities surrounding the programme's conception affected to the way it was received. Most young people wanted jobs, preferably with training, not training schemes. Consequently, YTS tended to be judged more as a poorly paid alternative to a proper job than as an extension of vocational education. These points are graphically displayed in the two accounts that follow, the first about a group of girls training for 'care' work and the second of boys training to be building operatives.

'Care' girls

This group of about 15 girls on a YTS 'caring' scheme generally met up in the mobile classrooms at the back of the college of further education which provided their off-the-job training. In winter they would huddle around a single heater; in summer they would often sit on the wooden steps in front of the mobile, tanning their legs. In general, they dressed inexpensively, in clothes often bought from market stalls. Nevertheless, sometimes the girls would proudly sport new gear such as a leather jacket, a see-through blouse, or travel bags. Most girls coloured their hair and new hairstyles were a frequent source of interest. The average 'care girl' was plump rather than slim and, while some were struggling to diet, food habits, lack of breakfast and the cheapness of such meals meant that they frequently opted for chips and buns in the canteen at lunchtime.

Working with this group involved making relationships with a hostile, conflict-ridden group split into factions. The everyday story of the group was one of feuds or trouble 'brewing', expressed, for example, in constant threats and assertions, 'I'm not speaking to her no more'; 'I'll get her back'; 'just you wait!'; 'we're gonna have it out with her'. Anger was directed mainly against other girls on the scheme who had caused offence; course tutors, who could find themselves faced with mutiny if they asserted the need to work; the liaison officer responsible for finding work placements, who was sometimes accused of showing favouritism towards individual trainees or towards other schemes; some staff on work placements, who 'give you all the dirty jobs'; and, at times, family members. Group members themselves in moments of conscious recognition of the turbulence and tension of life on the scheme described it as 'like a soap opera', with constant 'bitching'. Less humorously, individual girls would say 'I simply hate coming to college'. Nevertheless, a year after the course finished, trainees had warm memories of the course and many kept in touch with one another, suggesting the complex and multi-layered nature of their reactions.

At the outset of the research widespread dissension and bitterness were the most striking features of group life. Viewed in terms of social integration, the girls could be seen as poorly assimilated and reacting against most of the situations in which they found themselves. In so far as these situations involved elements of socialisation, these processes were certainly not operating smoothly. They were meeting resistance on every front, resulting in convoluted efforts on the part of their tutors, their peers and their families to accommodate the resulting friction.

Family and educational background

The group contained a number of girls not dissimilar from the fifth year 'wenches' vividly described by Davies (1984) who were similarly contemptuous of much of what the education system offered. The 'care' girls, however, were older and the experience of two further years of enforced 'schooling' appeared to have intensified their resentment. Mixed with these 'wenches' were 'little mice'. These were more conformist girls, who from their accounts had been quiet, rather than 'difficult', in school ('I were like a little mouse'; 'I used to dread speaking to a teacher') but who, like the 'wenches', had not performed well in tests and exams, despite diligent attendance. Both 'wenches' and 'mice' joined the scheme without any O-level equivalents, though most had passed some CSEs.

Detailed information on the occupations of parents revealed that they all came from working-class backgrounds, with fathers mainly in semi-skilled or skilled employment and mothers often employed in paid domestic work. The girls described family life mainly in terms of stressful relations with its various members, for example: a 'mum' who might nag them to help more with housework; a 'dad' who might work long shifts and come 'crawling home' to collapse exhausted on the sofa; a brother who would typically 'treat the house like a hotel'; and a resented sister who might constantly 'nick me hairspray'. Major conflict zones were: rules about times to be in at night; amounts of housework expected; and paying board. Arguments about coming home at night were intensified by parents' anxieties about 'murderers and rapists'. Parents often collected daughters from night club outings, even at 2 a.m. Coming home by taxi was acceptable only if they did not travel alone. Coming in late could cause 'scenes'. As Lisa explained: 'When I got in [late] they'd been up, they'd not gone to sleep, I'd made my dad right ill, he'd been out looking round the back of buildings and under the bushes for us.'

Some girls played the role of surrogate mother at home, undertaking considerable amounts of housework and childcare. The subjects of arguments about housework, for example, over obligations to hoover, dust, clean windows and 'wash pots' suggested that they were living in 'respectable' rather than 'rough' working-class families in which keeping up 'decent' appearances was important and household chores could not be allowed to 'slide'. In time off at home girls tended to live on the edge of the family, in bedrooms awash with gear and inaccessible to hoovering, and much time was spent watching television. Social change and more 'equal opportunities' during the 1980s seemed to have made little impact on girls' habitual recourse to a lifestyle based on 'bedroom culture' (McRobbie, 1978).

The need to leave home was experienced by most girls in varying degrees. However, there were both financial and emotional constraints and, consequently, living with a boyfriend or marriage were seen as the best chance of escape. For example:

My brother, he'll say, 'Why don't you leave home? You've got all these pressures on you, just leave, just turn your back and leave', and I says to him, I says, 'I can't turn my back on my family, it's all right for you'.

The generally oppressive quality of life at home, together with parents' expectations that they should pay board, appeared to sharpen desires for rapid entry into secure, relatively well-paid employment as a means of achieving a measure of independence. A job as a care assistant in homes for the elderly could be seen as satisfying these criteria while at the same time meeting parents' aspirations that they would enter a 'decent' job.

Experience and perspectives

One welcome feature of going to college for the purposes of off-the-job training for these girls was that it provided an opportunity to get away from home and mix with friends and 'enemies'. Here its perceived benefits stopped. The official modularised curriculum, consisting of a mixture of 'caring skills', science, communications, social studies and 'options', was regarded as irrelevant and reminiscent of school, which the group had already rejected: 'When I finish I'm gonna get all them modules, put them in a bonfire and burn the lot.' Time in college was valued as time to be with friends, to argue or 'have a laff' and 'fool around'. Set tasks in lessons were performed in a tokenistic way (four or five lines of writing in a one-hour session) and much time was spent instead on doing one another's hair, passing around mail-order catalogues, reading magazines, trooping off early to coffee and coming back late. On the whole resistance to college was expressed indirectly, with girls simply getting on with their preferred activities. If tutors pressed trainees to work, a semi-mutinous atmosphere could develop, or an 'almighty row' between tutor and trainee, which might well continue to fester after the event.

Interestingly, and revealingly, the one element of the curriculum which was invariably well received by the group was a course in first aid provided by an ex-nurse. Its appeal appeared to rest upon its obvious practical value, particularly in relation to the trainees' work placements. In distinct contrast with other sessions, trainees listened keenly to this tutor's instructions and hands would shoot up around the room to answer questions (e.g. 'What do you do if you think someone's having a heart-attack?' 'What do you do if you think someone's taken an overdose?'). This example of an apparently successful vocational curriculum suggested the possibility that resistance to training in educational institutions is not, as it often appears, an entirely intractable problem. In order to motivate such students it may be important to recognise that vocational 'relevance', broadly defined, will not suffice. 'Really useful knowledge' in the eyes of this group was that which has direct and immediate application within their currently preferred occupation.

The impact of YTS was deepened by the attendant peer-group interaction. While trainees valued the social aspects of coming to college, their relationships with other girls on the scheme were extremely fraught. Entire lessons could be spent with two girls 'at each other's throats'. As Sarah explained: 'They wind you up until you feel like exploding, scratching their eyes out.' The larger group of about 15 trainees divided roughly into three subgroups. One group centred on Mat, an extremely dominant and aggressive trainee who prided herself on her general toughness and experience of life. The group around her 'went with lads'; were from all accounts sexually experienced; enjoyed crude jokes; went out to pubs and, when they could afford it, one of the 'rougher' nightclubs in the city. In contrast, Sarah's group were quieter and viewed themselves as more mature. They objected to the aggressive remarks made by members of Mat's group but tried to ignore such incidents and 'brush it off'. They also went out with 'lads' but tended to prefer slightly more 'respectable' venues. The third group were the 'mice', two or three girls who were generally much quieter than the rest, saw themselves as shy, and as yet had no experience of boyfriends. Less socially and sexually experienced than other girls in the group, they easily became the object of jokes and were generally 'egged on' to 'get with it'. These three groups tended to have a stable core of about two girls, but beyond this there was some shifting of allegiances in the course of the various feuds.

The tensions on the course appeared to be fuelled by competition between group members relating to sexual attractiveness and job success, and, more broadly, the search for status. New clothes, new hairstyles, and reports of outings to the smarter nightclubs could provoke derisive comments, as could the kinds of 'lad' other girls went out with. One girl commented: 'Oh, everything that you do they pull you down for it. Just if I wear something they'll say "Oh my God, you look a state in that".' Jealousies over career success centred on progress in relation to work placements. Some girls managed to get better placements than others, in sites more likely to lead to jobs, for example, and were alleged to be 'sucking up to the supervisor' in such placements.

Unpleasant comments from group members could be seen as explicit and critical moments within what was in part a constant process of cultural preparation for a certain type of working-class womanhood. It was a culture which promoted, for example, glamorous 'dressing up' for special occasions; early sexual experience; getting engaged; an expectation of being married and away from home by the early twenties; a two-phase career (juggling paid domestic work with responsibilities at home and returning to work part-time or full-time as children grow up); physical toughness; a degree of emotional insensitivity; a preference for bluntness, for example, a capacity to give and take sharp-tongued remarks; and a superior, verging on scornful, view of males and male sexuality (e.g. 'I asked him if it were his 'dick' or a packet of polos!' – general laughter). Dominant peer-group pressures of this sort were not uncontested but resulted in the formation of protective subgroups which asserted other values.

Vocational identity and socialisation

While officially the YTS 'Caring' scheme provided training for a variety of jobs in the field of institutional care, the main occupation which trainees entered was that of care assistant in homes for the elderly. Most work placements were in such homes, including both local authority and private establishments. Through work experience the girls soon discovered the physically and emotionally demanding nature of such work. Their everyday tasks involved constant 'shit-shovelling' (cleaning up floors and beds soiled by the incontinent); cleaning commodes; bathing and re-dressing; changing catheters; 'getting belted' (by the senile); managing patients ('you have to ram the wheelchair behind her knees so she bends to get her to sit down'); and sitting with the dying. The work involved socially inconvenient hours and low pay. At the start of the course many trainees expressed intense dislike and sometimes fear of their work placements. As Di explained: 'To start with I thought "God, this is the pits, I'll never stick this."' Most had not expected to enter work in this field, having perceived 'caring' as working with children, the handicapped and perhaps the elderly.

However, after about six months on the scheme, while a few had dropped out and two were still determined to work with children, most had overcome initial reactions of dread and disgust and had developed an acceptance of and eventually pride in the job. Sally, for example, echoing the local liaison officer who monitored their progress, concluded: 'I've adjusted right well, I like it now.' Joanne enlarged on this: 'there are just parts of the job you have to try and get used to and overcome'. Moreover, while trainees generally complained bitterly about going to college, they often came to appreciate their placements ('I don't enjoy college, but I enjoy my placement'; 'I like it so much I could stay there all week'). By the end of the year the majority of the group were keen to find employment in this field, and hopefully to be kept on in their preferred placements.

How did these girls come to adjust to a job which, in terms of dominant cultural values, could be seen as highly undesirable? Among the groups studied the transformation of attitudes towards employment which took place among these girls was perhaps the clearest example of the impact of socialisation processes occurring between 16 and 19. These processes have been analysed more fully elsewhere (Bates, 1990; 1991b). In brief, it appeared that the YTS scheme provided an effective form of surrogate occupational social-isation, in the course of which not only were other career aspirations 'cooled out', but also the girls adjusted to the occupational culture of institutional care. Their adjustment was facilitated by previous cultural preparation within the family context. This orientated them in the direction of working-class gender-stereotyped jobs, as evidenced, for example, in the girls' accounts of their home lives which were heavily laden with stories of domestic work, nursing, physical violence and a variety of other forms of family oppression. The experience of the YTS scheme reinforced this preparation and filtered out girls who were not 'tough enough'. This process of continuous screening, within a buyers' market for labour, appeared to transform what might have appeared an undesirable job into a much sought prize, and most trainees 'buckled down' and fixed their ambitions upon being 'taken on' as a care assistant.

Building operative 'lads'

The study of 'labourers' was based on a group of lads on a building operatives YTS scheme training for unskilled and semi-skilled work in the construction industry. Lived experience ('havin' a laff', 'muckin' abawt', 'havin' a good time') was not something that happened to them but a happening daily accomplished. Silence was rare, visible only in the face of impersonal authority – for example, the police, the college principal, or employer. Generally, among themselves there was a ceaseless repartee – a battle of wits, banter, horseplay, leg-pulling, 'noises', wind-ups, all liberally spiced with expletives and humour. Theirs was 'strictly a consummatory group, devoted to the maintenance of patterns of self-entertainment' (Roy, 1973).

In the face of 'the outsider', there was massive group solidarity and cohesion. However, the group was characterized by differentiation along a 'being smart and streetwise' continuum. Some were much tougher than others; some had greater physical and sexual prowess; some had greater verbal dexterity than others. As such, there was often within the group a merciless verbal and physical abuse by 'the lads' of 'the mongs' – special needs students integrated with the mainstream and other ordinary students and regarded as inept. One day one such 'mong', 'Drippin', was thrown down a trench and 'the lads' attempted to urinate over him. 'Mongs' were constantly physically attacked. However, at the interface between the group and the wider social world, 'mongs' would be protected and incorporated.

Family and educational background

In many ways these lads were like those of Willis (1977), but two or three years older. They had next to no educational qualifications: 'School were a fuckin' waste of time, weren't it?' All came from unskilled or semi-skilled working-class backgrounds. At one end of the scale, there were those whose parents were in permanent employment, who were charged little or nothing for their board and were given other luxuries like clothes and holidays. At the other end, where there was parental unemployment, the group member could be a significant breadwinner, making a major contribution to the household economy. Somehow or other, in such a situation of tight finances, money was additionally made, begged, borrowed or stolen. Opportunistic theft was routine. All tended to be members of informal local networks which bought and sold televisions, videos, hi-fis, and so on, at significantly reduced rates, 'no questions asked'. In such a money-making situation, one could either be a 'principal' or a 'middle man'.

Group members tended to be serviced by their family. 'Ma' or sisters provided meals and laundry. None of the group claimed to undertake major regular domestic duties. They were beneficiaries of an indulgent 'boys will be boys' attitude which required only *ad hoc* domestic activity. Little conflict seemed to exist between parents and sons ('the old gal' had a special place in their affection), so long as 'trouble' was not brought home. As soon as it was, conflict tended to be between father and son and could get violent. One boy, Wolf, had a fight with his father because he was in trouble with the police, and was thrown out of the house. Overall, home was very much seen as a hotel, mainly reserved for sleeping and eating only. If they stayed in, it tended to be towards the beginning of the week, watching television when money was at its shortest.

Experience and perspectives on the Building Operatives Scheme

Generally the group liked coming to college ('It's fuckin' better than bein' sat at home on ya arse doin' nowt, ain't it?'), even though they often arrived late and left early. However, it was the informal group which was the motivation for attendance. The official curriculum, including communications, information technology, building theory and 'practical vocational projects', was experienced as 'a waste of time' and to be resisted. The college day was characterised by an utter indifference to all teacher instruction and a lack of any productivity, but very rarely amounted to outright warfare. In the face of desparate attempts on the part of teachers to extract a modicum of effort, the group could, in blistering and sweat-inducing activity, compress a day's supposed activity into minutes, usually under the condition that they could then go home. The rest of the day would be spent 'soldiering', for example, havin' a fag, listening to the walkman, leanin' on a shovel, throwing wire wall-ties into the insulated ceiling, bouncing a wheelbarrow as high as possible, switching off the cement mixer, going to the 'bog', sabotaging others' work, interspersed with the appearance of effort if any stranger should pass by. In other words, it was spent on 'the biggest occupation of all – how to pass the time, the dialectics of doing nothing' (Corrigan, 1979).

It was impossible for teachers to extract written work from the group, which never once manifested any positive commitment to the YTS course. In such a situation teachers had effectively withdrawn their teaching, a strategy grounded in a reasoning which stressed a 'pathological deficit' view of the group. The whole YTS programme, and by extension the teachers, were sapped by the group from within. Teachers filled the college day with a ritualised pedagogy, going through the motions in a situation where the group informally controlled the working day's time and space. An example was information technology. Here the trainees were officially supposed to be doing such things as spreadsheets, databases and costings. In order to keep the peace and minimise the destruction, the teacher allowed computer games to be played instead. The only valued part of the scheme was work placement, for this just might bring the possibility of 'real work', and could produce extra pay for overtime and Saturday working and the occasional 'backhander' from a generous employer or workmates.

The group's concern with sex and sexuality was central to their affirmation of selfhood. One of the rewards of college was the opportunities for 'chatting up the birds'. During the breaks, the lads could readily be observed sharing a single cigarette over hushed intimacies on the college corridors or in the pub. The rest of the time, when moving in convoy, they would chant 'Open your flaps!' to passing female students and teachers. Videoed and printed hard and soft pornography was a staple diet which was either vividly described or shown to those who had not seen it. Prostitution, what was available at what price and where, was discussed: 'You can have a sauna and a blow for ten quid, let's all go this Sata [Saturday].' One or two of the lads had a regular 'missus' but most were always looking out for 'tarts' who were 'good for a fuck'. If successful, by Monday morning they would be ignoring, ridiculing or insulting 'the slag'. 'Mongs' were simply voyeurs to all these activities and discussions.

If not 'chasing birds', then alternative 'fun' was sought – having a game of brag for pennies, or blowing up and exploding a condom in the refectory, spitting into someone's can of coke when they weren't looking, turning on all the taps in the toilets, going down to the chip shop and hanging around the street corners or going to the pub. At various times, the college authorities were thrown into a moral panic when there were outbreaks of urinating in the corridors and letting off fire extinguishers.

Much of the group's cultural offensiveness was especially reserved for black English students, particularly those whose origins were in the Indian sub-continent. All were subsumed under the rubric of 'Pakis'. Shouts of 'Get back home, you fucker' were commonplace and imaginary machine guns were fired. Physical violence was never far from the surface. One particular day, there was a smouldering 'Mexican stand-off' between the 'Pakis' and white youths (of which the YTS group was a part). Fifty or sixty people were involved in a shifting scenario. Any attempt at mediation was met with a hostile 'You don't fuckin' have to live with them, do ya!'. The specific origins of the conflict were obscure but seemed to have originated in a fairground the previous night and involved racial abuse of a white youth. There were skirmishes, pushings, shovings and threats throughout the college day and suggestions that knives were in the possession of both sides, but warfare did not break out. However, resentments were harboured for another day. The group insisted that the reason for their reluctance to participate in open conflict in college was they would be thrown off the YTS, lose their pay and the possibility of finding work through work placement.

In the evenings most went out. At the beginning of the week, this tended to be on the streets, or at a friend's home, 'hangin' around doin' nowt'. This was associated with vandalism and petty crime. For example, one group member, 'Graffiti', was intent on putting his 'tag' on every bus in the city. His paint was usually stolen. One evening he broke into the bus pound and sprayed every bus in sight. Friday, Saturday, and occasionally Sunday, were the 'big nights out'. These required 'smart gear'; the group would go on a pub crawl and then on to a nightclub. Alcoholic saturation was the desired state, often combined with soft drug use. If you had a car, or your mate did, this might be followed by cruising around the city looking for 'some action'. This would be followed by a takeaway, possibly vomiting and crawling into bed in the early hours. With a bit of luck, they might have 'got off with a bird' or had 'a bit of a ruck' outside the club. The next day would be spent in bed recovering. Monday was a favoured day for college absenteeism.

Some might go to a football match on Saturday afternoon; others went fishing sometime over the weekend. Several played football in a Sunday league. A big weekend might very occasionally be a 'great weekend' by car to London, or the seaside, sleeping rough for a drinking and 'bird-finding' weekend. All aspired to own a car at the earliest possible moment ('I want a black Capri, ya can't 'alf get the birds!') and usually 'informal' lessons were negotiated from a friend, neighbour or relative. Towards 17 pre-test formal lessons had to be budgeted for.

When pressed on the subject of politics, all the group insisted that they were Labour supporters. However, the group had many contradictory opinions on major political developments: they were, for example, supportive of the killing of IRA suspects in Gibraltar by the SAS, which occurred during fieldwork. This was tempered by a cynicism regarding all politicians: ('They're all out [for themselves], aren't they? None of them care about us') which might result in apathy with regard to Parliamentary politics at a later date. As such, if politics is seen as knowledge of and participation in the political system, then the group could be seen as apolitical. In the broader sense of 'politics' the group acted with considerable 'political' acumen in their effective resistance to the demands of vocational training.

Vocational identity and socialisation

Thus, the Building Operatives YTS unofficially reinforced the survival of working-class 'machismo'. At the end of the day workers or, more precisely, workers-in-waiting, were reproduced. Ironically, the more the lads resisted, the more they prepared themselves for dead-end jobs and subordinacy. They were constructing a subjective career trajectory, socialising themselves into becoming labourers – one kind of male, working-class career. In terms of the occupational hierarchy, these lads were ultimately going into 'dead-end' jobs, not into open-ended careers. What they were informally achieving was a potent and enjoyable anticipatory socialisation in the YTS 'way station', waiting for the road to 'real' work eventually to open. They knew, through all the informal social networks in which they were enmeshed, that they were not responsible for the demand for their labour. Their social network was their source of information about the state of the job market. Mates, relatives and neighbours were informants on its local conditions. They 'wagged off' YTS to go to the Careers Office, knowing they would be told there was no work.

Alternatively, they traipsed the streets, calling on any possible employer, leaving their name and telephone number, hoping for the return call that never came. They knew the YTS did not create employment opportunities and they themselves informally supplied the necessary cultural currency which would get them through their teens and the rest of their lives.

However, while on YTS, the lads would not take just any job that came along. They resisted 'shit work for shit pay'. The YTS was conceived by them as a minimal 'safety net', inseparable from the wider labour market. It gave them in the second year £35 per week and 'mates'. They knew that they were now in a kind of state-sponsored holding pen – an artificial secondary labour market. The YTS group was an informal Jobcentre which mediated the passage (or non-passage) to work. If the overall 'mates', 'money' and 'manhood' calculation was unfavourable, they stayed on the YTS, preferring its informal social relations and economic returns until real work came along. 'You must be fuckin' mad goin' to the steelworks for that pay, you, mad.' 'You 'ave to work, ya pinhead.'

Yet, ultimately, most were prepared to take any job offered. As Willis (1977) noted, 'particular job choice does not matter too much to the lads'. Work was central to their adult identities. During the scheme, one became a sign writer (his father getting him the job), another a van driver's mate; another took a job in the steelworks. Only one went into the building industry. The majority experience after YTS was unemployment. One lad was sent to a detention centre for mugging from a car and was reported as saying 'I'd rather be in prison than have no job'.

BTEC National Diploma students

These two studies focused on courses leading to Business and Technical Education Council (BTEC) National Diploma awards. Such courses fall within the Initiative's 'non-academic' or vocational trajectory which covers students who were not taking A levels but were nevertheless continuing their full-time education beyond 16. BTEC National Diploma courses are intended to be of high quality, vocationally relevant, and nationally consistent. Curricula must be specified in terms of 'competencies', or the intended outcomes of student learning. They lead to National Vocational Qualifications at level 3, cover most vocational areas and are one of the most extensively used systems of vocational qualifications in Britain. The normal entry requirement for a National Diploma course has been four O levels, although alternative qualifications are increasingly recognised. Given the close relationships between social class and educational achievement, these entry requirements tend to screen out students from the least privileged backgrounds, as can be seen in our two studies.

It was apparent from our initial review of BTEC courses that, while they all shared a strong emphasis on industrial relevance, not all awards could be translated with equal ease into employment opportunities. Therefore, our studies focused on two courses representing routes into contrasting labour markets: the expanding hotel and catering industry; and the more limited labour market in fashion design. The courses also differed from the point of view of the proportions of male and female students involved. On the hotel and catering course, which was the more secure and lucrative career route, there were roughly equal numbers. On the fashion design course, which turned out to be a much more precarious route to a secure and interesting job, the majority were female. We were interested in the ways in which both gender and the differences in students' employment prospects affected the ethos of the courses and the management of student aspirations.

BTEC fashion designers

The everyday lives of BTEC fashion design students were more privileged than those of YTS trainees in a variety of respects. Whereas YTS trainees resented their schemes and would have preferred real jobs, young people on the fashion design course valued their student status and many were seeking to use their BTEC National Diploma to enter art and design courses in higher education. Whereas YTS trainees were often despised as 'dregs' by other college students, fashion design students were more likely to be envied and labelled as 'weirdos', 'arty-farty', 'trendies' or even 'Sloanes'. The superior status of the fashion design course derived in part from the fact that it was a well-established, full-time college course leading to the BTEC National Diploma. In addition, however, entry into fashion design seemed to be valued as much for the cultural, social and, ultimately, marital capital expected to accrue from a career in this field as from the job itself. As Angela explained, looking back on starting the course, 'You think you're going to go to London and meet all these famous people and have a studio and all that ... '.

Their relative advantages did not, unsurprisingly, figure prominently in BTEC students' definitions of their situation. While they generally thought they were on a 'good' course ('It teaches you how really serious you've got to be if you want to get on'), they were by no means a contented group but frequently 'moaning and groaning' to one another. However, unlike the YTS trainees who were more aggressive and combative, fashion design students were less spirited in their expression of dissatisfaction and conflicts were more subterranean. Resentment was more likely to be expressed by 'bursting into tears' than through anger and, whereas, among YTS trainees, 'open warfare' frequently broke out, in this group names were called 'behind backs' and the appearance of civility was more often maintained. In college students were often found 'lounging' over work (from the tutors' perspective), bemoaning the endless pressure of assignments, worrying about what they would do after the course and about their lack of money. For the purposes of this research this prevailing mood of worry and discontent was explored in terms of its possible relationship with the group's experience of vocational training and the implicit processes of occupational socialisation.

Family and educational background

First impressions of fashion design students suggested that they came from rather more affluent and comfortable homes than the YTS trainees. However, details of parents' occupations revealed that both groups were recruited largely from the working class, although the fashion design group was more socially heterogeneous, drawing students from 'upper' working-class and 'lower' middle-class backgrounds. In Julie's words: 'There are no roughs and no really brainy ones. We're sort of in-between.'

The crucial difference in family circumstances between the two groups was the possibility of family sponsorship, or, in other words, the extent to which families were able to support students, both psychologically and financially. Fashion design students spoke of mothers and fathers who 'don't want me just to get a dead-end job' or were 'behind me all the way'. Parents provided financial support in the form of continued maintenance beyond 16, paying for college trips and expensive equipment. They provided physical space for students to work and appeared able to tolerate the sort of untidiness suggested by Tracy's account of working at home: 'I start off in my bedroom and when things get too cluttered in the bedroom I come and clutter the rest of the house.' Moreover, they were not expected to contribute greatly to housework in view of the demands of the course: 'I walk the dog, wash the pots occasionally, keep my room clean or at least I'm supposed to.' Interestingly, however, while parents of students in this group seemed keen to invest in their careers, they had little knowledge of opportunities in fashion design and could not assess the value of the course or the realism of their children's goals. In this respect they contrast sharply with the parents described by Roker (1991), in her study of private education, who were well informed about the routes to high-status careers.

Family sponsorship was critical not only at the stage of entry into the BTEC course. Variations in family support could be seen to affect student performance during the course and career routes thereafter. At one end of the spectrum were the more affluent students who sometimes incurred the resentment of others: 'There's Vera, for example, she didn't bother when her Dior glasses broke and she expects driving lessons. She wouldn't dream of getting a job.' At the other end, students with financial difficulties sometimes took several part-time jobs, and consequently their work suffered. For students who found the course a financial struggle, the attractions of higher education were offset by the prospect of continued poverty and the limits which this placed upon their social lives, growing debt as a result of loans, and the feeling of being a 'burden' on parents. The need to obtain loans in order to fund higher education was an emotive issue among all students. It was notable that those who could not expect any further financial support from home were the most reluctant to consider taking their training further to Higher National Diploma level.

Experience and perspectives

At the outset of training many students viewed the fashion design course as a route towards a glamorous, creative and lucrative career. While brought up in the 'Socialist Republic of South Yorkshire', they were not exactly 'Thatcher's children', but their ambitions had taken on something of a Thatcherite hue. Conversation was laced with talk of London studios, Jasper Conran, Helen Storey, making 'loads of money', working on top magazines and of becoming 'an amazing designer'. Some saw themselves as already having resisted the advice of careers officers or parents to do something more 'realistic'. As Jean explained: 'My careers officer, she said "you're living on cloud nine"'. Most were students who did not want to be 'stuck in an office' and were, at the very least, hankering to do 'something different, not just work in Kwiksave'.

This characteristic orientation towards individualistic career success in a group of young people, mainly female, whose academic qualifications rarely exceeded four O levels, or a BTEC first certificate, was problematic. Judging from the occupational destinations of previous students, few, if any, were likely to become successful fashion designers in their own companies. Most would work, at least for a spell, somewhere within the garment industry in jobs ranging from designer and assistant designer to pattern cutter and machinist. The aims of the BTEC course were to provide a realistic introduction to opportunities within this industry and to develop some of the necessary vocational skills. The gap between student aspirations on the one hand, and labour market opportunities as mediated through the course on the other, resulted in an underlying tension between student and tutor attitudes.

Student complaints centred on three related themes: the industrial emphasis within the course; the amount and standard of work expected; and 'crits' – the evaluation of coursework by tutors. The industrial emphasis was seen as limiting the scope for creative design: 'Industry, that's your whole thing, you can't do anything one off. It's just for industry, you've got to do everything, even a lay, like you would do it in industry.' The curriculum was indeed explicitly industry-led, as is increasingly the case with vocational courses within the 'new' further education. Tutors placed constant emphasis in teaching on encouraging awareness of the constraints of the market and production processes. Students characterised them as only caring about the 'three Ps': punctuality, presentation and pattern-cutting.

A closely related issue was the volume of work which was expected: 'I didn't expect anywhere near this amount of work.' The course was based on continuous assessment and the completion of assignments was a constant source of worry: 'You could work 24 hours a day and never finish everything that needs to be done', one girl complained. The tutors' emphasis on keeping to deadlines was justified as a form of preparation for work within the garment industry and this rationale was to some extent recognised, at least by some students. Nevertheless, they felt that work demands were at times excessive.

The other major concern focused on 'crits' and tutors' evaluation of students' work generally. 'Crits' was the term used for critical evaluations of student work, which tutors carried out regularly and often in public. Such 'crits' were considered unnecessarily harsh and destructive:

> When they saw my first design they said the designs were wrong for the inspiration, the inspirations were wrong for the season and the fabric was wrong as well ... they just tore it all to pieces and they did this with quite a few people.

'Crits' were justified by tutors on the grounds of teaching students 'the ropes':

> In industry they can be quite cruel. The woman I worked for thought nothing of showing you up in the middle of the design room, pulling things to pieces and throwing them at you ... It can be quite horrible ... there's no nice cushioned welcome and showing you what to do. You have to be very tough to get anywhere.

By the end of the course students were more habituated to the ritualistic public denigration of work which was not up to standard. Vera enlarged on this:

> To start with, I was thinking 'Oh God' and getting really worked up about it and the more I got worked up about it, the worse I did ... now it doesn't bother me as much. If you think 'I am not going to get upset no matter what they say about this', you don't really get upset.

Students continued to object, however, to their tutors' constant 'nagging' over the quality of their work and related warnings that they would never get a job in the industry.

These various dissatisfactions with the BTEC course were viewed differently by the tutors involved. They were concerned that students were ill prepared for the labour-market opportunities actually available to them and were failing to channel their efforts into acquiring marketable skills. 'They are expecting to get jobs as fashion illustrators and designers. They don't want to work for Top Shop or Marks. It's too boring, not glamorous enough.' They were also doubtful of students' complaints about overwork: 'They think they're working [at home] but they're watching *Neighbours* at the same time.' At the classroom level these contrasting views resulted in a struggle over the definition of appropriate course content, pedagogy and related assumptions regarding student career prospects – the 'noise' of struggles over 'cooling out'.

Turning from work to social life and sexuality, the students' attitudes were less accessible than those of young people on YTS. Sexuality was a more private matter not, for example, for discussion in the dinner queue, reflecting broader differences in class cultural codes. General views on social life, boyfriends and marriage were, however, discussed. Lack of funds and pressures of work meant that many did not enjoy the lifestyle they would have preferred. Evenings tended to be spent at home, watching television and working on projects, sometimes with a friend round. When students did find boyfriends, these young men were often 'dropped'. The more ambitious students planned to marry in their late twenties, once their careers were established. Students planning to enter employment straight after the course were less willing to make these social sacrifices at this stage of their careers: 'You can be one of these people that everybody loves ... or you can be like a person that works, works, works, works.'

The group overall tended to divide into 'workers' and 'socialisers', and related cliques formed. There was a tendency for the more studious and committed girls to come from the more affluent backgrounds and 'socialisers' to come from less prosperous homes. Once cliques formed they tended to act as a further influence on vocational orientations, reinforcing the effects of family background. In this way vicious or virtuous circles were created which contributed towards the process of filtering students towards different occupational strata.

Vocational identity and socialisation

The BTEC fashion design course was perhaps the most uncertain career route of the five studied in terms of its likelihood of leading to related employment. It attracted students with high hopes of glamorous employment as designers, but few were likely to achieve this goal. At times there were hints that the hidden agenda for some students was glamorous marriage, suggesting the appeal of a 'yuppified' domestic career which would raise the status of the female stereotype. Social class, family background and gender were major factors influencing entry into this trajectory, operating through the provision of various kinds of family support, and through deep assumptions about appropriate female careers.

In the course of training the group could be seen as undergoing a fairly intense period of socialisation directed towards adjustment of their aspirations and the inculcation of marketable skills. These processes of socialisation also served to filter students towards different occupational strata and, in so doing, interacted with social class and family background. Thus the quality of 'family sponsorship' affected levels of individual performance within the course and career routes thereafter. On completing the course students moved in three broad directions. About a third were successful in gaining entry into higher education courses in the field of art, design and textiles. Another group entered work, finding low-paid jobs somewhere within the garment industry as pattern-cutters or machinists. At least another third became unemployed or entered quite different jobs, mainly in offices, shops and garages. Those who became unemployed sometimes attempted to become self-employed with the help of an Enterprise Allowance. Essentially they were dressmakers, working from home, often making bridesmaids' dresses and perhaps hoping one day to open a shop. This was probably the least lucrative and least secure career outcome.

The group were poorly adjusted to the labour-market opportunities available to them, and some remained so throughout the course. They were, however, relatively compliant in responding to the pressures of the course, certainly compared, for example, with YTS trainees, and there was little overt resistance. Protests, in so far as these were observed, were expressed as worry and discontent which could be seen as a result of the various stresses of the course. A number of reasons can be suggested for their compliance. First, their different cultural backgrounds meant that overt, aggressive conflict was not a taken-for-granted mode of expression and means of negotiation of differences. Second, these students valued, if only instrumentally, many aspects of their training. Third, from the students' perspective, significant career stakes were involved in the successful completion of the course which might be jeopardised by non-conformity to tutors' expectations.

BTEC catering and hotel management

This study focused upon a social class- and gender-mixed group in the second year of their BTEC National Diploma course at a tertiary college. The course was intended for students wishing to enter the hotel, catering and leisure industry at the supervisory level, or for those going on to BTEC Higher National Diploma courses or a degree, with a view to entering at a more senior managerial level. The majority of the students were from skilled working-class backgrounds, with a significant minority from lower-middle-class backgrounds.

The college was in a strong 'buyer's market', given the unemployment pool in the city. The official entry requirement for the course was five O-level equivalents, but most students had considerably more than this. Patterns of selective recruitment favoured the well-qualified, behaviourally conformist, ambitious, socially and geographically mobile 'respectables'. The course was 'marketed' on the basis of the employment prospects for students. Indeed, throughout the 1980s employment in the industry outpaced that in the economy as a whole. In 1989 a joint report was published by the Hotel and Catering Board and the National Economic Development Office regarding ways of maintaining recruitment and retention in the context of the projected reduction in the numbers of 16–19-year-olds in the 1990s. Tutors and students were wise to the labour-market opportunities. The students stressed repeatedly: 'There are jobs in this industry, that's why I'm doing it'.

Experience and perspectives on the BTEC Catering and Hotel Management Course

Against the recent history of economic depression in the city, many students emphasised the excitement, glamour and romance of their chosen occupational field. They did indeed believe this course would make the 'world their oyster', giving them the opportunity to leave home, to travel extensively, to eat well, to meet interesting people and, generally, to have 'a good time'. 'I'm hoping to get a job on the *QE2*, it's the Ferrari of cruise liners, isn't it'. Their overall orientation was highly instrumental. They had an acute awareness that the BTEC qualification would definitely lead to a 'good career', rather than a mere 'job'. This instrumentality provided the key for understanding the lived experience of the college course by the students.

The college had a strong tradition of vocational training in hotel management and catering. Among its amenities were simulated hotel areas, and an 'haute cuisine' restaurant open to the public. The corridors, kitchens and refectory of the college were filled with students, some in mufti, others dressed in freshly laundered chefs', waitresses' or waiters' uniforms. Students looked freshly scrubbed and presentable, their hair at a 'suitable' length. There were no symptoms of any distinctive 'youth culture'. They conformed to all the traditional requirements of 'top' hotels and restaurants. Restaurant customers were impressed by the courtesy, confidence, articulateness, demeanour and accomplishments of the students.

The students found the college demands in terms of attendance (five days per week with some free time between lectures), combined with continuous assessment and examinations, onerous as they juggled college with work and leisure. All had experience of part-time jobs. Indeed, among themselves they informally ran a 'Job Shop', specializing in 'job hopping', as they managed their progress through the course. There was no paucity of such jobs and, as hotel and catering students, they were favoured in the marketplace. Indeed, the college facilitated 'job shopping and hopping' with a well-used 'situations vacant' board and the encouragement of contacts with, and visits by, would-be employers. Further, the students justified the part-time work in terms of evidence of work experience for their curricula vitae, which were quite professionally put together.

The main reason for part-time work was instrumental. It was a material means to see them through college, financing their social lives and reducing dependence upon their parents. Indeed, there were no visible signs of material deprivation. As was found in the case of fashion design students, home backgrounds were mostly very supportive, providing the facilities for meeting college demands. Leisure was primarily pubbing, clubbing (usually 'the better venues') and cinema-going, serving as 'oppositional' (Parker, 1974) recuperation from the demands of college and work.

During the course, the students operated a sophisticated 'pick and mix' regarding paid jobs, college work and 'having fun and a social life'. The emphasis given to each varied with current work demands. The most common pattern was that all students worked, usually full-time, during vacations; most 'retired' or 'went on short-time' during examination and revisions periods; and all combined work and college during 'normal' college time. Leisure was then fitted in around these demands.

This work experience strengthened pre-existing commitments to the course, gave practical expression to the students' aspirations and kept their knowledge of the subtleties of the labour market up to date. Indeed, many could have left the college and immediately worked full-time but were aware of the distinction between 'job' and 'career' and wanted the latter. Offers of work, when they finished the course, were often made by their employers but were accepted only by a minority who did not wish to go on to higher education.

Not surprisingly, there were manifestations of physical fatigue in college. It was quite possible for a student to be in college all day, dash home and do some homework, then work in the evening and go on to a club until the early hours. In such a situation, students questioned not only the sheer quantity ('It's homework, more homework, assignment, assignment, test and test, isn't it?') but also, more importantly, the quality of the curricular provision. Much of the course was perceived – paradoxically, given its vocational slant – as irrelevant, impractical and of doubtful utility. 'Common sense' and work experience led many students to view certain course contents as trivial and a waste of time (for example, making beds and cleaning glasses):

> I got a distinction in waiting. I am a waiter at the Imperial, I'm a good waiter but you are bound to be after about 18 months doing it, aren't you? I mean, Christmastime last year I was waiting 60 hours a week! So that aspect of college is a waste of time really, isn't it?

Further, as students' career interests developed, different students gave different meanings to what was relevant. As was noted in our other studies, definitions of vocational relevance were highly specific. For example, what was relevant to a would-be hotel manager was not relevant to a would-be chef. Yet both were undertaking a common syllabus. Also they felt that certain vocational subjects (such as, computing and bookkeeping) were taught in irrelevant ways. In particular, they were not applied to the hotel and catering industry. Consequently, these subjects were experienced, like traditional academic knowledge, as 'abstract, compartmentalized and external' to the learner.

> Bookkeeping is relevant because you have to do it in a hotel but the way he does it! He never mentions hotels or catering, he doesn't apply it in any way. He's mad about bookkeeping and he can't make sense of anyone who isn't. He's a right plonker!

More criticism was made by the students of their teachers. They were often bored by the largely one-way transmission in the classroom, where students were expected to 'bank' notes – copy from blackboards, from overhead transparencies or accept endless dictation. The biggest source of complaint was that 'the teachers just do not care about us'. Students also questioned the apparently arbitrary and random teacher differentiation and evaluation of their work, which was based on assignments, preferring the neutral criteria associated with external public examinations.

Within this overall context of curricular and pedagogical dissatisfaction, combined with extra-college work and leisure demands, there was a high rate of student absenteeism. This was often of a strategic nature; students knew the dangers of being labelled a 'bad' student, and often used absenteeism to undertake pressing college work, as well as to recuperate from work or leisure. Similar strategic absenteeism was noted in the study of fashion design students.

Despite all this general discontent, the classrooms observed were characterised by student passivity and conformity. Teachers had no overt disciplinary problems. Any 'outside' observer would identify a harmonious learning environment. The conflict between teacher and taught was sublimated and latent, and made manifest in student-only arenas.

In such a contradictory situation, of high student instrumentality combined with college discontent, 'making the grade' (Becker *et al.*, 1968) with the minimum of effort became important to the students: 'The only thing that gets me to college is to get that grade basically because you want to do whatever you want to do after college.' Grades were the desirable 'currency', passports to higher education and good jobs, which explained much of the student passivity: 'You get into a situation where jumping the fence is more important than real learning.' Students knew that the granting of grades gave teachers a great deal of power and felt that grades could be used malevolently against them (cf. Werthman, 1978). Students in such a situation coped by employing various 'impression management' techniques, sometimes to the point of sycophancy, which confirmed the prevailing aura of conformity. There was an accommodation through ritual:

> One lecturer, I want to strangle her, I do, but I don't because, you know, you can't. So you smile and keep 'em sweet. People don't rebel. They'll go up to a certain mark but they'll not shout and scream and put their career on the line.

Vocational identity and socialisation

Notwithstanding the above scenario, the majority of students at the end of the course intended going on to higher education. The students attached much greater significance to the extrinsic rewards of their education than to the intrinsic ones. They wanted the BTEC qualification without the BTEC 'training': 'I don't regret doing the course but I am just sick of doing it.' In fact, most students went on to polytechnic, college, or occasionally university. A minority of students expressed the view that they were 'sick and tired of college and I'm having a rest from it' and easily found work, usually as trainee managers. Yet even these students, who had chosen to enter the labour market, did not entirely reject education and its credentials. Such students said they intended to pursue employer-led programmes, part-time education, or return later if there were not sufficient career payoffs in work:

> I'm tired of college work. I was all set for poly but I just changed my mind. I thought 'I am 19 now. I'll get a job and if I feel I am not achieving anything I can always go back to polytechnic. It is always going to be there.'

This overall student subculture, characterised by strategic compliance, impression management and a sublimation of overt conflict, formed a circle with the occupational culture the students had already entered or were about to enter, and with the wider 'respectable', deferential and aspirational parent culture in which they originated. All three cultures were complementary and characterized by a 'privatization' of any 'rebellion' or 'resistance'. The contradiction between public behaviour and private attitudes can be seen as 'corresponding' with the demands of employment (cf. Bowles and Gintis, 1976). Moreover, in this as in other service industries the public–private dichotomy was reflected in and indeed provided for within the architecture of the workplace – for example, the front and back regions of hotels and restaurants (cf. Goffman, 1961). One hotel, for example, where students had work experience had signs behind doors with the reminder: 'Smile, you are entering a public area!'

Paradoxically, the result of training was that students were exceptionally well equipped for the *self-presentation* aspects of their industry. There was 'stress and strain' (Roberts, 1984) in transition but it was not overt. As such, the students' lived experience of the BTEC course provided them with a 'practical', 'relevant', 'vocational' and 'utilitarian' preparation for the actual realities of work and life. Informally, the course was engaged in *occupational socialisation*, developing and handing on a range of 'transferable "life-skills"', to nurture a trajectory and establish an occupational identity.

Sixth-formers

The traditional education route after age 16 is to A levels and higher education. It ensures access to the routes to professional occupations, and though by no means all sixth-formers survive it, those that do constitute an elite. The study involved a mixed group of some 20 sixth-formers, all of whom were taking A levels. The sixth-form centre where the study took place was part of a consortium of four schools grouped together to provide a greater range of A levels. Most students attended classes in more than one establishment.

Family background

Whether relations with parents were perceived as harmonious or in conflict, they were the principal agents in maintaining the students' sense of self and identity. When they spoke about their family backgrounds, they did so in a way which suggested that they themselves felt at least partly if not totally immersed in their parents' world. This world was one in which, in the majority of cases, social mobility was a critical and relatively recent experience. Sixteen students had lower-middle-class fathers – self-employed craftsmen, owners of small businesses, foremen or white-collar workers in the commercial sector. Most of the fathers, and in some cases the mothers, had begun their working careers in skilled manual or other working-class jobs and had moved on to 'better things', usually, although not always, because they had been made redundant when a steelworks had closed down. Nearly all parents were perceived as aspiring and very concerned that their offspring should receive the 'good education' which they themselves had missed. For the most part both parents and children anticipated success in moving upwards and the 'ladder of opportunity' was an idea they appreciated and accepted as part and parcel of how things were. Thus their sense of self included the assumption that they were part of a social grouping which was in a relatively good position on the ladder and had a stake in society.

Students also recognised that, for their parents, the process of becoming fully-fledged middle-class people was far from complete, and that many were still culturally and emotionally attached to the working class. 'Our relatives and a lot of our friends are still from where we used to live' was a typical comment. Many still lived, and perhaps purposely chose to live, in private housing not far from their 'roots'. Others, however, by accident or design, had created considerable geographical and in some cases cultural space between themselves and their origins. The process of acculturation was incomplete and relentlessly ongoing: 'My dad doesn't go back there much now. He's even joined the golf club. I'm afraid he's bending with age!'

The point to note here is that being socially mobile and coming from families with 'roots' in the working class was a significant part of the 'framework of imagery' (Goffman, 1961) for judging themselves and interpreting their 'moral careers'. This contrasts with the findings of some previous studies of working- and upper-working-class and lower-middle-class girls (McRobbie, 1978; Frazer, 1988), for whom social class was not a relevant organising category.

Experience and perspectives

For most of these sixth-formers the overriding concern was to obtain good A-level results so that they could go on to higher education. Although they had some notion of what they would like to do eventually, specific career aspirations were not a major preoccupation at this stage. They felt they had taken 'sound advice' from teachers, backed up by parents: 'I'd sailed through O-level with flying colours ... teachers, mum, dad, everybody thought I should go on to do A level ... it just seemed the right sensible thing to do.' Of course, they expected it to be 'hard work', much harder than O levels, but they were prepared to 'knuckle down' and make a commitment. Some saw this as a 'sacrifice' ('I knew it meant I'd have no money and wouldn't go out much') but they were prepared to forgo these immediate pleasures for long-term gains and in any case life in the sixth form had some compensations: 'It's more like being a student than a pupil.' They expected to be treated as more adult and for the most part felt they were.

A key feature was the type of relationship which could be cultivated with teachers. Most said they had always 'got on well' with teachers, but now they were encouraged to see them as personal tutors, as career and academic advisers and even as friends. They were frequently involved in official social functions (such as trips and discos) organised by the staff–student committee. This was seen by staff as symptomatic of an important transition. As one teacher put it: 'You can see it happening during the sixth form. At first they're still dependent, always wanting praise. Then they start treating you more as equal.' As ideal pupils, they had always shared with teachers the formal values of school life and they now took this a step further by establishing informal personal relationships.

There was a degree of tension surrounding these new relationships. Teachers saw this in terms of role conflict: on the one hand being 'friends' and personal tutors, while on the other having to insist on conformity to meet examination board expectations. However, most students accepted this, which they saw as done 'for my own good'. In this respect they differed from BTEC fashion students, who tended to resist tutors' advice regarding their career prospects and to cling to unrealistic aspirations. After initial concerns about low grades for assignments, students were, in their teachers' terms, 'sensible' enough to recognise eventually their own 'strengths and weaknesses'; as they became more 'mature', they became more 'realistic'. A cooling out process was clearly at work here. Some would drop out before taking A levels; others were heading for failure or poor grades. But most of the group were optimistic about the future and the majority expected to end up in some form of higher education. Even if aspirations had to be toned down a little, they were still confident about ending up with a 'good job'.

Vocational identity and socialisation

The students' social world, while continuous with their parents', was being modified in subtle but significant ways. These transformations were partial and connected with moving up a notch or two on the social ladder to become fully-fledged middle-class people. The changes which occurred were not the same for all of them. All the students were 'rising' into the middle class, but their interpretations of what this meant differed and it was here that differences in emergent vocational and political identity could be detected. There were clearly some students who identified strongly with one aspect of their parents' world, namely petty bourgeois individualism. They made a conscious effort to remove whatever traces of working-class attributes were left in their own personalities and friendship groups, as they proceeded to cultivate middle-class friends and middle-class lifestyles. Their reference group were students whose parents could unambiguously be described as middle-class; who were, as one student put it, at the 'top of the spectrum' in terms of social background. This was not a large group but one which was overrepresented in the sixth form; its members tended to be cliquy, to belong to squash and tennis clubs, to go to certain up-market nightclubs regularly; they were the 'jet set' or 'pace setters', the ones with 'money behind them'.

Those students who positively identified with the 'pace setters' are referred to here as 'elitists'. Elitists were aware that they were not equal to 'pace setters' in terms of background and material resources, but aspired to a cultural affinity with them. The hierarchical nature of the social order was accepted as part of how things were, and was not perceived as a destructive force (see Robins, 1988). Some tended to talk disparagingly about the working class. Jo recalled having lived in a cheap private house near a council estate, but saw herself as having moved away 'from all that'. She felt that working-class people were unsuitable for many of the jobs which were currently available:

> Its going into the sort of tertiary, you know, private sector jobs and to be honest, a large proportion of the population won't be suited to that sort of job. I mean that rules out a lot of the working class to be honest.

Martin, originally from a school in a working-class area, described how 'if you were not careful your mates would drag you down'. He was referring to the working-class mates that he used to have; that is, 'if you could call them mates – they were always calling me "swot", you know, just because they weren't clever themselves'. Sexism was viewed as a working-class phenomenon; 'At some parties, they just treated the girls as "objects", like a can of lager! I don't go to those sort of parties – well there is a bit of that, but in the sixth form we tend to talk to girls more.' Like several of his contemporaries, he had made a conscious effort to cultivate middle-class friends. The only thing he now did with his old friends was go to football matches, and that not very often.

Like other elitists, this student expressed a negative attitude towards a group of YTS students (not those described earlier) who also used the sixth-form centre. It was evident that relations between these 'lads' and the sixth-formers were not good. There were complaints that the 'lads' were rowdy, smoked illegally and made a mess in parts of the centre where they were not supposed to be. Neil referred to the YTS group as 'looking like slobs, dressing like slobs and behaving like slobs'. Marie felt that, 'to put it frankly, they haven't got a brain between them', and Louise elaborated: 'They come in a couple of days a week and run riot, leave crisp packets all over the place, smoke where they like and just abuse it ... they're just yobs!'

When asked to explain educational failure, elitists were more likely to emphasise lack of ability than lack of family support. Their view of human nature tended to be that people were basically selfish and that the 'right' were more realistic in this respect than the 'left':

> Left wing is more helping less well off people in society, ... taking money from the richer people and giving it out to the poor ... Sounds pretty good, but I don't think it works like that. Right wing tends to give a more selfish impression, more go for what you can get and it doesn't matter about everybody else but I think that's what everybody is after anyway.

'Going for it' was a typical elitist phrase. They didn't particularly like Mrs Thatcher but she did at least 'go for it'. They perceived themselves as 'going for it' in terms of educational qualifications, but also in terms of earning money by doing part-time jobs, money which they spent on such things as driving lessons and skiing holidays. Their parents were comfortably off but not so well off that they could keep on financing their offspring's expensive leisure pursuits. In any case, going out to work and earning your own money was 'virtuous' behaviour; it meant you were not being a burden on other people. Provided it did not interfere with homework, it was all right to work in a shop on Saturdays. For some, money seemed to be a 'good thing' in itself. When asked about the best things in life, one said 'my family and my money'; another said 'my girlfriend who I love and my money'.

Jobs to which they aspired tended to be in the private sector – trainee managers, tourism, quantity surveying. They were aiming to go to university or polytechnic, but they did not value higher education for its own sake. If a really good job opportunity came their way in the near future, they would 'grab' it and forget about going on to higher education: 'If I got a trainee manager's job with Marks and Spencer, I'd go for it.'

Politically, this group tended to be Conservative or moving towards Conservatism. A few said they were not interested in politics. However, they were not perhaps as right wing as they thought. They supported state intervention in most things and did not believe in wholesale privatisation or the poll tax. The elitists were a minority, but they represented a cultural option for the rest of the group, some of whom were becoming more aspirant; others were oscillating between different perspectives and some were opposed to the elitist group, whom they described as 'yuppies'. Although they were a minority, one had the impression that elitists felt that they were swimming with the tide. And other sixth-formers knew this; it was only a matter of time before most of the others moved in the same direction.

This was certainly the view of those subscribing to another clearly definable perspective, who are called here the 'nostalgics'. This group saw themselves as a minority group of 'socialists' who, in contrast to the elitists, were swimming against the tide. They are described as 'nostalgics' because their attachment to working-class culture was retrospective and somewhat romantic. They felt that most of their colleagues, including even some of their closest friends, were becoming part of the 'yuppie generation' and were gradually becoming Conservative. 'The majority of them are Conservative. I get called Karl Marx and commie and things like that; it's only banter, but they're definitely right wing.'

If elitists emphasised the upwardly mobile, self-help aspects of the parent culture, nostalgics tended to identify with parents' affiliation to working-class origins. They saw their own movement into the middle class as problematic. The clearest expression of this perspective was provided by Julia, whose relationship with her father was conflictual precisely because she felt he was confused about his class position and voted Conservative, while she identified with working-class values. She felt her mother was still working-class, and so was the area in which they lived. Most of her friends were from working-class backgrounds and she did not try to distance herself from them. For her the 'pace setters' were a group whose lifestyle was in marked contrast to her own. She felt the majority of them came from middle-class backgrounds and 'set the tone' in the sixth form because they were the dominant group.

In general, the nostalgics adopted a more tolerant attitude towards the YTS 'lads' and considered the views of the other students 'snobbish'. One explained that the lads should not be 'blamed' for their behaviour and another felt they were 'all right once you got to know them'. There were also differences in their attitudes towards careers. For most nostalgics the aim was to go to university or polytechnic and they did not anticipate leaving higher education even for a 'job with prospects' before they obtained their degrees. If they had a career in mind at all it was to work in the public sector as a qualified professional – teacher, nurse, social worker, psychologist.

The group described themselves as 'socialist' but not in any 'counter-hegemonic' or revolutionary sense. They were not opposed to private property, and viewed state institutions like education as helpful to working-class aspirations. There was clearly a gap between their egalitarian rhetoric and the reality of their day-to-day social relationships. Although their friends were often working-class, the number was declining, even for those who still lived in areas which they described as 'poor'. They tended to spend their leisure time more quietly than elitists – doing homework, visiting friends, watching TV, reading or doing other home-based activities, with occasional forays to pubs and clubs.

Conclusions

At age 16 the vocational education and training young people receive becomes more obviously differentiated. GCSEs, and now the National Curriculum, give way to distinct vocational tracks which lead to different occupational and social strata. The occupational horizons of young people themselves are at first not very clear but become more visible in the course of training. There is increasing divergence between the outlooks of the various groups of young people and the emergence, in embryonic form, of different moral, political and occupational career perspectives. Social factors such as class, family background and gender can be seen to interact with education and training, creating vicious and virtuous circles, pulling young people towards different destinations. Within these circles individual identities spin, undergoing partial transformations as young people seek to come to terms with their transitions.

For all groups social class and family background were important in explaining the directions they were taking. However, the research also shows that to account for young people's career paths it is necessary to take account of quite subtle variations in the social position of their families. Although nearly all the young people studied had parents originating from working-class families, their characteristics differed. Parents of young people in the two YTS groups were predominantly in unskilled and semi-skilled employment. Parents of young people in the two BTEC groups were largely skilled working-class and lower-middle-class, often owners of small businesses. The parents of sixth-formers appeared not dissimilar from those of BTEC students, although there were a larger proportion of middle-class parents and many for whom upward social mobility was a particularly salient experience. Hence, once backgrounds were examined not only in terms of social class but also in terms of *social mobility potential*, clear relationships were evident between student origins and vocational directions. Furthermore, the research also suggested that cultural values acquired within the family orientate young people not only towards particular *levels* but also towards particular *fields* of employment – for example, in the study of YTS girls.

Social class and family background were, moreover, meaningful categories to the young people themselves, a finding consistent with our survey results and other recent research (see, for example, Marshall *et al.*, 1988). At one extreme there were sixth-formers who employed the concept of social class itself in interpreting aspects of their experience. On the other hand there were YTS trainees whose awareness of class cultural bonds was less articulate but still powerful, being typically expressed, for example, through the exclusion of members of other social groups on the grounds that they were 'not one of us'. However, while young people were aware of their social class, more subtle social differences between themselves and others whom they 'rubbed shoulders with' daily, such as the 'Sloanes' on the BTEC course or the 'dregs' on the YTS course, had more everyday importance.

The influence of gender was also readily visible particularly for those groups involved in vocational training. The growth of feminism and equal opportunities during the 1970s and 1980s seemed to have had little impact on an overall pattern of gender-stereotyped career choices. In so far as change has occurred in recent years, it seems mainly to have affected the better-qualified young women in the sixth form and in further education, some of whom saw themselves as future 'career' women, who would perhaps enter business or science careers. There was evidence, however, that even here what was contemplated was a two-phase career allowing a prolonged period of social and economic independence before settling down within a 'late' marriage, at which point the demands of a 'domestic' career were expected to prevail. In this way the potential role conflict for young women was distanced, but by no means resolved.

Gender was heavily intertwined with class cultural factors. Career choices expressed in terms of entry into particular vocational tracks were bounded by gender identity, but conceptions of appropriate gender identity were in turn influenced by social class and family background. It would have been difficult to imagine, for example, the male YTS trainees studied contemplating a career in the hotel and catering trade, even if they had gained the qualifications for acceptance for the course. Such jobs were, in their view, for 'poofters'. Smilarly, while both fashion design and 'caring' were largely female preserves, a career in fashion design would have attracted scorn from the 'care' girls, and vice versa. These linkages between patterns of gender attribution and class cultural factors could be seen as functional in sustaining the processes of social reproduction.

Social class, family background and gender were not simply part of the social inheritance of each young person but a continuing active influence on their progress through education and training. One way in which this influence operated was through complex, and often latent, processes of screening young people for what were deemed to be occupationally relevant characteristics (see also Bates, 1990; 1991a). In practice, the possession of the appropriate qualities appeared to depend more on social class, family background and gender than on individual abilities. These factors influenced young people's responses to the courses they were on, the ways in which they coped with and negotiated their transitions, and the ways in which tutors – acting as gatekeepers to occupations – assessed their suitability. Hence, screening for suitability implicitly involved screening for social attributes. Examples can be taken from each category of education and training. YTS 'care' girls depended on a certain toughness and stoicism forged in the family context for surviving the demands of their employment. Passage through the BTEC hotel and catering course was facilitated by values such as deference, the privatisation of dissatisfaction and skills in impression management nurtured in the context of cultural backgrounds emphasising respectability. Finally, sixth-formers, on upwardly mobile career paths, could draw affirmation from their parents' values and experience as they entered the ranks of elitists. Within any of these groups students who lacked the relevant cultural resources were likely to be among the less successful, or even to be 'cooled out'.

Family circumstances also influenced progress at age 16 in more material ways, that is, through the extent to which families were able to offer young people financial support. Most young people on YTS schemes lived in circumstances where the YTS allowance was critically important to the overall family budget. In contrast, in order to undertake a two-year BTEC or A-level course families needed to be able both to support their offspring and to be able to contribute to the expenses of the course. These findings suggest that the lack of grants to support young people in education and training beyond the age of 16 may be underestimated as a factor affecting post-16 participation rates.

The influence of education and training on socialisation operated not only through processes of mediation between social characteristics, such as class and gender, and occupational cultures. Its impact was also exerted through specific socialisation processes (Bates, 1990). Within each setting, such processes were manifested contextually in a variety of aspects of both the hidden and the visible curricula. For example, the quality of relationships between tutors and young people varied significantly between the groups, with sixth-form tutors cultivating egalitarian, friendly relations with their students and YTS tutors tending towards a despairing, depersonalising insulting relationship in which the groups were categorised as 'that lot'. There were related variations in pedagogy. Sixth-formers enjoyed considerable opportunities to develop individual projects, while BTEC students came under relentless pressure to tailor their work to labour-market needs. At the other extreme, YTS students, convinced of the irrelevance to their prospects of formal education, drew their main learning directly from the experience derived from work placements and from their social lives.

Within this landscape of inequality, what were the perspectives of young people themselves? How did they experience their unravelling futures on different paths through education and training? These studies have shown glimpses of a wide variety of perspectives and meanings: the YTS lads' definitions of 'having a laff', their racism, sexism, and total rejection of liberal educational values; the 'care' girls' struggle with their emerging occupational identities which is partly resolved by recognising and embracing the cultural values of 'toughness' and stoicism; the fashion designers' resistance to their tutors' emphasis on acquiring marketable skills and persistence in clinging to notions of a glamorous career; and the hotel and catering students' cynical but deferential compliance in the face of more secure and favourable career prospects. Finally, in the sixth-formers we perceive the emerging perspectives of the rising middle class who will themselves be eventually involved in the management and implementation of processes of 'cooling out' (Quicke, 1990). Here the problem of defining a 'moral career' for oneself (Goffman, 1961), and reconciling origins and destinations, is perhaps most explicit.

In making sense of these various perspectives, it is apparent that what they have in common is that they all involve coming to terms with career paths and emerging vocational identities. These carry implications for future social position, which further enhances the significance of the identity stakes involved. The young people studied did not, on the whole, don their new identities easily, but rather struggled to achieve them within the network of structures in which they found themselves. Much of what was happening to them was disliked and resisted. Their social lives provided important respite, a time to 'moan and groan' and 'let off steam' and find other sources of satisfaction and achievement. They were sustained on their career paths by a sense of the future – 'the light at the end of the tunnel' – and by their own creative, identity-salvaging responses. Neither escapism nor resistance, however, altered the general direction their careers were taking. Such strategies appeared to perform the social function of reconciling young people to their future occupations rather than reconstructing them.

Chapter 6   SELF AND IDENTITY

Introduction

Education and training help shape identity, but, as we saw in the last chapter, the foundations of identity have deeper roots in family background and peer culture. The YTS lads, 'care' girls, BTEC and A-level students, bring with them to their post-16 education and training a set of values and expectations which are reinforced and deepened by the experience rather than challenged by it. Education is an affirmation of a set of values, a means to an end, or an irrelevance. Life outside it may be a relaxation from the 'hard graft' that aspirations dictate or the means of achievement itself where group solidarity is reinforced and self-esteem is sustained.

Occupational destinations, therefore, are only one element of the developing adult identity that is shaped by a career; the other elements express the relations between the individual and the wider social structure. Gender roles and political affiliations are examples of other elements which both interact with and help shape careers and identities.

But where does individual agency fit into this picture? Does the young person merely respond blindly to structural and situational influences or does he or she do anything actively to control them? Are there choices to be made or merely directives from cultural roots to reproduce the same lifestyles, values and aspirations that have gone before? How are competing pressures accommodated or resisted and the dilemmas they present resolved? 'Identities are negotiated, created wilfully out of the raw material provided by social relations and social circumstances' (Breakwell, 1987).

In this chapter we try to uncover something of this personal component in identity: what individuals perceive their attributes to be, what characterises their 'self-concept'. People carry images of themselves which encompass what they believe to be their personality traits. For example, some see themselves as timid; others believe themselves to be irritable. Such self-attributive traits form an important part of the self-concept. They have the power to motivate action; for example, people who think themselves confident and assertive are more likely to act that way. This is true even when their assumptions about their levels of confidence and assertiveness are based on fragmentary or false evidence (Collins, 1982).

But a self-concept is not just a collection of self-definitions in terms of social roles and relationships or psychological characteristics. It has embedded in it an evaluative process: it is reflexive; it assesses its own worth. This process generates the sense of self-esteem or self-satisfaction that characterises the individual. Achieving a mature sense of self-esteem is supposed to be a vital task for adolescence (Rosenberg, 1965).

This chapter will examine a number of features of the self-concept. First, we shall look at an attribute which has attracted considerable attention in recent years: enterprise. Were young people seeing themselves as enterprising and were there differences between groups? Second, we consider where young people see the origins of their self-definitions to lie and how important the views of others are to them. We then move on to consider two broad and well-established components of the self-concept, one concerned with personal control and the other with alienation: self-efficacy and estrangement. We then examine the relation of these attributes, first, to performance at school and in the labour market, and second, to family background and social and personal life.

Enterprise

In each of the three surveys, respondents were asked how they thought and felt about themselves in relation to a number of attributes. In the Swindon area interviews these questions were pursued in greater depth. The information collected in both types of study led to similar conclusions.

In the late 1980s there was much talk about the need for people to become enterprising. Many educational initiatives were launched with this end in view by the government which maintained that the economic success of the UK lay in the hands of enterprising individuals capable of turning ideas and limited investment into profit. The defining characteristics of 'enterprise' are arguable, but might be expected to include: a strong desire to accomplish things; taking initiative and seeking responsibility; preferring moderate and calculated risks; having lots of drive and energy; having lots of determination and a desire to get on with jobs and work; and setting your own standards of success. In 1988 we asked our respondents in all areas to tell us how far they saw themselves as the sort of person who had each of these characteristics.

Perhaps the most significant feature of the responses was that most young people claimed to have these characteristics and that they were highly consistent across the groups. Most young people saw themselves to be accomplished, tenacious and determined, three-quarters said they set their own standards and had drive and energy, and a majority said they took initiative and took moderate and calculated risks. Only on this last item was there a substantial sex difference, more boys than girls claiming to be risk-takers. There was also a small cohort effect for this item, with older respondents tending to endorse it more often. Surprisingly, there was little evidence of area differences. Swindon was marginally ahead on most items, but nothing like its boom-town image might have led us to expect. Living there was not engendering enterprise attributes to any greater extent than anywhere else.

The relatively high frequencies for all the enterprise items may, of course, simply reflect the fact that the enterprising image is seen by teenagers as desirable, and that they were answering questions in such a way as to impress. For this reason differences between groups are where our main interest lies, because they point to possible influences on the self-image over and above any such 'halo' effect. Some differences of this kind are apparent when the responses are analysed by career trajectory (Table 6.1). Those in the full-time academic trajectory were more likely than all the others to see themselves as having a strong desire to accomplish things, wanting to take initiative and accept responsibility, to take moderate and calculated risks and, in particular, to set their own standards of success. At the other extreme, more of those in the YTS/unemployment group acknowledged lacking these characteristics. However, the differences were generally not very large and for two of the characteristics, 'lots of drive and energy' and 'lots of determination to finish tasks', the school-to-job group and the YTS-to-job group were higher, suggesting that the work experience of these groups might have enhanced this aspect of their self-image.

Table 6.1 Enterprise attributes by career trajectory (all areas, 1988)

% answering 'very much' or 'quite a lot'	Academic	Vocational	Job	YTS–Job	YTS/ Unemployment
Strong desire to accomplish things	89	84	79	77	83
Take initiative and seek responsibility	68	69	70	69	62
Take moderate and calculated risks	61	52	52	50	44
Lots of drive and energy	68	75	78	74	72
Lots of determination to finish tasks	79	84	87	84	84
Set own standards of success	83	77	73	75	69

Sources of self-evaluation

People devise a sense of their own worth in a number of ways. They can establish it by earning social approval from people whom they consider important, such as friends or family. They can calculate it by comparing themselves with appropriate others, and where they think themselves better – spiritually, physically or socially – they can acquire self-esteem. They can also derive self-esteem from succeeding and achieving self-determined objectives.

We were interested to know how far our respondents were concerned with what other people thought about them and how far they were absorbed in their own opinions of themselves. In 1987 they were asked to say how far they agreed with the statement 'I am more concerned about how I feel about myself than about how other people think of me'. Two-thirds said they were concerned with impressing other people and only a fifth said they were not. Similarly, half agreed that what their friends or family thought about them was important, compared with a quarter who denied this. However, the desire to impress others was less important for the majority than what they felt about themselves. Nearly half said they were more concerned with what they felt about themselves than with what others thought about them; only 30% disagreed.

These views about the importance of other people in establishing self-evaluations were not related to gender, cohort, area of residence or career trajectory. The only exception was that those on the academic trajectory were slightly more likely than the others to agree that they were concerned about the impression they made on other people.

The picture was extended through the interviews carried out in Swindon, where respondents were asked to rank order all possible sources of self-esteem: 'feeling good about myself', 'feeling others think I'm good', 'feeling consistent over time' and 'feeling unique and different from other people'. 'Feeling good about myself' was rated most important followed by 'feeling consistent over time', then 'feeling others think I'm good'; 'feeling unique' was rated least important. As one 17-year-old girl said: 'it matters what other people think about you but what really matters is what I think about myself'. A 19-year-old boy reflected in the interview: 'I feel happy with myself when I'm with my girlfriend, what my mates think about me counts, but I know who I am myself and you have to hold on to that.'

The finding that consistency was more valued than uniqueness is interesting. Even those interviewees who reported feeling happiest with themselves when standing out from the crowd or doing something different from their friends, emphasised how important it was to maintain the same self-image over time. One fashion-conscious young man pointed out: 'I got a reputation to keep up, I can't go around changing what I look like or what I do, no matter what other people think'.

Self-evaluation

We wanted to measure how satisfied the young people in our sample were with their self-concepts. In all three surveys, respondents in all areas were asked to describe themselves in terms of a number of statements which had clear evaluative connotations. One group of statements clustered around whether they felt they had could handle people and problems effectively. The other group focused upon whether they were happy with who they were and with life in general and confident that they understood the rules and expectations of society around them.

Table 6.2 shows how they responded at each stage of the survey. The most striking feature of the responses was that a positive self-image emerged on almost all the items at all three time points. Most young people felt competent to perform tasks, and said that they found it easy to make friends and deal with social situations and to work to new rules and regulations. They felt that they knew what was going on in the world and were generally content with themselves. There were only three exceptions where a more substantial minority of young people held a more negative view. 'I cannot but wonder at times if anything is worthwhile' was endorsed by a third in 1987 and 1988 and a quarter in 1989. A fifth also endorsed the item 'I am troubled by emptiness in my life' and one fifth at waves 1 and 2, falling to a sixth at wave 3, said that they would like to be a different person if they had the chance.

Clearly the majority of the young people, because of the 'halo' effect, were likely to be presenting themselves positively. This is why the small number who had a less confident and satisfied view about themselves are of particular interest. Such young people were to be found in much the same numbers in all four areas. More of them were male than female and there were more in the younger than in the older cohort. They were also most frequently to be found in the most disadvantaged groups, especially school leavers who had failed to get permanent employment.

Self-efficacy and estrangement

The self-evaluative statements in the questionnaire fell into two broad clusters identified with two of the main dimensions of the self-image. One cluster of six items reflected a well-established personality attribute – perceived self-efficacy. This was an expression of belief in the ability to handle problems, achieve goals and deal with people effectively; it is represented by the single-starred items in Table 6.2 (Sherrer *et al.*, 1982; Bandura, 1977a; 1977b; 1989). The other cluster of seven items measured aspects of what has been called 'psychological estrangement' a sense of worthlessness, and meaninglessness akin to alienation; it is defined by the double-starred items in Table 6.2 (see Seeman 1959; 1972; Hammond 1988). Self-efficacy and estrangement scores were, not surprisingly, negatively correlated with each other in all waves of the survey, with correlations ranging from -0.43 in wave 1 up to -0.55 for the same individuals in wave 3. This suggests that the differentiation of the self-concept into these two components becomes weaker as people approach adulthood – an aspect of the tendency, as we shall see, for efficacy to increase and estrangement to decrease marginally with age.

Table 6.2 Self-evaluations in 1987, 1988 and 1989 (%)

	1987		1988		1989	
	Agree	Disagree	Agree	Disagree	Agree	Disagree
* If I can't do a job the first time, I keep trying until I can	91	2	90	2	93	2
* I avoid trying to learn new things when they look too dificult for me	11	89	11	88	10	80
* I give up easily	9	82	9	83	8	83
* I seem to be capable of dealing with most problems that come up in life	79	6	82	5	5	87
* I find it easy to make new friends	77	9	76	10	77	10
* I do not know how to handle social gatherings	13	63	13	65	10	71
** I feel unsure about most things in life	15	67	13	70	12	73
† I find it easy to adapt to new rules and regulations	69	14	68	13	74	11
** If I could, I would be a very different person from the one I am now	22	61	19	61	16	66
** I find it difficult to know what is going on in the world	16	67	12	72	11	75
** I am happy to be the person I am	79	9	77	9	78	9
** I sometimes cannot help but wonder if anything is worthwhile	35	44	32	48	26	57
** I am often troubled by emptiness in my life	22	62	21	63	19	68
** I feel that I am as worthwhile as anybody else	82	5	81	6	84	5

* = self-efficiency item   ** = estrangement item
† not included in either scale

Thus both self-efficacy and estrangement represent two components of an individual's overall sense of self-esteem, one positive, the other negative. In some respects they echo what Rosenberg (1985; 1989) labelled 'positive self-esteem' and 'negative self-esteem'. As we shall see, the degree of independence between the two points to different socialisation processes at work between the ages of 16 and 19.

As we saw in Chapter 1, adolescence, extending over the period of the early to the mid-teens, presents certain developmental tasks for young people which they have to resolve successfully in the move towards adulthood. These include coming to terms with sexuality and the opposite sex and a new relationship with parents. On this basis it would be predicted that as conflicts recede a sense of efficacy would increase across the latter part of the teens and that estrangement would decrease (Kroger 1989; Coleman and Hendry, 1990). However, this prediction will only be borne out if individuals have made the earlier transitions successfully and if by the end of their teens they are able to cope with the challenges that later transitions represent. Conflicts surrounding personal antonomy and relations with parents – the last developmental task of adolescence – can continue well into the late teens. Some domestic and occupational changes, especially those that are unavoidable or socially stigmatised, might also be expected to threaten self-esteem. For example, repeated bouts of unemployment might be expected to block the rise in self-efficacy and possibly reinforce the sense of estrangement.

Figure 6.1 shows the means scores on self-efficacy and estrangement by sex and cohort across the three surveys. Extending what we found from the item responses, males and females had much the same scores for self-efficacy. This is somewhat surprising since most studies of self-evaluation show that girls are more critical of their own abilities than are boys. Our data suggest that the girls had initially marginally higher self-efficacy scores than the boys and that they maintained these at much the same level throughout the period of the study. In contrast, the male self-efficacy scores rose marginally, reaching the same level as that of the females by the age of 19. This pattern appeared irrespective of cohort: the younger cohort had lower self-efficacy scores throughout. It should be noted in interpreting these trends that the data applied to those who stayed in the study throughout. In fact, those who dropped out after the first stage scored significantly lower on self-efficacy and higher on estrangement than those who stayed in.

For estrangement there was the expected gender difference: females were consistently more likely to demean their own worth and to claim a sense of alienation from society's rules and expectations. The younger cohort reported greater estrangement. There was an overall decline in estrangement during the study, revealing the expected developmental trend during the 15–20 age range. As they reached the end of their teenage years, our respondents were coming to feel that they could understand more of what was going on around them in the world, felt happy with themselves and with life in general and were more certain about and happier with their role in life.

It is interesting that the predicted gender difference in self-evaluation occurred in relation to estrangement but not to self-efficacy. The gender difference actually revolved largely around the items concerned with self-doubt and self-criticism. It seems that girls were as willing as boys to recognise and express their positive capacities, but were also more willing to acknowledge their weaknesses.

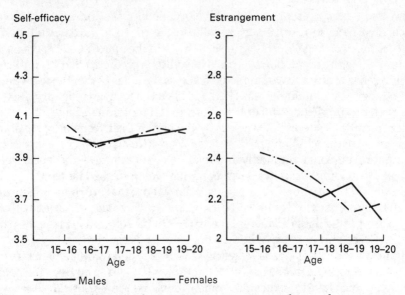

Figure 6.1   Self-efficacy and estrangement, mean scores by age, by sex

We might expect area of residence to have had an effect upon efficacy and estrangement. It could be argued that where you live acts as a cipher for the amount of opportunity available and the possibilities for achievement to be rewarded which might affect self-efficacy and estrangement. In fact, no direct or indirect impact of area on self-evaluation was detectable. This may be because in each area estimates of self-worth reflected opportunities which were differentially available across individuals.

Self-evaluation and career trajectory

There has been considerable debate about the effects of experiences in the education system and in the labour market upon aspects of the self-concept. Self-esteem has been found to be positively correlated with educational attainment (Rosenberg, 1989) but the causal direction is unclear. Is self-esteem a by-product of success at school or one of its determinants? There is probably a complex chain of interactions between the two over time and especially during the early school years. Later experiences in the labour market are also known to be associated with changes in self-evaluation. For instance, unemployment changes self-esteem, but its impact is moderated by situational variables, its length, and the availability of a social support network. Its effect is also moderated by how committed the unemployed person is to employment (Breakwell *et al.*, 1984; Warr *et al.*, 1985; Breakwell, 1986a; Hendry and Raymond, 1986; Banks and Ullah, 1988).

Educational attainment in our sample was correlated positively with self-efficacy in each wave of the survey, but the size of the correlation was small (0.13 in wave 1), and declined over time, presumably as educational success became a less important criterion for self-evaluation. Performance at school was more closely (negatively) related to estrangement (–0.18), and with slightly less decline over time (falling to –0.15).

Current status and the self-concept

Mean scores on self-efficacy and estrangement were calculated for each occupational status for the whole sample at each wave of the survey (Table 6.3). Basically, at each age, those who were unemployed had the lowest levels of efficacy and highest levels of estrangement, followed by those on YTS; those in full-time jobs and in full-time education had much the same scores throughout. It should be noted that the unemployed group did not constitute the same people throughout. Young people who were unemployed at all three data collection points were relatively rare.

Table 6.3 Mean scores for self-efficacy and estrangement by occupational status and age group

	Younger cohort		Older cohort		
	16–17 W1	17–18 W2	17–18 W1	18–19 W2	19–20 W3
Self-efficacy					
Unemployed	3.83	3.88	3.88	3.90	3.98
YTS	3.95	4.00	3.88	3.92	–
Full-time education	3.95	4.00	4.10	3.92	4.00
Full-time job	4.03	4.03	4.11	4.07	4.05
Estrangement					
Unemployed	2.56	2.35	2.52	2.42	2.42
YTS	2.46	2.38	2.34	2.58	–
Full-time education	2.28	2.16	2.24	2.06	2.01
Full-time job	2.25	2.14	2.17	2.16	2.11

Nevertheless, as Table 6.3 shows, being unemployed was associated with the suppression of efficacy and heightening of estrangement at each age, though for estrangement the relationship weakened with age. This could be due to some habituation to the status on the part of some of those who were long-term unemployed. More likely, those who found unemployment most distressing had found a route out of it by the final wave. They were also more likely to have dropped out of the study after the first wave.

It is notable that the profile of those on YTS was more similar to the profile of those who were unemployed than it was to those who had full-time 'real' work. Estrangement was substantially lower among the groups in full-time education and full-time work, and declined in both of them with age.

Part-time work hovered uneasily throughout: self-efficacy levels for this group were not as low as for the unemployed, but not as high as for full-time workers; estrangement was not as high as for the unemployed and not as low as for the full-time workers. Such findings point to the significance of the role current status plays in the maintenance of self-esteem.

Career trajectory

Current status says nothing about the route taken to different occupational destinations and the longer-term effects these might have on the self-concept. Our next analysis takes such routes into account by comparing the mean self-efficacy and estrangement scores at each wave of the survey across the five career trajectories (Figure 6.2).

For both cohorts the rank ordering of trajectories in terms of self-efficacy and estrangement at wave 1 reflected the social status attributed to each trajectory. The YTS/unemployment group appeared to have least efficacy and to be most estranged, and the academic group had the highest self-efficacy and the lowest estrangement. The other trajectories had intermediate positions with again less efficacy and more estrangement being associated with obtaining

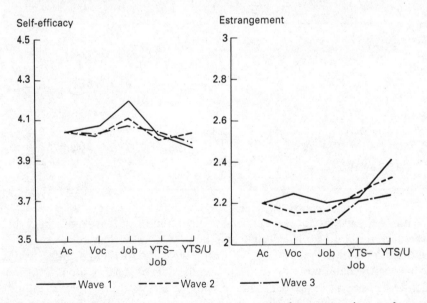

Figure 6.2 Self-efficacy and estrangement, mean scores by career trajectory, by wave

employment through a YTS scheme and direct entry into a job from school. There was a small rise in the self-efficacy scores between the group staying on at school and those going straight from school into a job, confirming what we found before, that the status of getting a job is just as positive for the self-image as is staying on. As to estrangement, however, there was no difference between the academic and the school-to-work group. Moving up through the age groups across the different waves of the survey, the difference in the self-efficacy scores between these two groups marginally increased. The school-to-job group were now marginally the better adjusted; those who stayed on were suffering more from self-doubt. In all waves, however, the YTS/unemployment group remained lowest in self-efficacy and highest in estrangement.

It has been suggested that unemployment may have a differential effect on the self-concept dependent upon locality. In high-unemployment areas it may be that unemployment is less stigmatised and less damaging to self-esteem. Our data provide equivocal evidence on this. For the older cohort there was no connection with area. But for the younger cohort, being in the YTS/unemployment group was associated with greater estrangement in Swindon than in the higher-unemployment areas of Liverpool or Sheffield. By 1989 the likelihood of that a young person in Swindon would be unemployed was half that in the other two areas. The interviews in Swindon showed that unemployment there was attributed to laziness or to a definite lack of ability. A young person who was without work was quickly told that it was his or her own fault. This contrasts with the political climate of the other two areas, where economic difficulties were believed to underlie unemployment. In Liverpool particularly there was also a greater tendency for young people to believe in an external economic locus of control (Chapter 3). This also helps to explain the greater estrangement that was apparently suffered by the unemployed young people in Swindon, particularly those in the younger cohort. They had no experience of a local labour-market recession, so clearly believed that if they were unemployed the fault lay somehow with them rather than with any external factors.

The self-concept and personal life

We expected that the personal situation of our respondents, their family background and their leisure activity, would be connected with their image of themselves. On the other hand, whether the more structural features of their backgrounds, such as family social class, would impinge on aspects of identity was more arguable. Although, early on in life, family background and identity may be bound up with each other, as adulthood approaches, the links might be expected to weaken.

As we have seen, career trajectories with strong social class antecedents do differentiate self-images, but the association was fairly weak. We compared self-efficacy and estrangement scores for three different family background characteristics – social class, occupational status, and whether parents were natural or adoptive. Working-class backgrounds were very weakly associated with estrangement scores, but the relationship grew weaker with age. There was no relationship between social class and self-efficacy.

With parents' current occupational status the situation was different. In 1989, we asked our respondents to tell us whether their parents were employed or not. In relation to scores on self-efficacy there was no difference, but for estrangement there was quite a strong relationship. Respondents who said that either their mother or their father was out of work tended to have the higher estrangement scores.

Sufficient numbers in the sample came from non-nuclear families to allow us to examine the relationship between self-efficacy and estrangement and belonging to a step-family or a single-parent family. Of all the family events which might be expected to influence identity, the break-up of parents is the most obvious. The analyses showed that self-efficacy did not differ across family type, but estrangement did. Both males and females from step-families or single-parent families reported higher estrangement. This finding may not be explained purely in terms of processes which go on inside the family. Children of step-families or single-parent families may experience a range of prejudices and difficulties to which other children are not exposed and develop a greater sense of alienation.

Social life

Educational and occupational pursuits are one source of self-appraisal. But, as we have seen in the previous two chapters, leisure is a major arena for establishing reputations and maintaining self-esteem.

Figures 6.3a and 6.3b compare mean self-efficacy and estrangement scores by frequency of leisure activities, where reasonably strong connections were revealed. Figures 6.4a and 6.4b examine the relationship with time spent with different types of companion. It is notable that a sense of self-efficacy increased and estrangement decreased not only for sports activity, which might be expected, but also for going to dances and discos and going to pubs. Remarkably, drinking alcohol, which bore no relation to self-efficacy, did relate negatively to estrangement, with those who said they never drank alcohol appearing to be more estranged than the others.

Either leisure life involving social contact with others was enhancing self-esteem or those with the highest self-esteem were succeeding more in achieving an active social life than the others. Both were probably happening, though the former relationship is decidedly more likely (Bynner *et al.*, 1981). The social isolation of those not participating was apparent. This finding extends to the different companions the young people spent most time with. Heightened self-efficacy and reduced estrangement accompanied frequent contact with a girlfriend or boyfriend, a close friend or a group. Frequent contact with parents or other family members bore no relationship to self-image. But for spending time alone, the relationship was reversed: the more time spent alone, the less efficacy was felt and the more estrangement.

Marriage and pregnancy

As we saw in Chapter 4, a small proportion of the respondents were engaged to be married and a smaller proportion actually married. More girls than boys had taken this step. There was a connection with estrangement which was substantially lower for the married group, with the biggest difference being for married girls. It is reasonable to see marriage in this context as representing a kind of achievement in the domestic career, which has positive benefits for identity.

Marriage may be one source of self-esteem. Pregnancy, even for married teenage girls, may not be. Perhaps the most extremely challenging personal event that can happen to a teenager is pregnancy. Here, surprisingly, the effects on identity appeared to be quite different. One per cent of the girls in the sample had a child at the start of the study; by the time of the second questionnaire 4% had at least one baby. These percentages parallel the national statistics. Earlier studies have suggested that women who have a child while they are teenagers have an unstable self-concept and lower self-esteem, and greater estrangement and self-doubt (Shiller, 1974; Zongker, 1977; Kiernan, 1980; Patten, 1981; Horn and Rudolph, 1987). However, research in this area is plagued by the absence of good random samples. Our study provided a rare opportunity to use representative samples to compare teenage mothers with their age peers. It also provided an opportunity to compare self-evaluation before and after the birth of the child. Teenage mothers reported lower feelings of self-efficacy than their peers. However, parenthood did not precipitate changes in self-efficacy; self-efficacy was not altered systematically by having a child. Low self-efficacy in teenage mothers was a precursor, not a consequence, of having the child.

In contrast, there was no difference between teenage mothers and their peers in estrangement. Our data indicate that those who had children early felt no more alienated than their peers prior to having the child and did not become so after the child was born. This was true despite the fact that they tended to come from the more disadvantaged part of the sample (lower educational attainment, poorer employment history, lower income, and working-class background). It has been argued that motherhood actually keeps estrangement at bay; it is an alternative career with rewards and status of its own. This hardly seems the answer for our respondents. Those with children reported less social support and lower self-efficacy. It may be that teenage mothers feel no

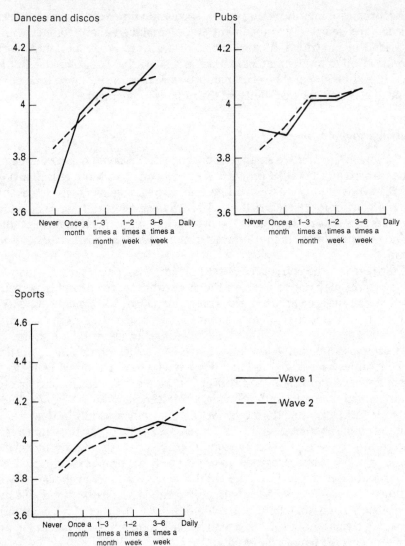

Figure 6.3a   Self-efficacy and leisure activity, mean scores by wave

less confused about societal rules than other teenagers, but they do feel less capable of exerting some control over their lives. In fact, this would simply be to recognise realistically their position. The more revealing finding from the study is that they tended to feel that they had less control even before the pregnancy.

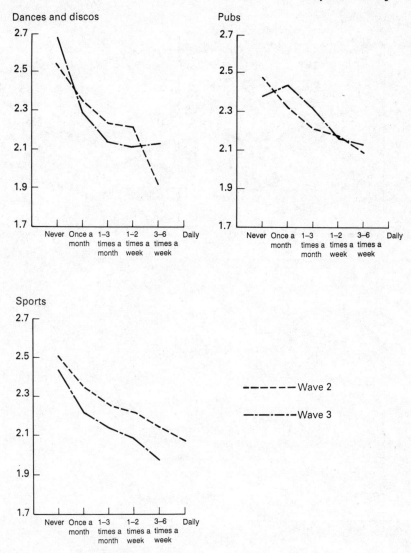

Figure 6.3b Estrangement and leisure activity, mean scores by wave

Conclusions

This chapter has probed the shaping of the identity as revealed by the diverse experiences of our sample. The majority of young people did consider themselves to be enterprising. The majority cared more for what they thought

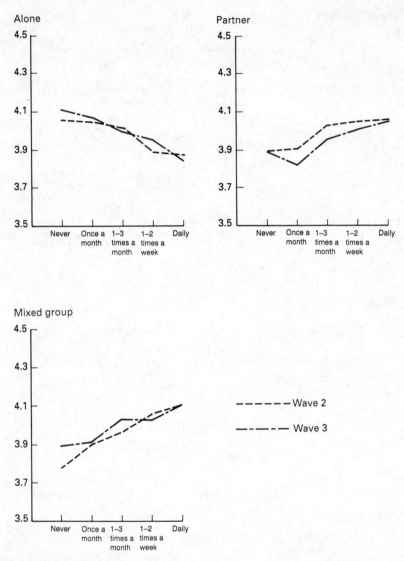

Figure 6.4a   Self-efficacy and leisure companions, mean scores by wave

about themselves than the opinion others had of them. The majority also had great confidence in their ability to handle problems and to deal with social situations. They also maintained that they understood societal rules and expectations and felt themselves worthwhile in relation to them. Yet there was a minority who could not be said to fit this rather positive self-image. The ones who deviated were predictable on the basis of their educational, occupational and domestic experiences. The data served to emphasise that the social

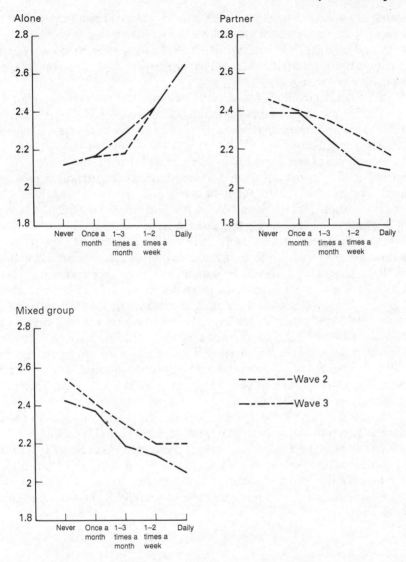

Figure 6.4b Estrangement and leisure companions, mean scores by wave

roles which determine social identities are bound to broaden beliefs about personal efficacy and feelings of psychological estrangement by the process of self-evaluation and appraisal.

It is particularly notable that although levels of self-efficacy and estrangement did not vary greatly across the late teens, major decision points to do with transition and highly significant personal events were related to changes in them. Thus at 16 staying on at school or going out to get a job means much the same in terms of self-esteem, but those who leave and are compelled to enter YTS schemes or become unemployed suffer from reduced feelings of self-efficacy and heightened estrangement. Similarly, those who experience family breakdown or the traumas associated with early pregnancy are likely to have less positive self-images.

On the other hand, family background factors have little importance for the self-evaluating aspects of identity as adulthood approaches. Only the problems associated with parents' unemployment and family break-up appear to have effects for our age group.

Other sources of self-appraisal in social and leisure life are evident, with the clear benefit of sport and active participation in teenage culture (pubs and discos) set against the estrangement accompanying social isolation. The connection between marriage and pregnancy and low estrangement points to their possible role in bolstering female identity.

We have emphasised the positive and negative aspects of experience in reflection to their possible effects on the formation of adult identity. In reality, as we have seen, against the slight increase in self-efficacy and reduction in estrangement across the late teens, there is considerable stability in these attributes. This underlines the point, as we saw in relation to teenage pregnancy, that self-attitudes are formed well before most of the experiences take place which are the concern of this study. In line with the ideas of agency, therefore, it is better to see self-efficacy and estrangement as contributing to as much as being influenced by the post-16 socialisation process. Personality is largely formed before the age of 16. What happens after then may damage or strengthen it, but only to a fairly small extent.

While the self-concept comprises identities derived from roles and relationships together with their evaluation and personal meaning, it also encompasses another dimension. Attitudes and systems of belief also serve the function of self-definition, locating oneself in a network of ideologies and values relative to other people. The expression of attitudes can become a major route for establishing a unique social identity. This is the subject of Chapter 7.

Chapter 7   BELIEFS, ATTITUDES AND VALUES

Introduction

Earlier chapters have focused on the role of post-16 education, entry to the labour market, and social and domestic life in the formation of adult identity. There have been pointers to particular views about the world associated with different entry routes. In Chapter 3 we discussed links between different education, training and employment experiences on the one hand, and attitudes to work and training on the other. Chapter 4 touched on the relations between domestic roles and gender-role attitudes and between personal relationships and sexual attitudes. In Chapter 5 we saw that YTS lads clearly had a different perspective on social and political issues from their counterparts on BTEC catering courses; 'care' girls and sixth-formers were some way removed from each other, not just in the political views they held but in whether they had any interest in politics at all. Finally, Chapter 6 examined the personal elements of identity, the way young people perceived themselves, especially their sense of self-efficacy and estrangement.

In this chapter we pursue differences in beliefs, attitudes and values much further, drawing on the survey data. We examine those facets of identity concerned with social and political beliefs and see how these relate to career routes and the characteristics that underlie them. First, we examine the opinions that young people expressed about a range of topics in the social and political domain. We then consider how these opinions relate to broader dimensions of attitude and value. Finally, we look at the relations between the attitude dimensions and the other features of young people's lives, especially the career routes they were on and the features of family background and educational experience which underpin them.

Teenage opinions

Many observers have commented that party politics in the conventional adult sense is of minor interest to most young people, even when they have achieved voting age. Elections clearly do heighten interest, by virtue of the media exposure they receive, and a general election like the one in 1987 concentrates attention on political matters. But the institutions of government and the political parties attract limited interest from young people, who see these as having little direct relevance to their lives. None the less, it would be wrong to conclude that young people are completely without concern for or do not have opinions about all matters political. As we shall see in this chapter, the pattern is rather more variable. Some issues do arouse strong passions and on occasion marked polarisation of views, while others fail to engage strong interest or provoke clear opinions.

The truth of our assertion that young people have little interest in politics can be seen from Table 7.1, which gives an indication of the importance our respondents attached to different issues. At each stage of the survey, sets of propositions about social and political issues were put to them and they were asked to indicate their agreement or disagreement. Table 7.1 shows the mean percentage who strongly agreed or strongly disagreed with statements about different topics. The list is headed by race and immigration, the roles of men and women and sexual behaviour. These are followed by the environment, youth training and education; then government services, spending and taxation, the police and law and order. The issues on which strong opinions were least often expressed were the family, regional inequalities, and last of all the political system. Thus, there would seem to be a degree of mismatch between the agendas for public debate in Britain and the issues which apparently concern young people. We shall see a further indication of this below.

A striking feature of most of the opinions to which Table 7.1 refers was their stability across the different waves of the survey and between the different areas in which the study was conducted. With a few exceptions, the numbers expressing support for or opposition to a particular proposition barely changed from wave 1 to wave 3; nor were there differences between cohorts or between males and females. Boys and girls from 16 to the end of their teens divided in much the same way on most issues. The main exceptions, which we have already encountered in Chapter 4, were attitudes to the roles of men and women and to sexual behaviour. Not unexpectedly, these showed more girls than boys favouring complete equality – though the majority of boys agreed with them – and adopting more cautious views about sexual relations. Boys also tended generally to express more hostile opinions about authority than girls. The younger cohort also seemed more favourably disposed than the older cohort towards training. But the similarities in opinions between groups were generally more striking than the differences. This does not mean that individuals did not change their opinions across time, nor, as we shall see, that nothing was influencing them after the age of 16. There was a slight tendency for some opinions to become less extreme with age but the overall distribution of answers generally held constant.

Table 7.1 Issues about which young people have strong feelings

*Mean percentages agreeing or disagreeing
strongly with statements about:*

Race	37
Roles of men and women	34
Sex	30
Environment	26
Youth Training	23
Education	22
Taxation, government services and spending	21
Police, rules, law authority	19
Family	18
Regional contrasts	17
Political parties, processes, and politicians	16

Equal opportunities and discrimination

The area of opinion in which young people felt most strongly covered sexual and racial discrimination. In relation to training, the workplace and the home, large majorities – approaching 80% or more of both sexes – supported equality of opportunity and obligation for men and women; barely any girls rejected these opinions and only a sixth of boys did so. Larger differences were apparent in relation to the role of women as mothers; more male than female respondents, for example, believed that the mother should care for a sick child and that childrearing was a full-time job. But even then the majority of young men disagreed with these propositions.

We found other evidence of anti-discriminatory attitudes, common to both sexes, in relation to race. Over four-fifths of both sexes believed that members of different races should be able to intermarry, did not mind working with people of other races, would not mind having a boss of another race and thought that the different races should live together.

Of course, some of these opinions could have been influenced by the strong equal opportunities policies in the mostly Labour-controlled areas in which the young people lived. However, even in Swindon, where the majority of young people were supporters of the Conservative Party, the same distribution of attitudes was evident. Most of the respondents were in favour of equality in all its forms.

The area of sexual behaviour provided one of our few observations of opinion changes over time. Against expectation, concern about AIDS, expressed through worry that a friend might catch it, fell from 35% to 25% between wave 2 and wave 3 of the survey. But there was also much sexual caution in the sample, with the majority believing that you should stick to one sexual partner, and disagreeing with the idea that sexual relations are 'okay after a few weeks' acquaintance'. Hostility to homosexuality was also apparent, especially among boys, with a majority asserting that homosexual relations are wrong. But in relation to one other contentious issue, abortion, liberal values were sustained, with three-quarters agreeing that a young girl getting pregnant should be able to get an abortion.

Authority, government and politicians

Attitudes to authority were generally positive and accepting, with the majority of young people agreeing that most policemen were honest, that they personally would not defy authority and that they would tell the police if they saw a break-in. Views were more divided about whether it was right to break the law to help a friend and whether the police were unnecessarily brutal. Other representatives of authority, such as teachers, were disliked by the majority, as were government and politicians. Over two-thirds of the sample felt that the government was too secretive, that they had no say in what it did, that it mattered little which party was in power, that politicians were only interested in votes, and that politicians did not care what people like them thought. Feelings were mixed about whether politicians were just in politics for their own benefit and whether political parties were of any help to young people. These attitudes reflect the general distrust among the British public of political institutions, a sentiment that has been observed in other surveys (see, for example, Heath and Topf, 1987). Although the majority of British adults vote in elections, and most of our young people expressed voting intentions, this does not extend to confidence in political institutions and politicians.

Political issues

Throughout the survey we canvassed opinions on a range of matters more directly related to the agendas of the political parties. Over the period of the survey, some values identified with 'Thatcherite' or 'radical right' ideology attracted support, but many others did not. Thus there was strong opposition to privatisation of public utilities and overwhelming support for increased public spending on health and education. 'Green' attitudes were also common, with large majorities agreeing that environmental problems were very serious and that governments should tackle them. On the other hand, there were similarly large majorities rejecting the idea that private schools should be abolished. Moreover, most believed that private taxation should not be increased (only 20% disagreed) and a large majority were in favour of the death penalty.

Opinions were more evenly divided on whether the police should be given greater powers, whether members of extremist groups should be allowed to teach in schools, whether war is preferable to occupation by a foreign power, and whether the church should give a stronger lead on matters concerned with sex. On many of these issues, particularly those about war and the church, large proportions said they were uncertain. Either they really could not decide or, more likely, these issues did not have sufficient salience for our young people to provoke an opinion either way.

Overall, what we found was not so much marked divisions on all political issues but rather three kinds of pattern, reflecting areas of consensus, areas of uncertainty or indifference, and areas of controversy, respectively. First, there were issues on which there was either a conservative consensus or at least a strong majority for an essentially 'conservative' position. Conversely, there were issues on which the consensus or majority was essentially liberal. In other words, many of the same young people had liberal opinions on some issues and conservative opinions on others.

There was a liberal consensus or majority on matters relating to equality (support for men and women doing the same jobs around the house, and having the same work opportunities), individual and civil rights (support for abortion and intermarriage, opposition to censorship), secular morality (unwillingness to concede authority to the Church on matters of right and wrong), and certain economic and welfare issues (opposition to privatisation of water and electricity, support for more funding for the health service), as we have already seen.

There was a conservative consensus or majority on law and order issues such as capital punishment and support for the police, on family life (one's greatest loyalty is to the family), and on sexual behaviour (one should keep to one sexual partner because of AIDS).

It should be said that on some of these issues there were significant minorities taking a contrary view, and doing so consistently from one survey to the next. There is always a problem in survey research of distinguishing 'true' opinions from more arbitrary and superficial responses. One means of making this distinction is to look for stability over time, on the grounds that true opinions will be less liable to change from one occasion to another. The difficulty is that true opinions can presumably also change.

Second, many of the issues that have figured in national political debates evoked no strong opinions, the most common response being 'uncertain'. These included issues of trade union power, national defence, whether MPs are in touch with ordinary people, and environmental protection versus economic growth.

Third, there were issues which did to some degree polarise our sample, issues on which a majority had clear opinions but on which those opinions were divided more equally for and against than was true with respect to the areas of consensus. This third pattern, therefore, reflects areas in which there is potentially more controversy (and possibly areas around which contrasting political loyalties might be expected to form). These more polarised issues included excessive police brutality, the pettiness of school rules, divisions of parental responsibilities, whether childrearing is a full-time job, whether politicians are motivated primarily by self-interest, whether teachers should have the right to strike, whether sex is all right after a few weeks' acquaintance, whether the church should give a clearer lead on sexual matters, whether homosexual relations are wrong, whether parents can tell you what to do while you are still living at home, whether adults understand young people, whether immigration should be halted, and, above all, whether life is so short that having a good time is more important than anything else.

If one examines this list, the areas of controversy are more to do with personal values and behaviour than with relations between groups that form the substance of most political argument. It is hard to see contrasting political loyalties defined in terms of many of the issues in the above list. And one is inclined to conclude that the choices of value commitment represented by the national political parties are not directly related to some of the most significant value divisions that exist among young people. Nevertheless, more deeply rooted orientations – egalitarianism, liberalism–conservatism, for and against authority – do run through them, as we shall see. It is the way that they are manifested in opinion that defines the political world of teenagers and in which there is a discontinuity with the political world of adults. So the difference may be more apparent than real.

Attitude dimensions

We have mentioned that one, albeit imperfect, indicator of true opinions is stability over time. Another is the extent to which opinions on one issue relate to those on another. If people lack clear opinions on issues, if their responses are largely random or whimsical, then one would expect little relation between their views on different issues. On the other hand, if they had worked out a point of view or reached conclusions about a specific issue on the basis of more general beliefs, then one might expect consistent relationships between opinions on at least some issues. So, for example, young people who disagreed with the sentiment that 'being successful at work is just a matter of luck' because they were committed to this view might also be expected to agree with the view that 'people who are successful at work usually deserve it'.

The origin of consistency in opinions is a matter of some controversy (see, for example, Emler *et al.*, 1983). Our working assumption, outlined in Chapter

1, has been that young people negotiate and construct identities and that their attitudes are among the ways in which these 'social' identities may be expressed. By examining the relationships between sets of attitudes we hoped, therefore, to learn something about the important dimensions of teenage social identities, the stability or changeability of these identities over time, and their links with the major categories of experience through which these young people were moving. We wanted to know whether their attitudes were related to choices about education, training and careers, and politics, whether they were associated with experience of unemployment, and whether they were influenced by patterns of social participation.

Ultimately, by the use of factor analysis, we identified a large number of attitude clusters or dimensions. They included: beliefs about gender equality (support for sex equality and support for the traditional female role), opposition to authority, political cynicism, sexual conservatism, environmentalism, conservatism, socialism, and support for race equality. They also included the scales discussed in Chapter 3: support for training, belief in the value of work, support for new technology, and belief in an internal economic locus of control. (The opinion items forming all the scales, together with their reliabilities, are shown in Appendix 2.) The labels are merely convenient verbal summaries of the constituent items' content and are not meant to imply that the attitude dimensions to which they refer have been covered exhaustively. In this section we will describe just some of the major attitude dimensions to emerge from the surveys. In each case we will describe the relation between the attitude dimension and gender, social class, education, and career trajectory (Figures 7.1 and 7.2). We will also comment on their stability across time and the degree to which attitudes change across time.

Beliefs about the roles of the sexes, sexual behaviour and race

As we have seen, 16–20-year-olds in Britain in the late 1980s were predominantly egalitarian in their views about the roles of males and females. The six questions we asked about aspects of male and female roles did nevertheless produce variations in opinion and these variations formed two clusters concerned with equality at home and in the workplace, and about women's maternal role, which proved to be interrelated. In effect, there were grounds for concluding not just that young people had differing views on various aspects of the roles of the sexes but that they had a position on sexual equality in general.

Females, not surprisingly, were more egalitarian than males, and sex-role egalitarianism was moderately related to educational attainment. However, this latter relationship diminished in strength between the first and third waves of the survey. Egalitarianism was also related to labour market position at 18, but principally among the males; boys who had left school and gone directly into employment were the least egalitarian, those remaining in full-

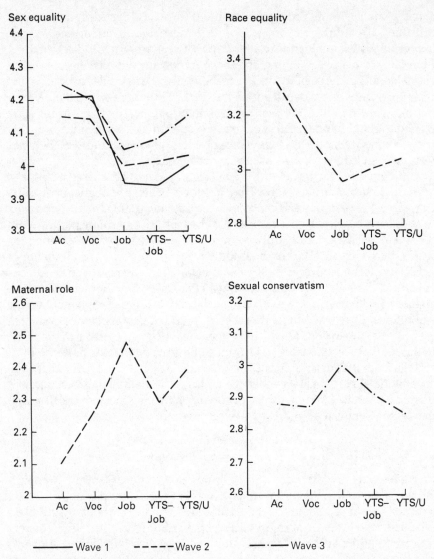

Figure 7.1 Egalitarian and traditional attitudes, mean scores by career trajectory, by wave

time education pursuing an academic track were the most egalitarian (Figure 7.1). As we have seen, in one area of equality, at home and in the workplace, both sexes were overwhelmingly in favour; in another, relating to women's role as mothers, they were much more divided.

Another attitude dimension, sexual conservatism, representing opinions for and against caution about sexual behaviour, was similarly endorsed by *more* females than males, but showed the reverse pattern with respect to career trajectory. Sexual conservatism was *lowest* in the academic and no-career groups and *highest* in the school-to-job group.

It seems that girls' greater endorsement than boys of gender equality is distinct from their views about sexual behaviour, where they take the more conservative position. Yet at the same time the more highly educated among both sexes were the most likely to endorse both equalitarianism and sexual liberalism, and those who had gone straight into jobs at 16 were the most likely to reject both.

Attitudes to race equality, which were assessed in the second wave of the survey, showed the same pattern as for sex role. Although both sexes endorsed 'antiracist' sentiments, the girls again were ahead of the boys. Those staying on in education were again the most in favour of race equality and those leaving the least in favour of it.

All the sex role attitudes were also relatively stable over time. That is to say, those young people who were most egalitarian at 16 were also likely to be among the most egalitarian at 17 and 18. At the same time, there was little indication of any overall changes with age or between cohorts' attitudes.

Attitudes to authority

We know from other research that teenagers differ in their attitudes to institutional authority generally; those who are most hostile to the police are also negative about the authority they encounter at school and the authority exercised by other state officials (Reicher and Emler, 1985; Emler *et al.*, 1987). There are distinct components to these attitudes; believing that one should always obey the law is not the same as believing that agents of the law are generally impartial. None the less, we expected that views on these matters would prove to be related, and indeed they were. The eight questions we asked about authority in the first survey formed a reliable scale, as did the six questions asked in the third wave.

In the case of this dimension also, young people expressed a generally favourable view of authority, though males were somewhat less positive than females overall. The relationship between opposition to authority and social background was quite weak, but there was a stronger relation between this orientation and the respondent's own likely social class position. Among the males, those following an academic route at 18 were most accepting of authority and those who had moved from school to employment were most hostile to it (Figure 7.2). Among the 18-year-old females, however, the most negative were those who had left school but had found no work. The relationship between this attitude dimension and educational attainment was particularly strong; higher levels of educational attainment were associated with more positive attitudes to authority.

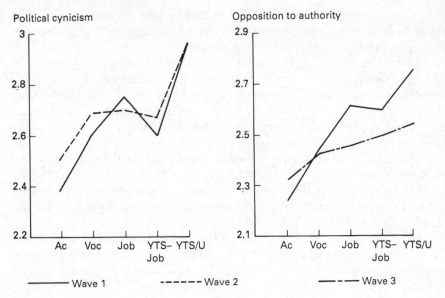

Figure 7.2   Alienation attitudes, mean scores by career trajectory, by wave

Political cynicism

We have already seen one reflection of the relatively low profile of political ideology in teenagers, lack of interest in politics. One attitude dimension to emerge clearly in the first wave of the survey was an expression of negative attitudes towards another 'adult' institution, politics. It was defined by views about the self-serving character of politicians, and by the belief that it makes no difference which party holds power and that none of the parties will do anything to benefit oneself. Following Marsh (1990) the dimension might also be labelled 'political cynicism', 'alienation' or 'distrust'. As might be expected, it was strongly and inversely related to expressed interest in politics. Anti-political sentiment was also related to career trajectory (Figure 7.2). It was lowest among the academic group and highest among the YTS and unemployed group. Finally, it was related to opposition to authority and belief in the value of work; anti-political sentiments were higher among those with negative attitudes to authority, who were also the most committed to employment.

The rise in opposition to authority and political cynicism accompanying the rise in the commitment to work in the school-leaver groups, which was sustained across the survey, also points to an increasing alienation of young people the further they are from the education system. This may seem paradoxical in that school leavers were entering adult society ahead of the rest. It suggests that the incentive to leave has more to do with money and social life than with a striving for adult identity in the wider citizenship sense, and, as writers like Willis (1977) and Meus (1989) argued, these 'teencentric' attitudes are partly what fuel the decision to leave in the first place.

The interesting aspect of all these relationships is that most of them persist long after the impact of post-16 career trajectory would be expected to have ceased. This suggests that whatever it is that prompts young people to embark on particular career routes at age 16, whether to stay on in education or to leave, is accompanied by distinctive values which do not decline and in some cases actually strengthen as they proceed along their chosen career routes: evidence perhaps of the relative impermeability of the British class structure and its values.

Socialism, conservatism and environmentalism

Research on adult social and political attitudes has quite consistently identified a broad left–right continuum underlying opinions on a range of issues (cf., for example, Fergusson, 1939; Eysenck, 1971; Wilson, 1973). So consistent is this finding that writers have argued that this dimension is the major organising principle underlying social attitudes. Moreover, position on this dimension is related to voting intentions and expressed party affiliations. It has thus been tempting to conclude that political socialisation will include the development of attitudes organised around this dimension.

In the first wave of the survey we failed to find a strong left–right dimension underlying a significant range of attitudes. This was reflected in the low reliability of the scale formed from those attitude items closest to conventional definitions of this dimension. The second wave of the survey sampled a larger number of overtly political attitudes but the scales that could be derived from these were still of relatively low reliability. Ultimately, we identified three distinct clusters from evidence collected in the third wave of the survey when respondents were 18 and 20. Because of the correspondence between the content of the items in them and broad ideological positions identified with the parties we labelled two of them 'conservatism' (for example, 'supports private medicine') and 'socialism' ('supports nationalisation of gas and railways'); the third cluster comprising expressions of concern for the environment, was labelled 'environmentalism' ('prefers environmental protection to economic growth'). Each was defined by just three items.

The sets of conservative and socialist items were weakly related, suggesting a degree of independence between them, but taken together they formed a moderately reliable scale (see Appendix 2) which may be identified with left–right ideology. However, for the purposes of investigating the origins of political identification, we treat the two sets of items as separate samples of, on the one hand, typical Labour Party beliefs and, on the other, typical Conservative Party beliefs. The items identified with environmentalism might be expected to lie close to the position of the Green Party, but in view of the recent espousal of green policies by all parties this identification might well be less clear-cut. We shall see how far this is borne out in actual party identifications

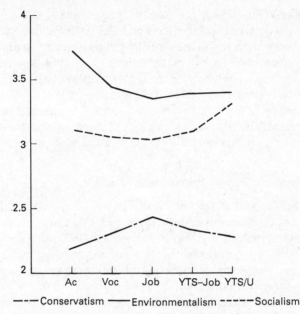

Figure 7.3 Political ideologies, mean scores by career trajectory (wave 3)

in the next chapter. Again, we stress the point that these labels are convenient descriptions and in no sense imply exhaustive coverage of entire ideological domains. Later we will consider influences on these attitude dimensions and their own impact on political behaviour.

As Figure 7.3 shows, the three types of attitude related differentially to career trajectory in the way we have seen for the previous sets of attitudes. Thus conservatism showed the same pattern of relationships as support for the traditional female role, with the highest scores in the school-to-job group. Socialism, support for sexual equality and anti-racism showed much the same pattern in reverse. Environmentalism related to career trajectories in the opposite way to opposition to authority and political cynicism.

For the moment we will note that the surveys failed to produce evidence that 16–20-year-olds in Britain either have or are developing distinct political identities defined by or expressed in terms of clear alignment with the ideologies of any of the political parties. Most of their social attitudes are not organised around political positions. One should not conclude, however, that the majority of 18–20-year-olds have no clear voting intentions, or that these are completely unrelated to the political beliefs they do hold. As will become clear in the following chapter, such intentions are both stable and predictable.

Teenage ideologies

It may be that broad ideological commitments emerge from 20 onwards or, more probably, that clearly articulated and generalised ideological positions will be found, if at all, only among relatively small political and intellectual elites. If so, then we are more likely to find attitude patterns that consistently resemble the polarities of conservatism and socialism among young people who remain in education after 16, who are interested in politics, who routinely discuss politics with others, and who define themselves and those around them in political terms. We have found some indication that this is the case (see for example, Emler, 1990) but at this stage it is a hypothesis that requires further exploration.

We can, however, say something about the interrelations between attitude dimensions – including those concerned with work discussed in Chapter 3. We have already seen that left–right ideology and environmentalism related differentially to career trajectory in the same way as other attitudes. Their commonality was investigated further through factor analysis. A factor analysis of attitude dimensions identified in the first survey produced two clear groupings. The first and stronger grouping included opposition to authority, political cynicism, support for new technology, and belief in an internal economic locus of control. The second included beliefs about the value of work, conservatism and gender egalitarianism.

A similar analysis of data from the third survey, though including some different dimensions, produced groups that differed slightly for males and females, though in each case three groups emerged (Figure 7.4). For the males, the first grouping included belief in an internal economic locus of control and socialism, with opposition to authority and support for new technology also loosely related. The second grouping included gender egalitarianism and environmentalism. The third and weakest grouping included orientation to authority, sexual conservatism, belief in the value of work, and conservatism. For the females, the first grouping linked together belief in an internal economic locus of control, socialism and opposition to authority but also conservatism. Unlike the males, the second grouping linked gender egalitarianism with work commitment. The third and weakest grouping included support for new technology and environmentalism.

We might conclude, first, that there are a few clear dimensions of social identity which emerge from our data; second, that a left–right dimension is not prominent among them, at least for males; and third, that these social identities are fairly well formed by 16 and show little major change thereafter. In other words, the period from 16 to 20 does not see any major reshaping or restructuring of social attitudes. On the other hand, we might expect, given this stability, that these attitude clusters or social identities are influences on the choices young people make between 16 and 20 and shape their patterns of social participation.

Attitudes and the self-concept

We had anticipated, and in the event we found, links between some attitudes and the self-concept dimensions examined in the previous chapter. Aspects

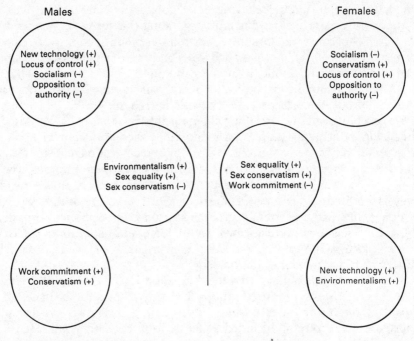

Figure 7.4 Attitude clusters

of the self-concept such as estrangement, self-efficacy and self-esteem have traditionally been regarded as influences on the development of attitudes
towards political institutions and social issues. Thus, it has been speculated
that estrangement, in so far as it reflects alienation in the Marxist sense, will
lead to political activism aimed at producing social change. On the other
hand, it might be argued that if estrangement reflects self-doubt it will be
associated with lethargy and withdrawal from social or political action.

The latter interpretation actually receives more support from our data.
Estrangement was positively correlated with political cynicism. In other
words, young people with strong feelings of estrangement were also more
likely to think they had no influence on political decisions, that the political
system is corrupt, and so on. Similarly, estranged youth were less likely than
the others to involve themselves in any kind of political activity, even of the
more passive forms such as watching party political broadcasts, and they
expressed less interest in politics.

Self-efficacy has also been linked to political protest. Marsh (1977; 1990) for
example, has proposed that even when people have a sense of grievance
against a political system this will not be translated into active protest unless
they also have a sense of their own efficacy. Empirical assessments of this
association have adopted measures of efficacy defined narrowly as ability to
achieve objectives in the political domain, thus more narrowly than in our

research. None the less, our more general measure was related to various indicators of political involvement. Young people with a relatively higher sense of their own efficacy were more interested in politics, less cynical about politicians and political institutions, and more likely to engage in the more passive forms of political participation.

Self-efficacy and estrangement were also related to social attitudes, but in different ways. Thus a sense of personal efficacy was associated with more egalitarian beliefs about sex roles, but feelings of estrangement were quite unrelated to them. However, both estrangement and a lower sense of self-efficacy were linked to negative attitudes to authority and to economic fatalism. They appeared to bear little relation to the ideological beliefs associated with conservatism, socialism and environmentalism. In other words, there seems to be little connection between efficacy and estrangement and political ideology.

Origins of teenage ideology

In this section, we return to the question posed at the beginning of the chapter. How do the strongly crystallised opinions on topics of importance to young people transform into the political values of adults, if at all? To answer this question we take the three attitude scales derived from the wave 3 data which approximate most closely to party-political ideology: conservatism, socialism and environmentalism. For each of these three scales we analyse relationships with critical variables measured at earlier waves of the survey. These include attitudes, self-concept measures, educational performance up to 16, whether the respondent stayed on in education after the ages of 16 and 17, and family background and personal characteristics, including social class, parents' education, gender and area – 26 explanatory variables in all.

To sort out the relationships involved and assess the relative impact of earlier experiences and attitudes on subsequent outcomes, we use the statistical technique of multiple regression. This provides an estimate of the correlation between a single outcome variable and a set of prior explanatory variables taken in combination. The contribution that each of the explanatory variables makes to the overall multiple correlation (R) is expressed in terms of a 'standardised regression' coefficient (ß) which indicates the strength of the relationship of the explanatory variable to the outcome variable, holding constant the effects of all other variables. To simplify the account, we shall examine the relationships via diagrams on which only the variables with significant contributions to the relationship are included.

Conservatism

As Figure 7.5 shows, conservatism had an overall multiple correlation with the full set of prior explanatory variables of 0.47, suggesting that about a quarter of the variation on this dimension could be explained by the variables we included (that is, $R^2 = 0.22$). As Figure 7.5 also shows, eight explanatory variables made significant contributions to the relationship. Note that the largest ß coefficients (the figures on the arrows) were for income at wave 1 and post-16 education. Staying on at school after 16 was positively related to conservatism, as was higher income. Interestingly, apart from living in Swindon – in terms of voting intentions the most conservative area in the survey – all other significant predictors were attitude variables, the most significant of these

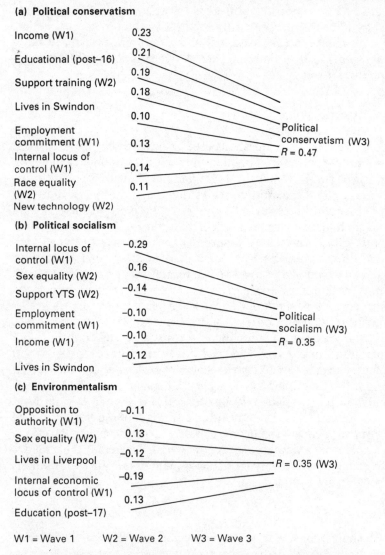

(a) Political conservatism

Income (W1)   0.23
Educational (post–16)   0.21
Support training (W2)   0.19
Lives in Swindon   0.18
Employment commitment (W1)   0.10
Internal locus of control (W1)   0.13
Race equality (W2)   −0.14
New technology (W2)   0.11

Political conservatism (W3)
$R = 0.47$

(b) Political socialism

Internal locus of control (W1)   −0.29
Sex equality (W2)   0.16
Support YTS (W2)   −0.14
Employment commitment (W1)   −0.10
Income (W1)   −0.10
Lives in Swindon   −0.12

Political socialism (W3)
$R = 0.35$

(c) Environmentalism

Opposition to authority (W1)   −0.11
Sex equality (W2)   0.13
Lives in Liverpool   −0.12
Internal economic locus of control (W1)   −0.19
Education (post–17)   0.13

$R = 0.35$ (W3)

W1 = Wave 1   W2 = Wave 2   W3 = Wave 3

Figure 7.5   Political ideologies, older cohort regression coefficients

being support for training. Others making minor contributions to the prediction were belief in work, support for new technology, and belief in an internal economic locus of control.

Socialism

It might be expected that as socialist beliefs are negatively correlated with conservative ones, albeit weakly, much the same variables would have featured in explaining both, and this was borne out by the statistical analysis. But although the multiple correlation was similar, a smaller number of explanatory variables were involved. Moreover, the strengths of the relationships were different. This time the belief in an internal economic locus of control had the largest (negative) ß coefficient followed by sexual equality. Other variables involved were support for training, belief in the value of work, and income, each of which showed *negative* relationships to socialism. Beyond the fact that income was the only non-attitude variable to predict socialism, each of the variables was in the economic domain, suggesting that, rather than embracing socialist ideology in a general sense, the socialism scale had picked up those aspects to do with the economy. In this sense, a broader socialist alternative to the new right radical conservatism would be better defined as the bottom end of the political conservatism scale, that is, support for protective economic policies but also opposition to conservative positions on social affairs.

Environmentalism

The growth of 'green' politics among young people in particular in all Western European countries made the antecedents of this scale particularly interesting. Another quite different picture emerged. The multiple correlation was lower at 0.35, but more variables had significant relationships. The strongest was for locus of control at wave 1 which, as for the previous scale, was negatively related to environmentalism (which is interesting, given the lack of relation between the latter and locus of control as assessed at wave 3). This was followed by living in Liverpool (negative), support for sex equality, non-opposition to authority, and staying on in education after age 17.

The picture that emerges of the young environmentalist is one of a socialist type of economic attribution, but without the early opposition to training, coupled with egalitarian views on gender roles – consistent also with the factor analysis described above that grouped environmentalism and gender egalitarianism – and a positive orientation to authority. Most interesting of all, however, is the connection with staying on in education after age 17. This is the first example we have of a connection between attitudes and post-17 education operating over and above staying on at 16. Is seems that young people with 'green' attitudes are likely to be concentrated in upper sixth forms and in higher education. In the absence of a prior measure of environmentalism at age 16, we cannot say with certainty whether the attitudes were formed by or help to form the 'green' ambience. But again it is plausible to consider the relationship a two-way one: like-minded young people influencing and reinforcing each other's values in a 'green' direction.

Origins of the 'origins'

With the possible exception of environmentalism, it appears that political attitudes are more a product of perspectives formed prior to age 17 than of subsequent experiences. Particularly notable also is the absence of relationships with other variables – most notably self-efficacy and estrangement, and political cynicism. As to pre-17 perspectives that do influence ideological commitments, we might look to social background and educational experience.

Figure 7.6 shows the multiple correlations and ß coefficients for all of the explanatory variables featuring in the previous analyses. In the analyses represented in Figure 7.6 these explanatory variables are now treated as outcome variables. The 'explanatory' variables included here are now restricted to the father's social class as defined by occupation, parents' education (as defined by school-leaving age), sex, area and educational attainment up to age 16 and earlier measures of attitudes. It is noteworthy that in every case except belief in an internal economic locus of control, gender egalitarianism, and support for training, the strongest predictor is pre-16 educational performance as defined by GCEs and CSEs (O grades and Highers in Scotland). Frequently coupled with educational attainment is the mother's education, clearly more significant than the father's. Also of interest is the significance of area in the foundations of many of these explanatory variables. Thus we can see clearly the effects of living in Swindon – higher income, more egalitarian gender-role beliefs, belief in the value of work, but also a greater likelihood of quitting education by age 17. And living in Kirkcaldy was associated with support for race equality, belief in the value of work, positive attitudes to new technology, egalitarian gender-role beliefs, but also with staying on in education after 17. The depressed state of Liverpool is reflected in its association with economic fatalism – the belief in an external economic locus of control.

A final analysis (Figure 7.7) traces influences one step further back by examining possible antecedents of educational performance in family background and personal characteristics. Here at last we find social class as reflected in the father's occupation exerting an effect. It turns out to be the most significant influence on educational attainment, followed by the mother's and then the father's education. These latter variables could also be regarded as indices of family social class. Gender, too, comes into the picture here, with girls tending to be the higher performers.

It is useful at last to have an indication that structural factors might play a part in the formation of political ideology, albeit indirectly. Indeed, it would be tempting to conclude that there is a line of influence, beginning with social

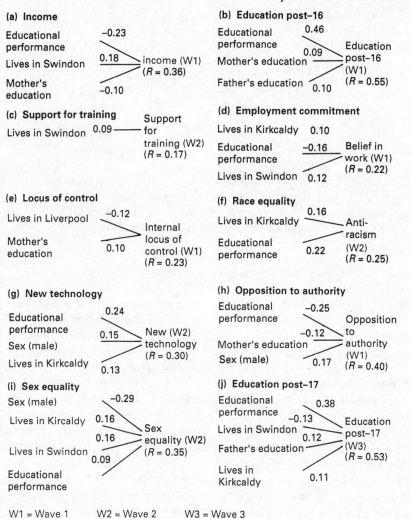

(a) Income

Educational performance −0.23

Lives in Swindon 0.18 income (W1) (*R* = 0.36)

Mother's education −0.10

(b) Education post–16

Educational performance 0.46

Mother's education 0.09 Education post–16 (W1) (*R* = 0.55)

Father's education 0.10

(c) Support for training

Lives in Swindon 0.09 Support for training (W2) (*R* = 0.17)

(d) Employment commitment

Lives in Kirkcaldy 0.10

Educational performance −0.16 Belief in work (W1) (*R* = 0.22)

Lives in Swindon 0.12

(e) Locus of control

Lives in Liverpool −0.12

Mother's education 0.10 Internal locus of control (W1) (*R* = 0.23)

(f) Race equality

Lives in Kirkcaldy 0.16 Anti-racism (W2) (*R* = 0.25)

Educational performance 0.22

(g) New technology

Educational performance 0.24

Sex (male) 0.15 New (W2) technology (*R* = 0.30)

Lives in Kirkcaldy 0.13

(h) Opposition to authority

Educational performance −0.25 Opposition to authority (W1) (*R* = 0.40)

Mother's education −0.12

Sex (male) 0.17

(i) Sex equality

Sex (male) −0.29

Lives in Kircaldy 0.16 Sex equality (W2) (*R* = 0.35)

Lives in Swindon 0.16

0.09

Educational performance

(j) Education post–17

Educational performance 0.38

Lives in Swindon −0.13 Education post–17 (W3) (*R* = 0.53)

Father's education 0.12

Lives in Kirkcaldy 0.11

W1 = Wave 1   W2 = Wave 2   W3 = Wave 3

Figure 7.6 Family background, personal characteristics and education experience, older cohort regression coefficients

class background, which shapes educational performance up to age 16, this in turn influencing both subsequent experiences and prospects (how much post-16 education a young person has, if any, and what he or she earns on entering employment) and attitudes and values, each of these finally feeding into ideological positions.

However, our last analysis explains only 14% of the variance in educational performance. Class, after all, does not explain everything about educational attainment, which suggests that other variables not included in the analysis

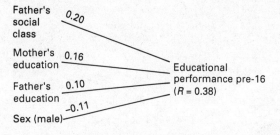

Figure 7.7   Educational attainment, older cohort regression coefficients

have a part to play, not to mention personal choice grounded in prior experience. Among the other variables are variation in ability (which is independent of class background) and possibly variation in attitude (also unrelated to class background). This brings us to the final section of this chapter.

Some repercussions of teenage ideological commitments

In Chapter 1 we suggested not only that the years from age 16 to age 20 were a significant period in the formation of identity but also that identities would shape and direct the choices made by young people in the course of their careers. Thus if attitudes are expressions of identity we should regard them not only as among the products of the socialisation process but also as predictive of various decisions and choices. In Chapter 4 we saw that beliefs about sex role equality did not relate to contributions boys made to housework, whereas for girls it did. Possibly this is because housework is a matter about which boys experience rather more real freedom of choice than girls. Here we will mention two other central choices of late adolescence, concerning how long to remain in full-time education, and which political party to support, if any.

The first of these has been examined in the previous section. Clearly it is influenced by prior educational performance and to that degree is probably a real choice only for some. However, we must also allow the possibility that some of the attitudes which are correlated with educational performance are themselves important influences on choices about educational career. We should remember that many of these attitudes proved to be highly stable across the period covered by the surveys and were particularly significant at wave 1 in predicting later ideological commitment; it cannot be assumed, therefore, that they are simply products of educational attainment.

Predicting leaving school between 16 and 18

Explanatory variables from wave 1 were selected on the basis of their correlation with the point at which young people left full-time education between 16 and 18, as indicated by the answers they gave at 17 and 18. Some of these individuals at 18 were, of course, still in full-time education. The predictors included five indices of social background: father's occupation; mother's occupation; father's age on leaving full-time education; mother's age on leaving full-time education; and nature of housing, that is, whether owner-occupied or rented. We also included the following attitudes and perception variables: opposition to authority; support for training; employment commitment; support for new technology; belief in an internal economic locus of control; sex equality; perceptions of the difficulty of finding work locally; and expectations about moving out of the area to find work. Increasingly, in each of the four study areas slightly different patterns emerged (Table 7.2).

Table 7.2 Origin of decision to leave school: regression coefficients

	Swindon	Sheffield	Liverpool	Kirkcaldy
Father's education	0.23	0.27	–	–
Mother's education	–	–	–	0.26
Support for new technology	0.21	–	–	–
Father's class	–	–	0.29	0.13
Mother's class	0.20	–	0.18	–
Emploment commitment	–0.19	–0.14	–	–0.15
Intention to move to seek work	–0.17	–0.18	–	–0.24
Owner occupier	0.14	0.19	–	–
Opposition to authority	–0.14	–0.32	–0.26	–0.31
Support for training	–	–0.17	–0.29	–
Political cynicism	–	–	–0.15	–

Various features of the analyses represented in this table are worthy of comment. First, social background in some form and orientation to authority figures in all four areas were independently related to length of time in full-time education after age 16. Employment commitment appears in three. Second, certain other variables only exerted a significant effect in some areas, such as support for new technology in Swindon – where it was the strongest attitude predictor. It is tempting to speculate that the character of the local economy reinforced a link between support for new technology and decisions to pursue further educational credentials. Support for training emerged as a significant (negative) predictor in both Liverpool and Sheffield. Third, Liverpool is the only one of the four areas in which expectations about leaving the area to find work were unrelated to post-16 education.

Remembering that these attitudes and perceptions pre-date the decisions they have been used to predict in this analysis, and cannot themselves be 'explained' by educational attainment, we can conclude that something more than prior educational attainment lies behind decisions to stay on in education beyond age 16.

Predicting political party preferences

Finally, do attitudes predict voting intentions? The answer seems to be that they do. Moveover, we find here evidence that political choices do, after all, continue to be ordered on a rough left–right dimension. Significant attitudinal correlates of voting intentions at wave 3 included political ideology, economic locus of control, orientation to authority, and gender egalitarianism. Interestingly, environmentalism was not correlated with voting intentions except in relation to voting Green. Multiple regressions, taking voting intentions expressed in wave 3 as the outcome variable, identified left–right political ideology as the strongest explanatory variable $R = 0.55$ (for 20-year-olds, $ß = 0.52$, $R = 0.55$; for 18-year-olds, $ß = 0.46$, $R = 0.53$). In each group educational performance and father's occupational category independently made significant but much smaller contributions, as did economic locus of control. There is again, however, a difficulty about the direction of causality here. Political ideology may itself be shaped by such choices as voting intentions.

Party preferences will be examined in more detail in Chapter 8. But we will note here that area differences in social and political attitudes were relatively small, whereas area differences in voting preferences proved to be quite large. If this suggests anything, it is that forms of political participation among young people such as voting are not shaped by attitudes and ideologies alone. Where young people live in Britain may have as much influence on how they plan to vote as does what they believe.

Teenage and adult ideology

In Chapter 1 we argued that the political terrain for young people is defined more in terms of the issues of immediate concern to them in their daily lives than in terms of the policies of the political parties. Thus the exercise of authority at home, at school or outside is a salient 'political issue' for a teenager living at home, as is everything to do with sex and relations between the sexes and between different races. We have also seen in this chapter how staying on in education is critically related to the attitudes held, and that leaving school to enter a job is often associated with oppositional attitudes to authority and strong work commitment. It is notable that those closest to adulthood in the sense of getting full-time employment at the earliest possible age are least supportive of equal opportunities standpoints; those staying on tend to be most egalitarian and liberal.

Interesting, too, is the finding that the group closest to the young workers is not the one comprising those who have entered jobs via YTS schemes, but those who have never experienced much of anything else. This last no-career group tends to be at the extreme opposite end of the spectrum to the academic group in political cynicism and opposition to authority. Though also tending towards socialist beliefs, they are least attracted to environmentalism, tending more towards hostility and alienation.

We have seen that these value positions feed and in a sense underpin more recognisable ideological systems such as conservatism and socialism, which themselves relate to expressed political affiliation of the conventional party kind; they also relate to future location in the class structure as reflected in the decision whether to stay on or leave school. The novel feature of this ideological domain is environmentalism. Clearly related to staying on in school and to educational attainment, it seems to hold a distinctive place in young people's political thinking which may gather strength as more young people stay on. Ecological movements and the Green Party may well have an increasingly receptive hearing.

Chapter 8   POLITICS

Why politics?

I'm not into politics. I'm not sure what I think of any of them.

I've never got into it. I don't think any of them will make much difference. In my eyes none of them are worth a light.

If you put it in front of me on the telly, I watch the news, but I don't exactly look for it there or in the papers. I think they're all a load of rubbish. I don't like the Conservatives. Also I don't like Labour; they're not up to scratch enough to be the government. The others are just a farce. I voted for the Greens last year mainly so as not to support the government of the moment.

I think I'd vote Labour but I don't follow politics much. Sometimes it seems just too hard to understand.

Politics was not a central interest for most of our respondents. When interviewed, some were vehement in proclaiming disinterest. Few considered themselves well informed about political parties, personalities and events. Many held low opinions of all the parties and of most politicians.

The previous chapter has covered topics that were of much greater interest to most of the young people we studied. We argued there that such issues as racial discrimination, sexual equality, training and the proper bounds of authority at home and elsewhere defined the political world of young people, but continuities with the political ideology associated with party preference, though tenuous, do exist. In this chapter we take the topic a stage further. What interest and involvement was there in politics of the conventional adult kind? What party affiliations were expressed and how did these relate to earlier circumstances and experience?

To set our findings in context, we need to record the changes in young people's circumstances and the government policies that might be expected to have influenced the stance they were adopting. As we saw in Chapter 1, the government response to the collapse of youth employment in the late 1970s was to encourage more young people to stay on in education or to change their status from that of worker to that of trainee. Chapter 3 showed that although the traditional route for early school leavers of direct entry into employment persisted, especially in Swindon, for the majority the new arrangements were dominating the transition to work. In 1988 young people also lost earlier adult entitlements such as social security from age 16, extending their dependency on parents. Yet at the same time they were being asked to pay the poll tax and, if they were students, to top up their maintenance grants by taking out loans.

In the early 1980s there were concerns that unemployment would nurture political disaffection and reaction (Unesco, 1981; Lenhardt, 1984). Urban riots in Britain lent credibility to such forecasts. Governments were said to have broken their side of 'the implicit social contract' (Turner, 1984). In high-unemployment areas, a 'passive alienation', spilling over into destructive vandalism and confrontation with the police, was detected (Ridley, 1981). Cochrane and Billig (1982b) also noted the rise in National Front membership among young people over a three-year period in the West Midlands. However, the later part of the decade did not bring any further evidence of such trends. Although, as we saw in Chapter 7, those young people out in the labour market, but least successful in getting jobs, were the most estranged and politically disaffected, they were characterised more by political apathy than active hostility to the status quo.

Our samples were born when Margaret Thatcher was Secretary of State for Education; they spent their secondary school careers and became voters while she was Prime Minister. They were 'Thatcher's children', but what did they make of her values? Again our evidence from the previous chapter suggested that Thatcherism had achieved mixed success. The majority of our respondents were opposed to raising taxes and were supporters of private education, capital punishment and the police, but they were also opposed to the privatisation of public utilities and services.

In relation to political affiliation and voting, some commentators have argued that the government's policies of expanding home and share ownership and extolling the virtues of 'enterprise' have strengthened the longer-term trend, based on rising working-class affluence and increased social mobility, towards 'class dealignment' (Robertson 1984; Franklin, 1985). Until the 1960s social class was the best single predictor of voting preference, giving each of the main parties a solid bedrock of support. Subsequently middle-class voters' attachments to the Conservative Party weakened, while Labour working-class support likewise became less dependable (Sarlvick and Crewe, 1983). The manifestations of dealignment are said to include more violent swings of the political pendulum and greater opportunities for centre and other alternative parties to capture 'floating voters'.

Some political scientists reject the dealignment hypothesis (Heath *et al.*, 1985; Weakliem, 1989), and even its supporters acknowledge the continued significance of social class in voting. Moreover, if British politics is becoming less class-based, it is not clear what its new foundations will be. Some argue that the sectors, public and private, in which people are employed are becoming more important, not only as a source of votes, but also as sources of the main parties' activists (Dunleavy, 1989; Saunders, 1978; 1981; 1990). Local political cultures are also said to be becoming more varied and influential as determinants of party choice (Goodwin, 1989). Another alleged trend is towards 'issue voting', where a preference is expressed, for whichever candidate takes the appropriate stand on the policy or policies the voter judges the most important. Clearly, in the age group represented by our respondents we can investigate these issues only to a limited extent. Nevertheless, if there is a case for dealignment we might expect to find signs of it among the next generation of voters. Some of the older cohort were old enough to vote in the general election of 1987 and all of them had reached voting age by the time of the European Parliament election in 1989.

Young people are said to be idealistic and receptive to new political messages. We might expect them, therefore, to be more easily detached from class-political affiliations. The relation between their social class and their expressed political preferences is, therefore, of particular interest. One of the difficulties, however, in assessing the evidence for class dealignment in young people is to decide which class they belong to. Educational attainment moderates the effect of family social class on future class status, which is what we are primarily interested in. The solution, following Jones (1988), is to allocate young people to four 'class trajectories' combining family social class as defined by father's occupation and their own educational attainment: middle-class high attainers; middle-class low attainers; working-class high attainers; and working-class low attainers. The two extreme groups can be defined as on 'stable' class trajectories and the two middle groups as 'mobile'. Besides comparing young people in terms of their cohort, sex, location and career trajectory (as defined previously), their class trajectory is also used extensively in this chapter. Most of the analyses are based on the group who completed all three surveys, so that longitudinal changes in the same group of young people can be assessed.

Political interest and cynicism

In all three surveys the young people were asked how interested they were in politics, to which they gave one of four possible responses: 'very', 'quite', 'not very' and 'not at all'. Interest was also assessed by whether they said they intended to vote for any party in a general election and, if so, which party. Furthermore, they were asked about their involvement in a range of political activities, from talking and reading about politics to attending meetings and campaigning. Together with the political cynicism measure we considered in Chapter 7, all these measures are interrelated (Bynner and Ashford, 1990); in other words, a young person who was not interested in politics was also more likely to be cynical about political institutions, less likely to intend to vote, and more likely to be politically inactive. Table 8.1 presents respondents' answers to the questions on interest, intention to vote, cynicism and involvement, by cohort, sex, area and class trajectory. The table shows a modest but steady growth in political interest and voting intention with age, with interest rising from 34% among 15–16-year-olds in wave 1 to 41% among 19–20-year-olds in wave 3. Males were also consistently more interested in politics than females – a well-established sex difference that has been found in many previous investigations (Stradling, 1977). There were barely any area effects except that interest was marginally higher in Liverpool, a reflection perhaps of the high-profile Militant politics of the local Labour Party and City Council which gained much media attention at the time. Intention to vote in a general election was far more prevalent than interest, starting at three-quarters and rising to over 90% in the older groups.

The sharpest differences were among class trajectories. Levels of political interest were similar and low among low achievers in middle- and working-class homes. Political interest was substantially higher among those in the higher-attainment groups, an effect which appeared to override home background, though interest peaked among the high-achieving group from middle-class families. Just over half of this group described themselves as interested in politics, compared with between a quarter and a third of the other groups. But the largest increases in interest occurred among the least successful. The class gap in political interest is likely to have been at least partly due to the lower achievers being the slower to develop political concerns.

In contrast, voting intention did not differ much between class trajectories, a finding which is in line with similar conclusions for adults (Heath and Topf, 1987). It seems that although interest is strongly based on social class and on attainment, the act of voting is not. Most people of all classes believe sufficiently in the value of universal suffrage to wish to exercise their right to vote even though they may have little interest in the politics that surrounds it.

Mean scores on the political cynicism scale reflected those for interest. Cynicism was most common among the low-attaining groups, and was more closely related to educational achievements than family backgrounds. But, unlike interest, it did not change at all with age, suggesting that the basic pattern seemed to have been 'set' by age 15–16, which was not the case with interest in politics.

Most of the young people were consistent in expressing interest or lack of

Table 8.1 Political interest and involvement by cohort, sex, area and class trajectory

| | | Cohort | | Sex | | Area | | | | Class trajectory/Family background | | | |
| | | | | | | | | | | MC Ed Att | | WC Ed Att | |
		Y	O	M	F	Sw	Sh	Li	Ki	High	Low	High	Low
Very or quite interested (%)	1987	34	37	42	30	36	35	36	34	53	24	41	23
	1988	39	43	47	36	40	42	44	39	60	33	43	31
	1989	37	41	45	35	40	39	44	36	55	32	44	29
Would vote in general election (%)	1987	72	75	79	69	74	71	75	74	78	66	73	69
	1988	85	89	86	87	85	87	86	89	90	85	87	85
	1989	90	91	90	91	88	97	89	88	90	93	94	88
Political cynicism (mean score)	1987	2.79	2.76	2.80	2.74	2.73	2.74	2.86	2.77	2.50	2.90	2.60	2.90
	1988	2.78	2.74	2.77	2.75	2.67	2.72	2.85	2.80	2.50	2.80	2.70	2.90
Political participation													
a Communicative (mean score)	1987	1.86	2.11	2.05	2.00	2.00	1.89	2.07	1.92	2.45	1.83	2.04	1.56
	1988	1.76	1.91	1.86	1.79	1.82	1.77	1.91	1.80	2.29	1.60	1.94	1.44
b Action (mean score)	1987*	0.66	0.59	0.61	0.65	0.57	0.53	0.71	0.71	0.71	0.77	0.53	0.56
	1988*	0.33	0.39	0.35	0.37	0.29	0.34	0.42	0.36	0.49	0.42	0.35	0.29

*A slight wording change in 1988 makes the figures not strictly comparable with those in 1987.

MC = Middle class; WC = Working class; Ed Att = Educational attainment; Y = Younger; O = Older; M = Male; F = Female interest, but, as we shall see, their party loyalties were far more fickle. Among those who answered the relevant question in all three surveys, 46% were consistently not very or not at all interested in politics, 24% were consistently very or quite interested, and only a minority (31%) changed sides.

Factor analysis suggested that the political activities formed two distinct groups which could be represented by scales; the first of these, with a range of 0 to 3, were 'communicative' activities, which included discussing politics with one's friends, reading about politics in the press and watching party-political broadcasts. The other scale, with a range of 0 to 4, involved political action and included signing a petition, taking part in a boycott, contacting public officals and attending a meeting. The mean scores on both of these scales for each group are also shown in Table 8.1. Again, it was clear that both forms of activity were strongly related to class and education, with substantially higher scores in the stable middle class than the stable working class. Although this distinction was clear for the communicative activities it was far less marked for political action, which was extremely low in both groups.

Despite this picture of relatively little interest and even less activity among our respondents, this did not necessarily mean that they considered politics unimportant. A relatively small minority on all class trajectories argued that it was not important to know about politics. In the interviews it was common for individuals to explain that they regarded their own lack of interest as a temporary phase: 'I still don't know much about politics but I think it is important'; 'I don't have time to read the papers but I watch the telly'; 'I have got a vague idea of what's happening'; 'I wish I was more involved'. Also, around two-thirds of respondents expressed a party preference in each survey. And, as we have seen, this was one measure of involvement which was unrelated to the sample's class trajectories.

Figures 8.1 and 8.2 return to the career-trajectory variables as a basis for comparison. Their significance in this context is that they represent most clearly the consequences of the labour-market changes and of government policies as they impinged on young people. Two types of trajectory, as defined in Chapter 3, are used in the analysis: the five trajectories that were identified for 16–18-year-olds (Type A) and the four trajectories, identified for the 18–20 age group: higher education, other kinds of education, continuous employment, and substantal experience of unemployment.

As we might expect, the members of the younger cohort who followed the academic route – who were the most interested in politics to begin with – were the only group whose interest rose substantially between ages 16 and 18. So at age 18 they were even further ahead of the rest than at age 16. Individuals who followed education routes between 18 and 20 remained the most politically interested throughout, with those in higher education well ahead of all the others. At age 18, two-thirds of higher education entrants described themselves as interested in politics. However, their interest declined slightly from then on. There was a parallel decline on the other education route. In

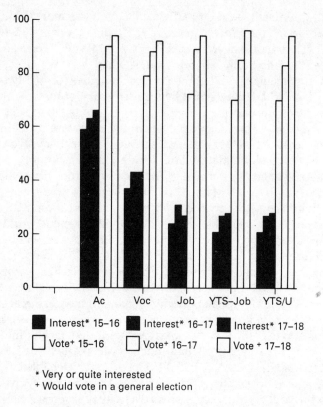

Interest* 15–16   Interest* 16–17   Interest* 17–18

Vote+ 15–16   Vote+ 16–17   Vote + 17–18

* Very or quite interested
+ Would vote in a general election

Figure 8.1   Interest and participation in politics, by career trajectory, (15–18) by age

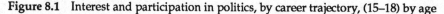

contrast, on the employment and unemployment routes political interest rose marginally. According to this evidence, students in higher education in the 1980s were the most politicised members of their age group, but it is important to recognise that this was not because higher education itself was arousing them politically.

Higher education entrants were a selected group of those staying on in education post-16 so their raised interest and reduced cynicism was established well before 18. In fact, some of the university students who were interviewed explained that their interest in politics had declined since their sixth-form days. 'In the sixth form I was very definitely interested, but I am not so interested now. I have become a bit disenchanted that even through protest nothing gets changed'. Nevertheless, as full-time students, they were the only 18–20-year-olds in the sample who were moving daily in social networks where interest in politics was the norm. Their interest was being sustained, if not actually increased, through the experience of being students.

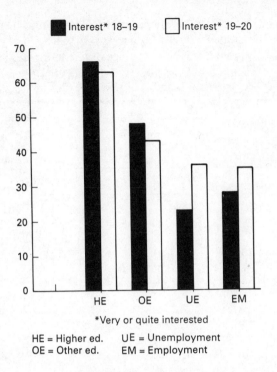

■ Interest* 18–19   □ Interest* 19–20

*Very or quite interested

HE = Higher ed.   UE = Unemployment
OE = Other ed.   EM = Employment

Figure 8.2   Interest in politics by career trajectory, (18–20) by age

Who would you vote for?

The following question was asked in all three surveys: 'If there was a general election tomorrow and you were able to vote, which political party do you think you would be most likely to support?' Table 8.2 gives the younger and older cohorts' answers in 1987 and 1989, with those who 'did not know' or said that they would not vote ignored. Around a third in each survey did not express any party preference, which is roughly in line with the rate of abstentions in UK general elections. Only individuals who responded in both surveys are included in the analysis on which Table 8.2 is based. So the shifts in opinion in Table 8.2 were the result of the same individuals changing their allegiances.

That Labour was substantially the most popular party overall in all three waves of the survey is a reflection of the political complexion of the four areas in which the research was carried out. In all of them Labour had control of the Council, though not in Parliament. Swindon, for example, returned only Conservative MPs.

Party choices of the younger and older respondents were virtually identical in 1987 and 1989. This supports earlier research which suggests that political socialisation occurs early (see, for example, Easton and Dennis, 1969; Greenstein, 1969; Stacey, 1978). By age 16, young people's political choices were already patterned by such influences as place of residence and social class.

Table 8.2   Party choices by sex, area and class trajectory (%)

| | Cohort | | Sex | | Area | | | | Family Social Class | | | |
| | | | | | | | | | MC Ed att | MC | WC Ed att | WC |
	Y	O	M	F	Sw	Sh	Li	Ki	High	Low	High	Low
1987												
Conservative	22	21	26	17	40	19	14	15	33	20	19	14
Labour	46	47	41	52	27	53	62	45	26	44	49	67
Centre	27	26	27	26	31	26	23	27	36	29	27	15
Green	1	1	1	1	1	1	1	–	1	2	1	–
SNP	4	4	4	4	–	–	–	13	3	6	4	3
Other	–	1	1	–	1	1	–	–	–	–	–	1
1989												
Conservative	30	30	32	28	51	36	16	17	39	32	29	22
Labour	50	48	46	52	34	53	69	40	33	45	50	63
Centre	7	6	6	6	9	6	7	3	9	9	6	3
Green	4	5	4	5	5	4	7	3	7	3	5	2
SNP	9	10	11	9	–	–	–	37	10	10	9	9
Other	–	1	1	–	1	1	1	–	–	2	1	–

MC = Middle class   Y = Younger   M = Male
WC = Working class   O = Older   F = Female
Ed att = Educational attainment

Age was making no difference to which parties the samples supported, but a cohort affect was also evident, in that between 1987 and 1989 overall party support changed substantially, the direction of change reflecting the general tide of political opinion in Britain at that time. Both surveys were conducted in the months of April and May, so the 1987 inquiry was just before the June general election, while the 1989 investigation preceded the European Parliament election. The Conservatives won the 1987 general election comfortably, though in this election, as in 1983, the centre parties (the SDP/Liberal Alliance in 1987) polled quite strongly.

In our 1987 survey the centre parties were supported by around a quarter of all respondents who possessed voting intentions. Then between 1987 and 1989, at the time of the merger of the Alliance parties and the breakaway of David Owen's SDP, the centre parties' support collapsed throughout Britain, as it did within our samples. Our evidence reflects the national trend that in

1987 the centre parties were on the verge of a Parliamentary breakthrough. Over the next two years their support evaporated.

At the time of our 1989 survey, less than 5% said that they would vote for the Green Party which then went on to win 15% of the popular vote in the European Parliament election in June. Chapter 7 explained that 'the environment' was an issue on which our samples had reasonably consistent attitudes. Interviews with subsamples during the winter of 1989–90 indicated that support for the Green Party had risen substantially, and the European election campaign seemed to have been the catalyst which converted interest in environmental issues into support for the Greens.

Table 8.2 also compares the samples' party preferences in 1987 and 1989 by sex and by area of residence. The main sex difference was that Labour was slightly more popular among the females, and the Conservatives among the males. There are alternative ways of reacting to this evidence. Throughout most of the twentieth century women have been Britain's more Conservative sex, at least in terms of voting behaviour (Butler and Stokes, 1969). Was the reversal among young people in the 1980s due to Conservatives' failing to respond to 'women's issues' or to Labour failing to hold its traditional support among male workers?

There were even sharper inter-area differences. The Swindon sample contained the highest proportion of Conservatives, while only the Kirkcaldy sample gave any support to the Scottish National Party, which is unsurprising. We shall return to these inter-area differences shortly but, to anticipate, they are not attributable in any straightforward way to the young people's social class locations. In Swindon young people on all class trajectories were more likely to support the Conservatives than in any other area. Similarly, there was a 'Liverpool effect' favouring Labour in all social classes.

In both 1987 and 1989 the party preferences of the two socially mobile groups were fairly similar, whereas the party allegiances of the socially stable groups polarised sharply. In both years there was roughly twice as much support for the Conservative Party in the stable middle class as in the stable working-class group, and more than twice as much support for Labour within the latter. In 1987, when support for the centre parties was widespread, it was most prevalent in the stable middle-class group, and least prevalent among the young people on the stable working-class trajectory. Social class had certainly not become politically irrelevant. Indeed, it was among the best predictors of our samples' voting intentions (as also noted in Heath *et al.*, 1985).

A noteworthy feature of the evidence in Table 8.2 is that the same general political drift, away from the centre parties between 1987 and 1989, occurred in every subgroup – among males and females, in all class groups, and in every area. In 1987 the centre parties came second in terms of total support within our samples in all four areas.

Despite the same general drift away from the centre, there were some interesting variations between the sexes, areas and class groups in terms of exactly how their party allegiances changed between 1987 and 1989. First, the difference between the sexes in party allegiance narrowed. Second, the Conservatives derived most benefit from the collapse of centre party support in the areas where Conservative support was initially strongest – Swindon and Sheffield. In Kirkcaldy the main beneficiary was the Scottish National Party, while Labour benefited in Liverpool.

The differences between areas in the samples' voting intentions were comparable in magnitude to those associated with social class, and were certainly not due to the areas' different social class compositions. Table 8.3 compares the party loyalties in 1989 of two groups of young people in each area. First, we take young people from middle-class homes who remained in full-time education beyond age 16, then early school leavers from manual families. It is immediately apparent from Table 8.3 that, with social class situations held constant, there were still massive inter-area differences in the samples' party loyalties.

Table 8.3 Party preferences and level of education, 1989 (%)

	Middle-class students in full-time education				Working-class early-leavers			
	Sw	Sh	Li	Ki	Sw	Sh	Li	Ki
Conservative	46	40	21	26	50	35	11	12
Labour	30	41	58	29	37	59	80	46
Centre	10	11	7	7	9	3	6	2
Green	13	7	13	4	3	3	2	1
Scottish Nationalist	–	–	–	34	–	–	–	39
Other	1	1	1	–	2	1	1	–

We approached this analysis with the expectation that Scotland would be different, but in fact the contrasts among the English areas proved just as wide. Indeed, Kirkcaldy closely resembled Liverpool in the Conservatives' lack of local support among young people in all class locations. Even among young Liverpudlians from middle-class homes who remained in full-time education beyond age 16, there was nearly three times as much support for the Labour Party as for the Conservatives. Kirkcaldy differed from Liverpool basically in its anti-Conservative vote being divided between Labour and the Scottish Nationalists. In Sheffield, and even more so in Swindon, young people in all class situations were less likely to support the Labour Party, and were more likely to intend to vote Conservative than in Liverpool. In Swindon the Conservatives had more support than Labour even among working-class youth. In fact, working-class youth in Swindon were more likely to intend to vote Conservative than the area's middle-class young people.

All this evidence underlines the importance of local political cultures in shaping young people's voting intentions. In Kirkcaldy, support for the

Scottish Nationalists was related to a feeling that Scotland was relatively deprived, and unjustly so, compared with the rest of Britain. In Liverpool many young people shared a similar feeling that Merseyside was a disadvantaged area, but the result seemed to be a consolidation of Labour's position as Liverpool's dominant party. Levels of support for the different parties, and the directions of change between 1987 and 1989 in our samples, were being influenced by the relationships between their home areas and the local political cultures on the one hand, and the national political context, where the Conservatives were dominant, on the other. This seemed to be working to the Conservatives' advantage in Swindon and to a lesser extent in Sheffield, and to their disadvantage in Kirkcaldy and Liverpool.

Local trends in party support between 1987 and 1989 give some credence to such a geographical polarisation, and trends on the different class trajectories are consistent with the dealignment hypothesis. Between 1987 and 1989 Conservative support increased among respondents on all the class trajectories, whereas Labour support rose only within the group where it was initially lowest, that is, among those on the stable middle-class trajectory.

Table 8.4 charts the changes that occurred in the samples' party preferences between 1987 and 1989 according to three of the career trajectories that they were following from 16 to 18 and the four they were following from 18 to 20. The collapse in centre party support occurred in both cohorts, and among young people on all the career routes. Within the younger cohort Conservative Party support rose on all the routes, and likewise on all the career routes from age 18 to 20, with just one exception – higher education. Within the younger cohort the academic route was the only one where Labour Party support rose, while within the older cohort Labour support rose most substantially among the higher education students.

It is possible to present this evidence as further support for the class dealignment theory. With increasing age, within the cohorts that we investigated, cross-class supporters were comprising a growing proportion of all the Labour Party followers. Of course, there can be no guarantee that the 'middle class' members of our sample who switched to Labour while on educational routes between ages 16 and 20 would not swing away at later stages in their careers. Whether or not they were to do so, it could be that individuals who swung while students have always featured among the Labour Party's supporters, particularly its more active supporters. And it is worth bearing in mind that the changes recorded in our samples between ages 16 and 20 were making only minor adjustments to patterns of party alignment whose main contours were already pronounced at age 15–16.

Party loyalties

The net shifts in party support recorded in our samples between 1987 and 1989 are a poor guide to the number of individuals who changed their minds.

Among the older cohort, the centre parties' share of the vote fell from 27% to 7%, while the Conservatives' share rose from 22% to 30%, and Labour's from 46% to 50%. These shifts could have occurred through no more than a fifth of the sample changing their preferences. In practice, however, most individuals switched, often more than once. Just 8% of all respondents expressed support for the Conservative Party in all three years of the survey, and 20% for Labour. So under a third of the young people remained faithful to one of the two main parties throughout the two-year period. Another 2% of respondents consistently supported a centre party, a further 2% were constant in their support for the Scottish Nationalists, and 12% were consistent in not supporting any party. Fifty-seven per cent of the sample changed their party allegiances during the two years of the research. It is possible that a similar study of adults would have recorded greater party loyalty, though the substantial swings in the opinion polls in the late-1980s suggest that our 16–19-year-olds were merely reflecting the volatility of the entire electorate. Mobilising sufficient support to achieve office meant that any party would be dependent mainly on voters with floating loyalties. Among our samples, the main parties' bedrocks of staunch, reliable support were narrow. Most respondents were floaters.

Table 8.4   Change in party support by career routes, 1987–9 (%)

	Routes followed at age 16–18			*Routes followed at age 18–20*			
	YTS	*Acad.*	*Trad.*	*HigherEd.*	*Other Ed.*	*Unempl.*	*Employment*
	1987 (aged 15–16)			**1987 (aged 17–18)**			
Conservative	13	25	23	33	25	3	21
Labour	65	35	54	31	35	68	49
Centre	19	36	19	31	39	23	25
Green	1	1	–	3	–	1	–
SNP	2	2	5	3	2	5	4
Other	1	1	–	–	–	–	–
	1989 (aged 17–18)			**1989 (aged 19–20)**			
Conservative	22	33	30	32	34	14	33
Labour	58	40	57	39	38	67	52
Centre	3	7	5	11	6	1	6
Green	3	9	1	11	4	4	1
SNP	14	8	5	8	18	13	8
Other	1	1	2	–	–	1	–

In the 1989 survey respondents who supported any party were asked to select from a list the reasons for their support. Nearly all the supporters of both parties, on all trajectories, explained their choices partly or wholly in terms of believing that their preferred parties had the best policies, and agreeing with the parties' basic ideals. However, many of these young supporters did not rate their own political interest or knowledge highly, and, as we shall see, although they may not have realised this, substantial numbers did not agree with their parties' principal domestic policies. It is likely that these reasons for supporting the parties were often endorsed simply because the answers appeared the correct ones to offer.

Conservative supporters were more likely than Labour voters to say that a reason for their choice was that the party had the best leaders. Labour supporters were the more likely to give 'family' and 'sectional' motives.

Were the Labour and Conservative voters really as solidly behind their parties' policies as the young people's own reasons for their support suggest? As we saw in Chapter 7, the evidence was mixed. In the 1989 survey respondents were presented with four propositions which spotlighted major Labour–Conservative disputes on socio-economic policy. Labour was opposed to the privatisation of publicly-owned industries and services. Also, the Party believed that spending on public services should be maintained or increased even if this meant sacrificing tax reductions. Unsurprisingly, Labour supporters were more likely than Conservatives to endorse Labour's policies on these issues, but while most Labour supporters agreed that major industries such as British Rail and British Gas should remain in public ownership, only a minority, less than a quarter, agreed that personal taxes should be increased in order to pay for better public services. On both these policy issues support for the official Labour line was lower among the party's working-class than among its middle-class supporters. Labour appeared to be capturing middle-class support on the basis of its policies while failing to consolidate its 'natural' class support by educating these young voters to a similar level of agreement with measures that a Labour government would implement.

Our Conservative propositions were not drawn from stated government policies but represented Conservative new right or Thatcherite thinking and the most likely long-term implications if government policies of the 1980s were continued. The questions were designed to assess the extent to which the incoming generation of voters was Thatcherite in outlook in the sense of believing it desirable to reduce state dependency by paying welfare benefits selectively – only to the needy – and encouraging people to pay for their own services, including health care. In the event, the new right policies were endorsed by only a minority of the Conservative Party's own supporters. Just over a third agreed with restricting state welfare to the very poor, while less than a fifth wanted to reduce reliance on the National Health Service. More Conservatives wanted to keep industries such as gas and the railways under public ownership than to enlarge the role of private medicine. According to this evidence, Thatcherism had not even converted the majority of the Conservative Party's own young supporters, let alone the bulk of their generation. Among the Conservatives, support for new right policies was unrelated to class trajectories, whereas on the Labour side opposition to new right thinking was more prevalent among the cross-class supporters – further evidence that they were more committed to Labour policies than the Party's 'natural' class voters.

The general political orientations manifested through these opinion items were associated overall with voting preferences in 1989. Table 8.5 compares mean scores on our three political ideology scales – conservatism, socialism and environmentalism – between groups defined by party preference. It is clear that high scores on the scales were associated quite strongly with party preference, but with some interesting overlaps. Thus Conservative supporters tended to endorse conservative beliefs, Labour supporters socialist beliefs, and Green Party supporters environmentalist beliefs. But it was noteworthy that Centre Party supporters came second to Green Party supporters on environmentalism, while Green Party supporters came second to Labour Party supporters on socialism. There are signs in the figures of potential for detachment from Centre to Green and vice versa, a sign perhaps of the ideological 'softness' of the middle ground. Conservative and Labour supporters were equally far from the Greens on environmentalism, but on socialism the Greens and Labour came closer together. This might suggest that a much stronger commitment to environmental policies by Labour would weaken Green support. Conservative moves in this direction seem less likely to meet with success because of the bigger gap between the Greens and the Conservatives on conservatism – unless the Conservatives changed tack on Thatcherite values themselves.

Table 8.5   Political beliefs and voting preferences in 1989 (mean scores)

	1989		
Party Preference	*Conservatism*	*Socialism*	*Environmentalism*
Conservative	2.67	2.59	3.42
Labour	2.06	3.51	3.49
Centre	2.23	3.05	3.61
SNP	2.34	3.45	3.57
Green	2.06	3.21	4.32

These speculations are, of course, impossible to test any further with our data, which included measures of political beliefs only at wave 3. And in any event, the political context may change so radically that quite new types of common ground between the parties might supersede them. What they do serve to illustrate is the complexity and likely volatility of what are, at least for the bulk of this age group, fairly weakly formed political positions. Their interaction with party preference and voting extending to older age groups merits further investigation.

It came across very clearly in face-to-face interviews that our samples generally favoured political moderation. Tony Benn and Arthur Scargill were mentioned repeatedly and disapprovingly in this context (see Quicke, 1991). In 1988 the Liverpool respondents were asked for their solutions to their city's financial problems, which had become a national issue culminating in the disqualification from office of a group of Labour councillors and the leader of the Labour Party Neil Kinnock's repudiation of the Liverpool Militants. The solutions to their local council's difficulties that drew the widest support from the Liverpool sample were demanding more money from central government (86%) and encouraging tourism (85%). There was negligible support for cutting local services (2%) or the council workforce (8%), or raising more cash locally through the rates (4%) or council house rents (5%). Derek Hatton, the city's best-known Militant politician, was considered bad for Liverpool by far more respondents than offered the contrary opinion, and he was regarded as an extremist. Yet the policies that the sample endorsed mirrored the Militant position.

Conclusions

Some of the questions with which this chapter opened can now be answered unequivocally, and negatively. First, young people's new condition created by the gap between leaving eduaction and obtaining employment in the 1980s was not nurturing a new kind of political generation. We found no evidence of any 'sea change' in political culture (see also Crewe, 1989). The predicaments of 16–19-year-olds were not leading to a spread of disaffection, radicalism, conservatism or anything else. Possibly the most striking, impressive and consistent feature of the evidence presented in this chapter has been that the young people's attitudes were so little affected by whether they spent their late teenage years mainly in education, continuous employment, on schemes, or experienced substantial unemployment. In confirmation of our findings in Chapter 7 about the origins of political ideology, basic patterns of political involvement and partisanship had been largely set by age 15–16 and the patterns survived subsequent events. Our findings reinforce previous evidence that Britain's young unemployed in the 1980s were typically anti-Thatcher and pro-Labour, but otherwise uninterested and cynical (Breakwell, 1985; Coffield *et al.*, 1986; Banks and Ullah, 1987b; McRae 1987). Our longi-tudinal evidence shows clearly that the reasons why the young unemployed had such outlooks had more to do with the groups that already possessed these attitudes being the most prone to unemployment than with the experience of joblessness producing the attitudes.

Second, it is equally clear from our evidence that most new voters in the late 1980s were not Thatcher's children in an ideological sense. Her enterprise values had not become standard. There were few signs of a 'new realism'. The so-called 'British disease' was much in evidence. The young people did not want to contribute more taxes, but they expected to receive more in benefits and services from government.

Our respondents' party loyalties were mostly fickle. In comparison, individuals' and groups' levels of political interest and involvement were relatively stable. There were huge differences by age 15–16 related mainly to educational attainments. Thereafter the trends depended primarily on whether individuals remained in full-time education or became early school leavers. The political interest gap between those who remained in the academic mainstream and early school leavers widened between ages 16 and 18, but narrowed between ages 18 and 20, with the net result of little change in the original pattern except that all groups were a little more interested, though no less cynical than at the outset.

This class pattern supports earlier findings about young people's involvement in British politics (Dowse and Hughes, 1971; Stradling and Zureik, 1971; Zureik, 1974). Most young people derive their initial party affiliations from their families (Himmelweit and Swift, 1971; Jennings and Niemi, 1974), but other class differences are not so much accentuated by as reproduced mainly through education. The successful become the most interested and active, and according to our evidence this class difference was continuing in the 1980s. It was not formal school teaching about politics that had made the difference. The UK is one of the few countries where politics is not normally a timetabled school subject, and it remains outside the National Curriculum. In the 1987 questionnaire the younger respondents, who were still at school at the time, were asked whether they had been taught about a range of political and social topics. Only 30% recalled having been taught anything about local politics, 35% about political parties, and 42% about defence and the armed forces. Larger proportions recalled being taught about local industry (60%), AIDS (63%), the law (also 63%), unemployment (78%), drugs (80%), and contraception and abortion (83%).

The political education that some respondents recalled did not appear to have shaped their political outlooks decisively. We have previously explained that, with parental social class controlled, educational success was related to intention to vote Conservative, and low attainment to support for the Labour Party. These relationships were less likely to have arisen through the content of teaching than the manner in which educational success and failure were signalling to pupils the positions that they would occupy in adult society and the associated interests. Also, the ways in which high- and low-achieving pupils in Britain are typically divided for teaching purposes, which has some bearing on their friendships, would have resulted in the most successful being surrounded by peers among whom Conservative support was common, and likewise Labour support within schools' lower streams and sets. These processes would also have been congregating pupils with high and low levels of political interest, thereby in all probability accentuating each group's norms (Roberts and Parsell, 1988). The educational processes responsible were described in Chapter 6 which explained how success at school accompanied increases in young people's feelings of efficacy and reduced their feelings of estrangement. In other words, educational success was encouraging young people to feel involved in their society, able to understand its workings, and to act effectively within it (cf, Marsh, 1990).

Middle-class high achievers tended to score above average in all kinds of spare-time activity; politics was just one instance of this. However, political activity, apart from reading, talking and the like, unlike political interest, was abnormal even among middle-class high achievers.

Political activists who supported all the parties tended to be drawn from the same social group, namely, high achievers in education. Again, this is a time-honoured feature of British political life. In the late nineteenth century an elite group of public schools supplied most leaders in the dominant parties of the age, the Whigs and the Tories. Nowadays it is the universities and polytechnics that educate Britain's 'political class'. This produces a particularly sharp contrast among Labour supporters between the middle-class activists who tend to be aware of and committed to the Party's policies, and working-class voters whose loyalties depend more on family traditions and a general feeling that the Party represents people like themselves.

Class dealignment is the sole alleged trend that our evidence will not allow us to dismiss. As we have seen, some of the relationships between the samples' attitudes, party affiliations and class positions, and some changes that occurred between 1987 and 1989, were consistent with a longer-term trend towards class dealignment. However, we have also pointed out that the same evidence could be interpreted in alternative ways. Irrespective of any longer-term trends, class trajectories were good predictors of respondents' voting intentions. Although the centre parties were supported by around a quarter of respondents with voting intentions in 1987, this support had largely disappeared by 1989. It is also notable that over four-fifths of Labour supporters and over a half of the Conservatives gave 'It represents people like me' among the reasons for their party choices.

We found plenty of evidence of volatility, but in our view it is misleading to treat this as a sign of dealignment. Only a minority of the respondents in this survey had stable party loyalties from 1987 until 1989. Neither the longer-established nor the newer parties were inheriting or consolidating substantial bedrocks of reliable support among the new generation of voters. Their lack of loyalty is not difficult to understand, given that most of the young people felt neither interested nor well informed about politics. Many held opinions which conflicted with their preferred parties' policies. It was also the case that many of the young people possessed strong views on issues that were weakly related, if at all, to either their class trajectories or preferred parties.

New issues may draw voters away from what would hitherto have been their normal class-based parties without laying the foundations for a stable realignment. People's opinions on issues that influence their voting at particular points in time may be unrelated to their class situations and interests. Even so, these processes themselves could become class-based if the underlying changes in the economy, occupations and the class structure were weakening traditional loyalties, thereby leaving voters available for mobilisation around new issues. The expected outcome of such developments would be trendless fluctuations, with all parties experiencing sharper gains and losses among 'natural' and other supporters than in the past. These fluctuations would be around enduring class-based patterns, which was the case in our samples between 1987 and 1989.

The interviews and ethnography which were reported in Chapter 5 emphasise the powerful influence of families and peer groups on the political outlooks of individual young people. It is within their primary social networks that young people, as well as adults, become sensitive to issues and formulate opinions. The state of the economy, national political events and media stories do not impose themselves directly on the consciousness of individuals but are interpreted in everyday social intercourse. Thus it can be argued that effective political socialisation, in terms of individual outcomes, occurs at this micro level, and one predictable result is sharp contrasts between and within all areas and social classes. Such contrasts have probably always existed, even when party loyalties were more stable than today. Even so, much of the micro-political socialisation will be inconsequential at the societal level because the effects will be temporary, local and counter-balancing.

The overall evidence from this research suggests that the more stable features of political culture and action in Britain remain primarily class-based, and throughout the 1980s were being reproduced among incoming generations by age 15–16. Thereafter we can confirm that there is considerable change at the individual level, but the net outcome among our respondents was simply to reconstitute class-based patterns. There is no need to search for novel explanations for the persistence of these patterns. Britain's class structure may be changing, but different classes of people still have unequal life chances which give rise to enduring interests. Most young people's trajectories are clearly signalled by age 15–16. This means that the fortunes of political parties in the future are likely to depend, as in the recent past, in large part, on their ability to appeal to class-based interests.

Chapter 9   CAREERS AND IDENTITIES RECONSIDERED

Introduction

We have now taken the reader through a rich and complex account of the lives of 16–20-year-olds. In this final chapter we shall attempt to draw together the various strands of our inquiry and consider what general patterns can be discerned and what broader conclusions these suggest about the processes and outcomes of political and economic socialisation.

Throughout our research we have interpreted political and economic socialisation quite broadly. We have taken political socialisation to include not only the development of attitudes towards particular social issues such as racism, the equality of the sexes, and the environment, or the emergence of party loyalties, voting preferences and political identities, but also the emergence of active interest and participation in politics, and confidence in political institutions. Similarly, we have treated economic socialisation as a broad process in which individuals come to participate in different ways in the economic life of society – for example, in the market place as consumers, as well as in the labour market. We have examined the part family background, gender and local opportunity structures play in the socialisation process, in the formation of careers and in the development of adult identities. At the same time, economic socialisation is about the development of attitudes, whether towards work or training or towards inequality, and thus shades into political socialisation. Finally, political and economic orientations are likely to be anchored in the personal lives of individuals, and for this reason we have paid particular attention to the social relations and domestic circumstances of the young people participating in our research.

We shall return to the concepts of opportunity structure, career and identity and consider what sense they have allowed us to make of the processes and outcomes we have observed. Are there implications for theory or for future research agendas? Finally, we shall consider what general conclusions can be drawn for policy and for those involved at a practical level with young people.

Patterns of participation and patterns of meaning

To simplify somewhat, our inquiry has been concerned with two broad kinds of phenomenon. First, we have examined forms of participation in society, whether economic, political or social. In more detail, this category includes participation in different forms and levels of education, in training, and in paid employment. It also includes economic participation as a consumer of goods and services. It includes participation in the household economic system through financial contributions, contributions to household labour and via the use of household resources. It includes participation in leisure and recreational activities, such as holidays and sports – both as player and as spectator – in youth culture, in smoking and drinking. It includes participation in social life, in personal relationships of varying degrees of depth and intensity, in sexual relations, marriage and parenthood. Finally, it includes participation in the political life of society, through such activities as voting (or intending to vote), protesting, lobbying and organising collective political action, as well as more passive forms of participation such as reading newspapers and watching political broadcasts.

Second, we have examined subjective reactions and orientations in the form of beliefs, opinions, feelings, evaluations and judgements – or, in other terms, attributions of meaning, whether to the self, to others or to the social world more generally. This second category includes the identities in terms of which young people define themselves. The distinction is less clear-cut than it may appear; for example, these 'subjective' reactions and orientations may assume significance only inasmuch as they constitute social performances. People do not merely hold opinions, have feelings, assume identities, and make judgements as private mental events; they also express these overtly, before different kinds of audience.

The distinction between participation and subjective reaction, however, is useful in capturing the range of changes in the transition from adolescence to adulthood and their interrelations. We have been interested, among other things, in the influence of different experiences upon expressed attitudes, as well as the influence of attitudes on behaviour and, particularly, on critical choices and commitments on the path to adulthood. In this concluding chapter we will summarise the kinds of change that occur, the rate at which these changes unfold, and their consequences for the individual.

We look first at changes in patterns of participation, at the pace of transition, and at the various routes through which young people move towards adulthood.

Changes, transitions and differences

The period of life between 16 and 20 sees no major physical changes that would influence capacity for any of these forms of participation, certainly nothing on the scale of the preceding five years. Physical sexual maturity has typically been achieved. There are normally no further gains in physical stature. Moreover, most of the more obvious psychological and psycho-physical changes that began in infancy – visuo-motor development and coordination, first language acquisition, growth in intellectual capacity – have ceased, in most cases many years previously. Even the normal period for acquiring culturally promoted skills such as literacy and numeracy has passed. Yet we are inclined to regard the average 20-year-old as a more completely adult participant in society than the average 16-year-old.

One reason is perhaps that a degree of social and emotional development has still to occur. Coleman and Hendry (1990) identify relationships with parents as the major developmental task still faced by most 16-year-olds. The average 16-year-old also has little experience of life outside family and school, little experience of longer-term close relationships outside the family, and little experience of those moral responsibilities for others that we tend to associate with adulthood. Individuals at this age are still likely to report difficulties in handling a range of social situations, such as contacts with the opposite sex, making new acquaintances, starting friendships, and keeping conversations going (cf. Bryant and Trower, 1974). In addition, managing their own money, their time and their lives in general are not problems the majority will yet have faced.

Finally, though this is not a complete list, the average 16-year-old is not yet a complete adult because many aspects of adult identity remain as yet unformed. Erikson (1968) regarded adolescence as a period in which a stable personal and social identity is still in the process of formation, and Marcia's (1966) research, based on Erikson's ideas, supported the conclusion that this process is far from complete at 16. This is not to say that by 20 all developmental tasks will have been completed. But those four intervening years will bring discernible changes, partly through the deepening of existing experience, but also partly, and perhaps more importantly, because this particular period of life is likely to bring quite new experiences, new choices and new dilemmas.

So what defines adulthood? And where does it begin and youth end? Adult status is psychologically and behaviourally a 'fuzzy' category; it has many typical features but few that are naturally universal. Thus, the transition to adulthood in the late 1980s was typically accompanied by an end to full-time education, and an end to complete financial and material dependence on parents or guardians. It involved moving out of the family home and setting up an independent household, involvement in a long-term relationship, generally formalised as marriage and leading to parenthood. And, despite high levels of unemployment, it still ultimately meant for most people entry into paid employment. Quite evidently, sizeable majorities, legally adults, would not have fitted one or more of these conditions; for example, employment and financial independence can be delayed until well into the twenties for those who pass through higher education. Because sizeable minorities, even majorities in some countries, are still at these preparatory and transitional stages, the term 'youth' is often extended to cover the whole period; adulthood follows it.

The elements of the transition are significant in defining for members of the culture what is 'normal'; in this respect they exercise a social control function (Neugarten and Datan, 1973). People are disposed to judge their own and others' life courses in terms of the 'typical' pattern in two respects. First, do they conform to the timetable implicit in the image people have of it? It is commonplace for people to comment on their own and others' deviations from the normative pattern: 'I married late' or 'she left home early'. Second, did the relevant events occur in the expected order, or indeed at all? Data collected by Neugarten *et al.* (1965) suggest that these normative expectations are particularly strong for women and for young adults. The normative pattern also provides a framework against which we as researchers can ask about progress towards adulthood.

The timetable for transition to adulthood is, despite its normative character, constrained to certain limits by the institutional context. Indeed, what makes the years between 16 and 20 an important period on the route to adulthood is almost entirely a function of the institutional structure of society. In Britain in the late 1980s, the context of our own research, it was a period in which a number of significant changes occurred in the individual's legal status; most of the formal entitlements (and obligations) of the adult citizen were acquired by our respondents during this time. Most importantly, full adult rights were acquired in three central areas – economic activity, personal life and political action. At 16 our respondents acquired the right to seek and accept contracts of full-time employment or to run independent businesses. They became entitled to set up households independent of former legal guardians, to cohabit and to marry. And at 18 they acquired the basic political right to vote in public elections.

The entitlements of adult status are, however, exercised in different ways, at different times and to differing degrees. We anticipated in Chapter 1 (cf. Roll, 1990) that only a minority would have taken all the steps described above by the end of the teens, and so it proved to be. By 20, for example, only a minority of the participants in our research had left home, and an even smaller minority were married or cohabiting. A majority expressed little or no interest in politics and engaged in only relatively passive forms of political participation, while a significant minority expressed no voting intentions. More were in paid employment than not, but substantial numbers had either not yet entered the labour market or had failed to find work by 20. The patterns underlying participation in these different facets of life can be summarised in various ways.

We shall consider them in terms of four themes: transitions; careers; choices; and inequalities.

Accelerated versus protracted transitions

First, and much as anticipated, we found wide variations in the rate of transition from full-time schooling to employment. As noted at the outset, this transition has always been 'protracted' for a minority of the population, those taking a route through higher education, followed in some cases by further professional training, before entering the labour market sometime in their mid-to late twenties. By the late 1980s, however, it appeared to be only a minority who made an 'accelerated' transition, moving straight from school to full-time employment at 16. Among the majority making a more or less protracted transition there were two quite distinct groups. One passed through an intermediate stage of government-sponsored training schemes before entering the job market. Membership in this group was determined partly by lack of educational credentials and partly by local labour-market conditions. And the evidence by the final stage of the research was that the prospects of stable, well-paid employment for many in this group were poor. Those whose training was not part of, or leading directly to, employment often drifted into peripheral unskilled employment interspersed with unemployment. A second group deferred entry into the labour market with a further period of full-time education either in school or at a further education establishment or some combination of these. Membership of this group was substantially a function of social background and educational attainment up to 16. In the short term, early entry into employment did bring money and status. Beyond this, however, a more protracted transition in itself conferred no particular longer-term economic advantages or disadvantages. Rather it was the content of the training or educational experiences intervening between the end of formal schooling and entry into the labour market that appeared crucial.

Labour-market entry is not the only area in which varying rates of transition were found. Another was personal and social life. We found marked differences in the rates at which young people became involved in such activities as dating, commercialised forms of leisure (going to pubs and clubs), cohabiting, and marriage. In most of these aspects of life, the females were ahead of the males at 16, with the latter catching up, in some areas, by 20. However, there were also links between transitions in this area and transitions in the occupational sphere. Those making accelerated transitions into employment were also in advance of their peers in personal life transitions, an advantage which can be attributed in part to earning an income earlier on. Nevertheless, these differences again evened out with age.

Politics represents a third area of transition, but one in which the pattern was in some respects the reverse. Young people from middle-class backgrounds and with above average educational attainment developed political interests ahead of their peers. And while females were in advance of males in lifestyle transitions, they lagged behind them with respect to political participation. Although there was again some catching up by those groups making a slower transition, a substantial gap still remained at 20.

Historical trends with respect to these three spheres of life – economic, personal and political – have been mixed. With respect to work roles, the trend from the early nineteenth century onwards has been towards an increasingly protracted transition. Education and training have been progressively extended, accompanied, as noted in Chapter 1, by structural changes in Western economies which early in the century vastly increased the proportion of non-manual occupations available to adults, and more recently have reduced the size of the market for unskilled labour. The effects of new technology, deskilling, and Third World competition have all played their part in these trends. The timing of marriage and parenthood has not shown the same progressive pattern, with the result that these events now more frequently overlap education and training. Political participation has shown the reverse trend, with suffrage progressively extended down the age range so that now a sizeable proportion of the electorate is still in full-time education or training.

Britain remains behind most of the other established industrialised economies in the trend towards more extended education and training. But change was apparent even within the limited span of our survey, with higher proportions of the younger cohort remaining in education, but not training, after 16, and lower proportions, at least in Swindon and Kirkcaldy, entering directly into employment at 16. In so far as our research sheds any light on variations in the rate of transition to adulthood, it suggests that different kinds of transition – in economic role, in political participation and in personal life – are related to one another by their common links to education and to class background.

Careers

The transition to adulthood not only occurs at a certain pace, but also involves changes that may occur in a particular sequence and may additionally lead to different destinations. The concept of a 'career' captures both of these features of the transition. But can we identify sequences to patterns of participation in the social, economic and political life of society that characterise the life course of individuals? And if so, is it apparent that there were alternative careers available to young people in Britain in the late 1980s?

Labour-market careers

We applied the 'career' concept most directly to the transition from school to work, and it is in this area that it proved to work best. We identified some distinct education–training–employment career patterns from 16 to 18. This was a complicated task because of the legislative and labour-market changes that occurred across the two-year period separating our two cohorts and necessitated two versions. What follows describes the common features of both. They are interesting in two respects: first, as an indication of the variety of transitional patterns that now exist at the end of full-time compulsory education; and second, as determinants of subsequent positions in the labour market. The patterns were:

1. *Two-year education route.* This involved continuing full-time education for the two years between 16 and 18, followed by about one-third of our sample; the proportion increased between the two cohorts. The route included the traditional academic trajectory leading to A levels in England, in which two-thirds of this group were involved. The others were mostly on two-year vocational courses such as those leading to the BTEC National Diploma. In fact higher education was the most common destination for this group, but only for just over half of them. A minority (15%) proceeded to other kinds of education, while almost twice this proportion went into employment between 18 and 20.
2. *One-year general or vocational education.* A second route typically involved up to one year of post-compulsory full-time education, including repeat courses and one-year vocational courses such as CPVE, CGLI, RSA. About 10% followed this route, which was again attracting a higher proportion of the younger cohort. It led, in 85% of cases, to employment between 18 and 20.
3. *Education to work.* This was the traditional transition, straight from school at 16 into the labour market, without any intervening period on a training scheme or in further education. Substantially more were entering it in Swindon (30%) than elsewhere (10%).
4. *School to YTS to work.* About a quarter followed this route. It was strongest in Sheffield where a strong Council-led scheme had operated, and weakest in Swindon where direct entry to employment was available instead.
5. *YTS, education and unemployment.* This residual pattern was most common in Liverpool and Sheffield. It declined substantially in frequency between the two cohorts, and also varied in content between areas. Unemployment was more evident in Liverpool and, to a lesser extent, in Sheffield, as a major component, especially among the older cohort.

It can now be seen more clearly that protracted transitions took various forms; in some cases postponing the accoutrements of adult status was voluntary, in others rather less so. Thus, the delayed entry to the labour market of the YTS and unemployment routes would seem to have been largely involuntary, associated with immediate labour-market conditions, as we saw in Chapter 3, and associated psychologically with the most negative outcomes, as we saw in Chapter 6. The delay and extension to the transition involved in the academic and vocational routes would appear to have been more voluntary, to be associated with social class, educational attainment, and the character of post-16 provision, and to have had the effects psychologically of reinforcing a positive self-appraisal and orientation to authority and a weakened belief in the value of work.

A question for the future must be the consequences of these different transition patterns for the quality of any subsequent employment. At what level are the participants employed, in what sectors of the economy, with what occupational career prospects and with what stability of employment? As an influence on employment status between 18 and 20, of the institutionalised routes the YTS route would appear to have provided the least protection against unemployment, and the non-academic education route the best protection. However, the pattern between 18 and 20 was different from that of the earlier period for obvious reasons. Only three kinds of status were to be found: in full-time education (though this could be divided between a larger group in higher education and a smaller group in some other kind of further education); in employment; and unemployed (and in some cases not seeking employment). Employment and unemployment also became more distinctive categories after 18; between 16 and 18 it was more common to move back and forth between these statuses. Finally, the most important determinants of employment status between 18 and 20 were educational attainment at 16 and area of residence.

Political, social and domestic careers

Careers in the labour market involve a succession of qualitatively distinct forms of experience – schooling, training, college-based education, unemployment, full-time employment, and so on. This is not the case for political life, where for the great majority the changes are matters of degree rather than kind. Voting is such an infrequent event that it cannot be said to represent a distinct pattern of life, and only a tiny minority develop any serious daily involvement in politics of the conventional kind. Such changes as we were able to observe involved gradual increases in interest in political issues and in commonplace forms of political participation such as watching party-political broadcasts on television or discussing political issues and events with friends and family. The trend for more active involvement in politics was, if anything, the reverse. The elements of ideological beliefs appear to be largely established earlier than 16–19, though reinforced by later experience.

In contrast, personal and domestic lives go through changes that involve qualitatively distinct forms of experience: living with parents versus living alone, sharing accommodation with other non-family members or living with a partner; same-sex friendships versus dating; being a parent; and so on. Thus there would seem to be more potential for identifying careers in this area, though the first thing to be said is that there was little evidence of any stage-like progression through these various forms of experience. The normative pattern seems to be living with parents and associating with same-sex peers, the latter then changing to include increased heterosexual contact and then dating, followed by a move out of the parental home, setting up a household with a partner, and parenthood. This precise sequence may nevertheless still be a minority pattern, and anyway many of the significant changes – notably leaving home, setting up an independent household with a partner, and parenthood – would occur for most individuals outside the age frame of our research. We did, as already noted, observe some cases of accelerated transitions embracing these later changes, in which females figured more frequently than males. But for most of the participants in our research, personal and domestic careers involved mainly changes in degree between 16 and 20. Thus, as documented in Chapter 4, the emphasis shifted away from single-sex groups to more mixed-sex contact outside the home. Within the home, domestic responsibilities increased for both sexes.

The sharpest changes were in financial relations with the household. Many of our sample moved from a state of relative financial dependence to one in which after 16 they were contributors to the household budget. The obvious source of this change in relationship was entry into work or training. Overall, there was little difference between males and females either in the proportions making any financial contribution to the household or in the scale of the contributions, though males' higher wages were accompanied by slightly higher board payments. Finally, this particular role of financial contributor to the parental household may never arise for at least one group, those remaining in higher education through to tertiary level.

Gender careers

There are grounds for the conclusion that there are qualitative differences to gender careers which are more than a matter of the speed of transition to an adult status. Moreover, there are aspects of gender careers relatively untouched, except in terms of timing, by educational attainment or social background. Some of the differences began to open out as soon as full-time schooling ended. While girls and boys remained in the academic system there were few obvious differences between them. In terms of political interest and leisure activities they were little different, and their academic interests were only moderately differentiated, with girls specialising more in business studies and boys in technical subjects. But as soon as they stepped outside this system, whether at 16, 17, 18 or even later, the differences immediately became striking. Especially if they left school early, males and females headed for very different labour-market segments, mediated, where some form of training intervened by very different kinds of training experience, as we saw in Chapter 5. Just why this should happen is not clear, though it is likely to involve some combination of self-selection and social selection, probably with the balance tilted towards the former.

One significant difference between the social world of education, whether at school or in higher education, and those of training and work is that the latter are segregated by sex to a degree that the former is not. Thus, those who left academic education immediately entered into a different kind of social world. The social worlds of females were further differentiated from those of males in being less public on the one hand, and more extensively based in domestic settings on the other. The social contacts of females were less likely to occur in public places and more likely to occur in their own and others' homes.

Two further differences should be mentioned here. Females were less likely than males to benefit from certain household resources, particularly means of transport. One can see that this would have consequences for the control they could exercise over their own mobility. And females made more extensive contributions to household labour. These differences cut across social class background and educational attainment but were accentuated in working-class families. It would seem that in adolescence males and females were already extensively rehearsed for rather different roles in the household.

Choices and dilemmas

What determines the particular career paths along which young people move towards adulthood? For certain kinds of career, decisions made at particular junctures would appear to be critical. One such decision, and perhaps the single most important decision, occurred towards the end of compulsory schooling. The young people in our survey who left full-time education at this point were very unlikely to re-enter later on; only about 5% did so within the time period of the study.

It should be said that many other choices become available, or more readily exercised, between 16 and 20 that are far less irreversible in their long-term consequences. These include choices regarding party-political loyalties, leisure activities, patterns of spending, and personal relationships. Indeed, a body of theory and research has grown up around the idea that the reversibility of such commitments is a defining feature of modern adolescence. It is a period of life in which different identities can be tried out and different patterns of life explored without an irrevocable commitment to any one of them (Erikson, 1968). Adulthood arrives, psychologically speaking, when final choices are made.

We have seen that a whole range of choices in this age group were unstable and frequently reversed. Many young people in the sample left the family home only to return again. Some took jobs and then changed them or went on to training schemes. They also changed political loyalties or expressed voting intentions, only to abandon them later. The instability of political affiliation is, however, almost as characteristic of adults.

All choices occur within a context of limited opportunities, and some are undeniably more consequential than others. Choices about education, training, occupational goals, personal lives and political involvements can either accelerate or prolong the transition to adulthood, but these choices will also take the individuals who make them to quite different destinations as adults. So let us look in more detail at what we believe may be the single most consequential choice: what determined whether or not individual young people remained voluntarily in full-time education after 16?

Three things were likely to be critical: the opportunity structure; credentials; and identity. Choices are limited, first, by the range of opportunities available, and second, by those opportunities for which the individual qualifies. Thus the scope for genuine choice may actually be quite limited. Finally, we might expect that identity will influence decisions to the extent that those decisions represent real choices on the part of the individual concerned.

Opportunity structure

The options that were available at 16 to the participants in our research varied from one part of Britain to another, and indeed according to the year in which they became 16. Employment opportunities for 16-year-old school leavers varied considerably from one locale to the next. YTS changed from a one- to a two-year scheme during the course of the research. The quality of youth training schemes available varied across Britain, as did the nature of the post-16 educational provision. And in 1988, the rules relating to unemployment benefit changed, so altering the nature of unemployment as an option.

Labour markets had marked effects for those who left full-time education at 16. But interestingly, and contrary to expectations, local labour-market conditions had little impact on proportions staying in full-time education or leaving at 16 – the rates in Swindon and Liverpool were very similar, and they were similar in contrasting labour markets within a single study area. The most important factor underlying area differences in staying-on rates seemed to be the nature of the post-16 education available. More specifically, a higher proportion of the older cohort remained in some form of full-time education between 16 and 17 in Scotland than in England. One of the major differences between the two contexts is that the most conspicuous form of post-16 provision in England has for many years been orientated towards A-level qualifications, and these normally require a two-year commitment. Scottish Higher grades require only one year of study.

It would be nice to believe that teaching quality makes some difference. Secondary school teachers in Scotland tend to be more highly qualified than their English counterparts. But we have no direct evidence that this contributes to the differences in participation in post-16 education. One further comment here: the take-up of post-16 education was higher in the second cohort than in the first, but only in the English areas.

Another difference between localities was apparent at 18 where strong labour-market forces were operating. In the relatively affluent area of Swindon, many more young people with A levels entered jobs than in the other areas where higher education was the preferred option. But it was also more common in Swindon than elsewhere to return to (higher) education after a year in employment. Given differences in the range and nature of opportunities from one locality to another, what determines which individuals will take up which opportunities?

Credentials and class background

One set of factors relates to 'credentials', interpreted here as all those attributes individuals are judged by others to possess and which may be regarded as relevant in offering them, or encouraging them to take up, opportunities. In other words, credentials relate to those attributes of individuals which influence their treatment at the hands of others. These include objective paper credentials of the conventional kind but also visible attributes such as gender, race or accent, and other qualities that may be attributed to them on the basis of observation or reputation by, for example, teachers or potential employers.

The most significant form of credential to have emerged in our research has, not surprisingly, been educational. Young people in the highest educational attainment band were the ones most likely to remain voluntarily in full-time education at 16. However, beside this banal point also needs to be registered the fact that other kinds of 'credentials', such as gender, had only modest effects on the decision. As we saw in Chapter 3, females were slightly but not consistently more likely to stay on at 16. On the other hand, it should be emphasised that by no means all the variation in decisions could be accounted for by variations in attainment.

The divide at 16 clearly was related to social class background, but precisely why this should have been so is a more complex matter which our own evidence does not completely resolve. This complexity resides largely in the fact that social class background has a variety of effects. For example, class can in effect become a 'credential', something attributed by others on the basis of appearance or accent and influencing others' reactions at critical points. Class background is also part of what a person is as a public being, one of the things known about that person by others acquainted with him or her. Apart from these consequences, we anticipate that class background affects those material, social, and personal conditions of life that themselves influence the development of both abilities and attitudes. Social class membership might be expected to shape values and aims such as employment commitment, occupational aspiration, and desires for early independence and autonomy.

Our own data support the conclusion that the impact of class background is partly mediated by its influence on educational attainment, however that influence occurs; aspects of class background also exerted an effect independent of that exercised via their influence on educational attainment. In other words, young people with the same educational credentials were more likely to remain in full-time education after 16 if their backgrounds were middle-class than if they were working-class. At the same time, as we saw in Chapter 7, social class differences accounted for only a small proportion of the differences in educational attainment at 16. And we found little to indicate that class background influenced attitudes relevant to career decisions at 16.

Identities

The existence of a range of opportunities and the access given to any of these by a particular individual's credentials tell only part of the story. We have also argued that individuals themselves do make positive and negative choices; they have to pursue opportunities and to accept or reject those they are offered. There is, in other words, self-selection as well as social and institutional selection. And we assume that self-selection is influenced by – is, indeed, an aspect of – identity. That is, young people make choices and pursue goals that are consistent with their own notions of who they are and of what they are capable of. Potentially, social class is a part of subjective identity, as is attainment, and as such is an influence on how people define themselves and what choices they make as a consequence of such self-definitions.

To the extent that there was scope for individual choice about when to leave full-time education, there was some indication that it was related to how young people defined themselves in relation to institutional authority. Those with a more positive view of such authority and its legitimacy, and of adult institutions generally, were likely to remain longer in full-time education than those who were more ambivalent or negative towards education. Similarly, those with the strongest commitment to the idea of work were most likely to leave. However, there was also some influence of identification with locality, and some effect of area of residence itself. Young people more strongly identified with their locality in the sense, for example, of being reluctant to move to find work, were more likely to leave full-time education early. Positive attitudes to new technology were also associated with staying on in education, especially in Swindon.

We cannot claim that this captures all the significant influences on the decision at 16. But we will have to leave it to other research to reveal what additional contribution might be made by other, perhaps more strongly class-related, values and aspirations. Certainly, the ethnographies we reported in Chapter 5 point almost to an inevitability of career decisions based on class identities which it would seem very difficult to shake off. The two sets of attitudes most consistently associated with quitting education early – attitudes to authority and belief in the value of work – might be said to reflect an emphasis on a certain kind of autonomy and status, and dislike of the bureaucratic constraints of the school and value attached to having a job and earning a living. However, neither set of attitudes was particularly class-based.

Inequality

The transition to adulthood is a process in which differences of various kinds emerge or crystallise. Puberty produces a degree of physical differentiation within a population that had been up to that point much more homogeneous. Males and females become physically much more distinct than they were in childhood and at puberty differences in size and physique are amplified within each sex. There remains, however, a certain homogeneity of experience which persists up to age 16. Peer society is substantially age-segregated and a common denominator remains the experience of full-time compulsory education, even if the content of that education begins to diverge well before 16.

The watershed at 16 produces a differentiation in social experience. Individuals begin to move more decisively in different directions, into different patterns of life, and towards different positions in the social structure. In other words, social inequalities become both more visible and more exaggerated. Among the participants in our research an unequal distribution of desirable jobs and job prospects was in evidence well before 20. Also already evident was unequal participation in the political process, and from this we can probably extrapolate to inequality of influence in the political process in adulthood. We can also anticipate that the personal and domestic lives unfolding between 16 and 20 will progress to an unequal distribution of stable marriages, prosperous households, and compatible spouses, not to mention inequalities in the distribution of power and contributions within the households. Certainly, there is nothing in our data to contradict these expectations.

What our data do confirm is the centrality of educational career in the reproduction of social inequality. Observation suggests that different forms of inequality are correlated. More extensive participation in education, high-status jobs, high quality of life, successful marriages and more extensive political participation tend to go together. The links between educational attainment, participation in post-compulsory education and subsequent labour-market position are empirically well established. However, the present research reveals that the consequences of educational career may be much more far-reaching than this. In particular, education in our sample had an impact on social life and patterns of social contact, and other research confirms that it is powerfully related to mate selection. Educational career, whether defined as level of attainment or amount of participation in full-time education, was also the single most potent determinant of political involvement.

It is thus easier to see why various forms of inequality should be correlated with one another. Education has repercussions that are mutually reinforcing. Berger and Berger (1976) offer a useful analysis of social mobility in which they argue that individuals may improve their position in a stratified society by money-making, marriage, political action, self-presentation and education. But educational differences are likely to contribute to differences in each of these other activities. Thus, in so far as adults occupy relative positions in the structure of inequalities that are very little different from those occupied by their parents, the role of education would appear to be crucial.

Finally, we have already commented on the effects of social class background on adolescent careers. The deprivation associated with a less prosperous home background continued in the late 1980s to shape the adult destinations of young people. But the deprivation associated with a depressed local labour market was almost equally profound in its effects. And unequal opportunities for earnings had predictable effects on leisure.

Meanings, ideologies and identities

As young people make the transition towards adulthood, what kind of sense are they making of their society, what meanings do they attach to their place in it, and how do they define themselves in relation to this society? We interpreted all these as questions about identity, about the kinds of people 16–20-year-olds are or are becoming, both as personally experienced and as presented to the outside world. Thus, for example, the attitudes, opinions and commitments they display can be thought of as statements about the sorts of people they are or would like to be taken for.

We have seen that during this period of life individuals began to head more decisively towards different destinations in adult society. This movement was accompanied by increasingly differentiated forms of experience and would appear to have produced, or confirmed, a variety of social differences and inequalities. In a stratified society which nevertheless promotes an ethos of equal opportunities, it might be hard to avoid evaluating transitions as more or less successful. This inevitably raises certain kinds of question about the repercussions of change between 16 and 20 for identity. How did these young people react to their own fates; what consequences did different kinds of outcome have for their self-esteem or their views about the legitimacy of the social order? And were different careers and destinations associated with different values or perspectives on society?

Our answers to these and other questions about identity can be summarised as follows. First, we have looked at two broad components of identity – one that relates to self-concept and one that relates to social identity. The former includes such dimensions of the self-concept as self-efficacy, self-esteem and self-confidence, as opposed to depression, poor motivation and estrangement. The latter includes various attitudes, values, beliefs and commitments in relation to society and social institutions. So, for example, views about the value of work or of training are also statements about identity. We make this distinction because it provides a convenient way to organise the discussion; we do not wish to suggest that the two components are unrelated to one another.

Second, there are various changes in these aspects of identity that might be expected to occur as a consequence of the experiences which intervene between 16 and 20. Thus, is there any general growth in self-confidence or sense of self-efficacy that accompanies growing older, or simply accumulating experience? Do identities become more consistent and stable with age, or with movement into a particular occupation or career? Are self-evaluations affected by personal experiences of success or failure? Are attitudes, and particularly political beliefs and commitments, affected by personal outcomes, by where individuals end up, or find themselves heading for, in the structure of social and economic inequalities? A related question is whether beliefs and ideological commitments are affected by community resources for explaining individual positions and outcomes in terms of group positions. What do we find?

Self-evaluation

Sense of self-efficacy increased between 16 and 20, but only among the males. It should be added that this increase was very modest and that it occurred against a background of relatively stable individual differences. In other words, there were already well-established differences between individuals at 16, and, as compared to these, any subsequent changes were relatively minor. With respect to estrangement the picture was similar except that estrangement declined among females as well as males, but remained higher among females at every age level. Generally one might, therefore, conclude that there was some absolute improvement in self-image over this period of life but that there was little change in relative levels. Sense of self-efficacy seemed to be related to educational attainment, whereas sense of estrangement was more strongly related to social background.

The effects of particular kinds of change or experience between 16 and 20 on self-evaluation were similarly undramatic. Experience of unemployment depressed levels of efficacy and increased feelings of estrangement, and there was some tendency for experience of youth training to have similar effects, particularly on estrangement. If one considers careers, then the more full-time education there was in a post-16 career, the less estrangement was experienced. Finally, a lower sense of efficacy was associated with lower levels of social participation.

Though we tend to separate occupational, political, personal and domestic careers for analytic purposes, they deserve to be considered in relation to one another if only because the same individuals go through each of them. Coleman (1974) has argued that the temporal proximity of a number of different developmental tasks in adolescence increases the difficulty of coping successfully with any one of them. Simmons and Blyth (1987) present evidence suggesting that a number of life changes occurring close together can be associated with poor adjustment, something one would also expect from research on stress. Simmons and Blyth were able to demonstrate effects on both academic performance and self-esteem.

It would appear from our own evidence that for some young people a number of changes were clustered close together. At the extreme they may within the space of one or two years have left school, left the parental home, begun work, and become parents. At the other extreme there may have been long gaps between each of these changes. As yet we do not know the consequences of the relative timings of these various transitions.

Identity: content and stability

As regards the emergence of increasingly more consistent and stable identities between 16 and 20, our evidence points to the conclusion that many aspects of social identity – those reflected in particular sets of attitudes – were also well formed at 16 and were merely reinforced thereafter. Social identities emerged in this research as organised around such themes as relationships with institutional authority, gender and race equality, commitment to employment, and fatalism. These orientations were relatively stable between 16 and 20. Thus, for example, on the one hand there was little overall change with age in either attitudes to authority or to gender equality, and on the other hand individuals' positions relative to one another remained much the same. Orientations to authority, as we have seen, proved to be very strongly related to educational careers and attainments. Attitudes to gender and race equality were likewise related to education, but less strongly. The most potent influence on gender attitudes was gender itself Interestingly, neither orientation was strongly related to social backgrour.d; there was little indication that those from working-class backgrounds were more hostile to authority or more sexist.

Other and perhaps more 'political' dimensions of identity present a more complex picture. The clearest conclusion is that most of these young people did not have distinctive political identities in the sense of holding attitudes towards social issues organised strongly around party affiliations or underpinned by broader ideological commitments. Nor did they develop consistent identities of this kind much before 20. By then the traditional and newer forms of left–right divide were beginning to become apparent, as was the growing interest in environmental issues. In so far as party politics figured at all in their outlooks on the world it was largely in a negative sense. Many expressed either indifference to conventional politics or cynicism; these reactions were reflected in a lack of interest in politics and a lack of awareness of the politics of their peers.

This general lack of engagement with politics might seem to be contradicted by the willingness of a majority to express some kind of voting intention. Indeed, one of the more interesting findings to emerge with respect to political identity at this level was the strong effect of area on political preferences. However, this should be set beside the unstable character of expressed voting intentions. Only a minority of our sample consistently expressed the same party preferences across the three waves of the research, though preferences were consistently related to political attitudes. Whether participation in full-time education beyond 16 of itself contributes anything to the formation of political identities is not yet clear. There was some evidence of environmentalist beliefs being nurtured by educational experience, but the traditional left–right loyalties seemed largely unaffected by it. What is clear is that young people who displayed any engagement with political issues were already distinct from their peers at 16. From then on, extended educational experience was restricted largely to reinforcing the divide.

One particular experience that might shape or modify identities between 16 and 20 is experience of narrowing career options. In effect, relative class positions begin to crystallise. It might be expected that this would be reflected in attitudes that accord either more or less legitimacy to the status quo. In political terms those who emerge from this transition relatively advantaged in economic or status terms might be expected to support conservative values, parties and policies. Those who emerge relatively disadvantaged might be expected to support radical or left-wing parties and political agendas for the redistribution of power and advantage. Our findings suggested, if anything, a weakening of the traditional relationship between class position and political orientations. Voting intentions were related to class background, post-16 experience and educational attainment, but more strongly to social attitudes and to locality, and not at all to earnings. But there was another important divide – between those with an active interest in politics of any kind, a minority defined largely by class background and educational attainment, and the majority with little interest and few clear beliefs about political issues.

Those young people who could be regarded as having been relatively unsuccessful in the competition for opportunities in the labour market did display some clear differences in value from the more successful. Their attitudes to training and to new technologies were the most negative but their commitment to the value of work itself was the highest of any group. Paradoxically, it is as if those who could least take employment for granted were most committed to its desirability.

Vocational preparation did appear to shape identities. As we saw in Chapter 5, even objectively undesirable and poorly rewarded jobs could acquire positive value when there were few other choices. And the collective context in which many kinds of vocational training occurred helped produce these accommodations. Indeed, accommodation to and identification with occupational destinations seemed to be a more common response than resistance.

If occupations, actual or anticipated, emerged between 16 and 20 as sources of identity, locality was potentially already a feature of identity, and one that had repercussions for social and political attitudes. Young people differed in the strength of their identification with the areas in which they lived. And this in turn was reflected in party support. To the extent that they identified with their locality, they also tended to identify with the dominant political groups in that locality.

Some issues for policy makers

Of all the themes emerging in our research with most impact on policy, that of inequality is the most pressing. Young people's access to resources, occupations and domestic futures is critically influenced by career choices made in the mid-teens. These choices are themselves in large part, but by no means exclusively, bound up with identities, part social and part personal, established earlier. Policy needs to address two questions: why disadvantage is concentrated in groups defined by class, gender and race in particular localities, and why so many British young people's social and occupational values appear to be out of step with the demands of a modern technological society.

The problem needs to be addressed in terms of the inadequacies of curriculum and post-16 institutional arrangements not only in formal education but also in the world of employment training. The fundamentally selective nature of the education system reduces choice and stunts opportunity. To redress the balance a totally new post-16 curriculum blueprint is probably required, not only to ensure young people's successful progress into the transformed labour market of the twenty-first century but also to reinforce the foundations of active citizenship.

Perhaps the most disturbing aspect of our findings was the political apathy and the incoherence of much of the political opinion that our respondents expressed. Concentrated among early school leavers, this is to be seen as another form of inequality. Again, those proceeding with education have a sense of political self-efficacy which goes on strengthening as they stay on. Those who leave for the ostensibly adult world of the workplace are not only the most politically alienated but also likely to be the most politically impotent. Clearly, for a democracy to have meaning, it must be accessible to and understood by all its citizens. Even the act of voting was rejected by up to 15% of our 18-year-olds. It seems that the pre-16 school curriculum and education policy generally have been neglectful in this respect. Educational institutions offer numerous opportunities for enabling young people to gain understanding of and to exercise political responsibility at the classroom, school and community level. The curriculum, too, can be made more relevant and meaningful to young people by creating space in it for them to engage continually with current events. Most other European countries recognise the importance of such education for citizenship. The National Curriculum in England and Wales needs to recognise it, too.

But curriculum and institutional changes to help young people make the transition to modern adulthood successfully are only part of the equation. Equally important is financial support to extend the benefits at present accruing to higher education students to much wider sections of the population and to ensure that nobody is prevented through lack of means from staying on in education after age 16. Most pressing of all is personal support from adults, and advice and counselling on the choices that need to be made. No other modern system of education and training has anything like the array of routes, qualifications, institutions and destinations among which young people in Britain have to choose over the ages 16–19. Even the rationalisation being undertaken by the National Council for Vocational Qualifications will still leave myriad complexities to be resolved. The traditional labour-market networks that sustained 'like father like son' and 'like mother like daughter' attitudes are no longer there: what father and mother did is no longer likely to be what is available to son and daughter, and as time progresses even less so.

There is compelling evidence from our research that many young people and their parents are at sea with respect to what needs to be done to ensure their futures. The orientations of schools, colleges and employers are still fundamentally selective rather than facilitative, and career education is too frequently marginalised. Many young people are allowed, if not actively encouraged, to set themselves adrift in the labour market without adequate preparation. The essential antidote is to give career and personal counselling a much higher status, not only through the specialists involved in it, but also in the jobs of teaching and training themselves. Work with young people and their parents to optimise their opportunities should be given as high a priority as is at present attached to getting selected pupils through exams.

As more young people stay on in education and training, extending dependency for larger numbers over a much longer period of time, what other policy changes are needed to support them? A policy question that needs to be addressed is how to reconcile the autonomy that young adults need with their extended dependency on family and home. There is an irreversible pressure within households towards independent living arrangements. The desire to form partnerships and start families cannot be postponed indefinitely; nor is it in the interests of parents and children that it should be. Some recognition of these pressures is already there, with the acceptance that higher education is best pursued away from home; but again, this privilege is only extended to a relatively small minority, the 15% who go on to higher education. The rest are expected to stay at home until they are in a position to support themselves and their prospective families. For all young people to be given the opportunity to establish independence and achieve autonomy, affordable housing must be available and support available to ensure that this form of transition can be achieved successfully.

Should we be pessimistic about our young people's futures? Certainly, unless the necessary conditions for modern adult life are set in place, the vagaries of expanding and contracting labour markets and irrelevant conceptions of family life and independent living will continue to damage and demoralise. In this respect young people's generally positive evaluation of their own potential and confidence in their futures is their main insurance against the future. Society needs to ensure that their optimism is justified and that promises to the next generation of adults are honoured. Only then can we feel satisfied that all careers and identities have equal value and are equally fulfilling.

Appendix 1 METHODOLOGY

Area

Swindon

Swindon's reputation as one of the fastest-growing towns in Western Europe sits a little oddly with its recent industrial past. From the nineteenth century until the 1930s Swindon's growth and development centred on a single industry – the railway engineering works. At its peak before the First World War, the works employed 12,000 men out of a population of 50,000. From the 1960s the decline in the railways reduced the need for the works, but when it finally closed in 1986 there was a lot of other commercial and industrial activity in Swindon, much of it based on electrical engineering. The Swindon workforce actually doubled between 1951 and 1981, and unemployment was never a serious problem. By 1989 the unemployment rate had dropped to half the national average.

Swindon's development was aided by the construction of the M4 motorway and the growth of new-technology businesses and industries associated with it along the 'golden crescent' running from Bristol in the West to Cambridge in the East. Important private sector companies in Swindon included car-makers Rover and Honda, British Telecom, two major finance and insurance companies (Allied Dunbar and Nationwide Anglia), and two major electrical engineering companies (Plessey and Thorn EMI). At the time of the study Honda was setting up a car assembly plant. Public sector employers included Wiltshire County Council, Swindon Area Health Authority and Thamesdown Borough Council.

At the height of the railway engineering industry Swindon was a typical working-class community with an economy based on male manual work. The continuing diversification of industries created new employment and work cultures, especially the increased participation of women in the workforce through part-time jobs and shift work. In 1981, 63% of the women aged 16–59 were employed in the locality, close to the national average of 62%. Encouraged by the expansionist aims and policies of the town council, many new companies – some American-owned – flooded into Swindon, bringing with them organisation and work styles at variance with the shop-floor management practices of traditional British industry. Coupled with the agricultural tradition of the rural hinterland where most of the early workforce was recruited, trade unionism never established a very strong footing in Swindon.

Because of the relative buoyancy of the Swindon labour market, finding jobs for young people there was less of a problem than in those areas suffering industrial decline. In consequence, the traditional transition of direct entry from school into a job without the intermediate stage of a training scheme remained common in Swindon.

Like most industrial towns in the South of England, during the 1980s Swindon gradually broke with its traditional Labour Party affiliations in favour of the Conservatives. At the time of the research it had a Conservative Member of Parliament, but for most of the period since the Second World War Thamesdown Council has remained under Labour Party control.

Educational provision after age 16 was organised in the Thamesdown Local Educational Authority through two tertiary colleges: one specialised in A levels and traditional academic courses; the other offered a wide range of academic and pre-vocational qualifications such as CPVE, RSA, CGLI and BTEC. Because of the strong youth labour market, YTS was a relatively small part of the provision and was mainly focused on Swindon's popular Information Technology Education Centre (ITEC). Employers actively recruited young people into jobs direct from school, offering a package of good pay and training to induce them to leave. GCSE and especially A levels were attractive qualifications to employers. Vocational qualifications were also good currency for getting jobs with good prospects. Only a small proportion of young people, other than students, were involved in casual and unskilled employment.

Liverpool

Both the development of Liverpool and its subsequent decline are connected with its function as a port on the Lancashire coast. At the beginning of the nineteenth century Liverpool was the third largest city in England with 77,653 people. The city grew rapidly during that century and the early part of the twentieth and reached its maximum population, 857,247, in the Census of 1931. Throughout the nineteenth century, Liverpool was associated with a large trade in raw materials from the Colonies and the export of finished textile goods; sugar, tobacco and slavery were also prominent. After the First World War the port experienced a continued dramatic decline, as trade shifted from the Commonwealth to Europe, resulting in the increasing dominance of east coast ports. Between 1945 and 1971 there was an attempt to diversify and expand the economy; 94,000 new manufacturing jobs were drawn to the Merseyside area. In the economic collapse that hit most of the industrial North of England, large numbers of these jobs disappeared. Although since the 1960s there was some compensatory increase in white-collar jobs, the rate of growth of these was less than half their increase in Britain as a whole. Even in nationally expanding blue-collar employment (transport, communications and distribution and miscellaneous services) the fall in Liverpool over the period was 50%.

From the 1930s, Liverpool's population declined, with an average annual net loss of as many as 18,535 people between 1966 and 1971. The level of unemployment was consistently higher than the national level: twice the national average in 1989 and twice the national average for people remaining unemployed for more than five years. The vicious circle of population loss and economic decline produced poverty on a scale not found in any of our other areas.

Liverpool's political history has been dominated by religious sectarianism. The large influx of Irish Catholics in the nineteenth century polarised the population in terms of support for policies displaying positive or negative stances towards the immigrants. For over a hundred years, the Conservative Party dominated the City Council and did not lose control to Labour until 1955, long after the Labour Party had come to dominate most of Britain's other cities. Subsequently, political control of the city moved between the Liberal Party and the Labour Party, with a steady decline in Conservative votes. By 1987, of the seven parliamentary seats, six were in Labour hands and the other was Liberal. At the time of the first survey, Liverpool was at the centre of political controversy over the control of Liverpool City Council by the Militant faction of the Labour Party. Confrontation with the government over rate-capping and central government financial support for local government generally, were probably more accentuated in Liverpool than in any other industrial city. Finally, the Militant leadership of the Council was expelled from the Labour Party, and by the end of the project control of the Party had returned to mainstream Labour Party hands.

Liverpool is a large education authority controlling 39 secondary schools, 29 special schools for children with health or learning problems and four colleges of further education. Unlike many other cities, it had never experimented with tertiary colleges, offering a traditional pattern of schooling in 11–18 comprehensives, 15 of which were voluntary-aided Roman Catholic comprehensives. Because of the lack of opportunities in Liverpool for school leavers, Liverpool had a relatively high staying-on rate after age 16. Those who left typically entered YTS schemes rather than jobs, with non-firm-based schemes (college-based courses, training workshops and community projects) playing a major role. Although during the period of training young people were kept off unemployment records, at the completion of training a substantial proportion failed to get jobs.

Sheffield

If Swindon is a town that never really suffered from the slump of the early 1980s, and Liverpool is one where the slump simply accentuated long-standing decline, Sheffield is one that suffered greatly and then recovered. With an international reputation based on special steels, especially cutlery, and associated heavy and light engineering industry, much of it serving car manufacturing, the economic collapse of the 1970s was exceptionally painful. Hit by competition from the Far East and by new manufacturing methods, including automation, Sheffield was unable to compete and unemployment rose dramatically. The consequence was a city where a skill shortage in the 1960s gave way to an oversupply of skills in the 1980s, greatly in excess of the jobs that were available: in 1982 there were 151 unemployed skilled workers for every vacancy in the engineering, metal goods and metal manufacture occupational group. Perhaps because of Sheffield's 'skills bank', diversification into other businesses – especially white-collar work and services such as banking, local and national government and catering – was less difficult than in many other places. In 1984, manufacturing provided less than 30% of all jobs, compared with 50% in 1971, while in the service sector 13,000 more jobs existed in 1984 than in 1971. In 1985, with a population of half a million, Sheffield still remained the fourth largest city in Britain; unlike Liverpool, it never sustained major population loss. Despite its problems, Sheffield's unemployment rate did not exceed the national average until 1981; since then it has remained just above that level.

Because of its strong tradition of a skilled workforce, Sheffield made an early commitment to equipping its young people with the skills that modern industry demanded. Exceptionally among British cities, Sheffield embraced YTS enthusiastically with the City Council taking a significant role in organising it. There were 10% more young people involved in YTS in Sheffield than in any other area we covered.

Politically, Sheffield had a long-standing radical tradition based in an active Labour movement in its local industry, especially in the light steel trades and the heavy iron and steel sectors. During the First World War, an almost revolutionary stance was adopted in Sheffield through a particularly strong shop stewards' movement. Most of the time, however, Sheffield's trade unions operated through the orthodox political system, using the Labour Party as the means of pursuing their goals in supporting the interests of their workers. As part of the tide of radicalism that swept town halls in the early 1980s, Sheffield City Council established a reputation of being in the forefront of 'new socialist politics', picking up the title of 'Socialist Republic of South Yorkshire'. In company with other town councils that came into conflict with the government over 'rate-capping', Sheffield City Council conceded defeat and subsequently adopted a much more 'moderate' stance in relation to local government finance and relations with central government generally.

Sheffield, like Liverpool, is a large local education authority with 37 secondary schools, all of which, at the time of the study, were comprehensive and coeducational. There were relatively few voluntary-aided schools or private secondary schools, and most of the secondary schools served districts with defined catchment areas relating to a group of feeder primary schools. There were five colleges of further education, offering mainly vocational courses. In the mid-1980s, Sheffield put forward plans to transform sixth-form and further educational provision into a tertiary system. After an initial rejection by the Secretary of State for Education a modified plan was accepted which excluded six secondary schools from the reorganisation. However, at the time of the study, the post-16 education system was similar to that of Liverpool.

Kirkcaldy

Swindon, Sheffield and Liverpool are all metropolises of varying size. Our fourth area, Kirkcaldy, has a much more dispersed urban character. Though Kirkcaldy meets the definition of a labour market, with 80% of those living in the area also working in the area, it actually comprises a number of small towns, each very different in character. It is also distinguished by quite different cultural and political traditions from those prevailing in England, and by a different education and legal system.

Kirkcaldy is located in the region of Fife between the major cities of Edinburgh and Dundee, and it includes the town of Kirkcaldy itself, with a population of 140,000, the new town of Glenrothes, the Levenmouth cluster of Buckhaven, Methil and Leven, and the small towns of Kinghorn and Burntisland. In between there are villages and farmland.

The whole area had been self-contained economically, with little experience of immigration from overseas and no minority ethnic population to speak of. Employment there resides in long traditions in coalmining and manufacturing. Linoleum, bricks, textiles, paper, pottery, ships and whisky were also important products in the past, but, along with industry in other industrial regions in Scotland and England, these ran into difficulty in the late 1970s. However, at the time of our study a higher proportion of the workforce was still employed in manufacturing and primary industries than in Scotland as a whole, and a lower proportion was in the service sector. Decline in the traditional industries, concentrated particularly in the Levenmouth area, was compensated for to a certain extent by growth in new ones based in Glenrothes, where microelectronics flourished. The net result was that up to 1984 unemployment had remained at the same level as for the whole of Scotland. However, the unemployment level in Levenmouth was consistently higher, reaching a peak among males in 1982 of 28%, compared with 17% for the whole of Kirkcaldy district and 18% for Scotland as a whole. The collapse of the textiles industry hit women's employment in particular, but this was offset by the expansion of women's employment in the new industries developing in Glenrothes. In 1982 the unemployment rate was 18% for women in Levenmouth, and 12% for the whole of the area, the same as for Scotland as a whole. These unemployment levels have not changed much since.

Politically, Kirkcaldy has strong left-wing traditions, rooted particularly among the Fife coalminers, who had the reputation of being the most radical miners in Scotland. Apart from a period when it returned a Communist representative, it has consistently elected a Labour MP since 1931. But a reputation for political militancy had not discouraged the expansion of employment. Glenrothes, priding itself on its strike-free record and harmonious industrial relations, had attracted large investment. A survey of employers in Fife pointed to the 'quality of the workforce' as the single most important factor in attracting employers to the area. The absence of any sizeable minority ethnic population had given less prominence to issues to do with race, such as competition for jobs, ethnic identity and racism, than was the case in all our other areas. More significant were relations with England and the thrust of Scottish nationalism as an alternative to Labour Party affiliation. The introduction of the poll tax in Scotland one year ahead of its introduction in England had given prominence to nationalist strategies of opposition (non-payment) and policies (Scottish sovereignty) to which the Scottish Labour Party was having to respond. Use of what were regarded as Scottish oil revenues for English economic purposes was another dominant issue on which the Scottish Nationalist Party had made a strong appeal.

State education in the area was the responsibility of the Fife Local Education Authority. There are secondary schools and further education colleges in the area. Concern to improve young people's employment prospects led to early adoption of TVEI in all secondary schools, and early piloting of a new certificate, Standard Grades, to replace the O grades comparable to English GCE O levels. The introduction of the Scottish 16+ Action Plan accompanied by an academic Highers curriculum broader than its English equivalent (A levels), encouraged more mobility between the post-16 school and further education sectors than in England. Because of the relatively high youth unemployment rate, especially in the Levenmouth area, the Scottish variant of YTS was the destination of a high proportion of school leavers there at the time the study was carried out.

Sampling

Postal Survey Samples

The sample of young people in each locality was constructed in such a way as to ensure representation of all local education authority (LEA) schools (except special schools) and all parts of the area, corresponding as closely as possible to the designated labour-market (journey-to-work) area. In order to cover the required age range for the 16–19 Initiative, it was also decided to base the selected sample on two age cohorts: the younger cohort was in the last year of secondary school and 15–16 years old at the time of the first survey in 1987; the older cohort was two years older, having completed the last year of compulsory schooling two years previously, and was 17–18 years old in 1987 when first contacted.

To find the young people in each area, complete population lists of young people in the relevant age groups were compiled from LEA records. These varied from a completely computerised system in one area, to no system at all in another, with the need to build up the list from scratch by going to each school in the area. In drawing up the lists, we decided to exclude 'special' schools, with a view to studying the population that attended them in an 'associated study'. We also excluded private schools, partly because of the problem of obtaining permission to work in them, but also because, unlike the maintained schools, they were not centrally listed. In the case of the younger cohort, all still at school when first surveyed, the lists were reasonably up to date; in the case of the older cohort, where over half had left the education system, the lists were up to two years out of date. This reduced the response rate for the older cohort, but not disastrously. In planning the study, we had considered every other possible way the older cohort could be listed, including enumeration by interviewers and electoral registration. Our experience leads us to conclude that the method we adopted, school lists, is probably still the best, even for 17–18-year-olds.

We decided to draw random samples of 1650 young people from the school lists in each area – 825 for each cohort, making a target sample of 6600 in all. Because of a data-collection problem in Sheffield the numbers there were increased slightly to 855 for the older cohort and 895 for the younger cohort, respectively, raising the target to 6700.

Another strategic decision was to send questionnaires for completion to the young people in their own homes. Again, this had advantages and disadvantages. For those still at school it would clearly have been easier and more rigorous to collect the data in classrooms from the young people under supervised conditions. However, because we were not sampling whole classes, but individuals across all schools, and because for those who had left school there was no institutional setting which could be used for data collection, sending the questionnaires to the young people's homes was the preferred method. To satisfy the LEAs that no young person would feel compelled to complete the questionnaire, or would object that their name and address had been released, we first of all sent an introductory letter to all of them, inviting them to telephone or write to us if they did not wish to participate in the survey. This placed the onus on the young person or their family to refuse, but in the event less than 7% took the opportunity to do so. Questionnaires and a stamped addressed envelope were then sent to the homes of the remainder with a covering letter stressing the importance we attached to the young person's *own* views and the confidentiality of the data.

To localise and personalise the approach, the address used was that of the local university team with named individuals as contacts, rather than the London-based market research agency that carried out the data collection for us. The procedure adopted was for the questionnaires to be returned to the local university address and then forwarded to London where they were checked in and processed. Those young people who did not respond in the first round were sent a subsequent questionnaire, and if they still failed to respond to that a locally-based interviewer visited them with a further questionnaire and offered to help them fill it in. This procedure did a lot to maximise response. Less than half, for example, responded to the questionnaire when it was first sent to them; subsequent contacts raised the response rate of those who were contactable, that is, had not moved without a forwarding address, to 80%.

One unexpected result was the relatively large number of untraceables. This reached a peak for the older cohort in Liverpool where a large number of young people had left the area without trace, and the sample was 200 down on that in any other area. It meant that the sample at stage 2 was more depleted than we had intended, and there was a risk that at wave 3 there would not be sufficient numbers for analysis. To solve this problem it was decided to boost the sample at wave 2 by selecting further samples from the population lists to be added to each cohort in each area. The effect was to keep numbers up to sufficient levels at all stages. Overall up to 4830 young people participated in the study at wave 1, and by wave 3, including the boost, 2752 were still providing data.

The same procedure was adopted in each wave of the survey. Following precedents in other longitudinal studies of young people, to maintain contact between surveys and sustain motivation, a 'feedback' newsheet containing selected results from the survey was sent to all respondents twice: between the first and second waves and between the second and the third waves. The problem with this approach was that the danger of influencing young people's subsequent replies led us to select rather bland and innocuous information to feed back to them. We have no idea whether receiving feedback encouraged our young people to continue to take part; it may have actually put some of them off!

Table A1.1 shows the response rates for each area obtained at each wave of the survey, and table A1.2 compares the sample characteristics, sex, cohort, and family social class across the four areas. Table A1.3 gives a rough guide to the statistical significance of differences in means, percentages and correlations based on different sample sizes.

Interview samples

In selecting young people for interview, a 'stratified' approach was adopted for the older cohort and simple random sampling for the younger cohort. For the older cohort, well over half of whom had left the education system, five categories of post-16 experience, referred to in this book as 'career trajectories', were identified as defined in Chapter 3 academic, vocational, school to job, school to YTS to job, no career.

In each area 10 young people from the older cohort were selected from each of the first four of these trajectories and 20 from the fifth, making a total of 60 older-cohort interviewees. From the younger cohort a random sample of 50 were selected, making a total of 110 interviews in each area. Following a standard letter to each selected respondent explaining the interview, interviews were carried out by members of the local university research teams over a period of three to four months in the autumn of 1987, usually in the young people's homes. An appointment for the interview was made, whenever possible, by telephone. Doorstep approaches, the number of callbacks to be made and booking-in procedures were standardised in all areas.

Table A1.1 Response rates

		Wave 1			Wave 2			Wave 3		
		a	b	c	a	b	c	a	b	c
Swindon	NBOC	825	559	68	561	352	63	362	225	62
	NBYC	825	661	80	647	425	66	431	265	61
	NBTOT	1650	1220	74	1208	777	64	793	490	62
	BOC	–	-	–	251	87	35	73	45	62
	BYC	–	-	–	249	122	49	107	87	81
	BTOT	–	-	–	500	209	42	180	132	73
	OC	825	559	68	812	439	54	435	270	62
	YC	825	661	80	896	547	61	538	352	65
	TOT	1650	1220	74	1708	986	58	973	622	64
Sheffield	NBOC	855	529	62	549	350	64	408	265	65
	NBYC	895	691	77	698	499	71	558	365	65
	NBTOT	1750	1220	70	1247	849	68	966	630	65
	BOC	–	-	–	250	108	43	81	67	83
	BYC	–	-	–	250	131	52	110	80	73
	BTOT	–	-	–	500	239	48	191	147	77
	OC	855	529	62	799	458	57	489	332	68
	YC	895	691	77	948	630	66	668	445	67
	TOT	1750	1220	70	1747	1088	62	1157	777	67
Liverpool	NBOC	825	491	60	493	288	58	345	210	61
	NBYC	825	603	73	599	474	79	446	275	62
	NBTOT	1650	1094	66	1092	762	70	791	485	61
	BOC	–	-	–	262	87	33	66	51	77
	BYC	–	-	–	261	134	51	100	84	84
	BTOT	–	-	–	523	221	42	166	135	81
	OC	825	491	60	755	375	50	411	261	64
	YC	825	603	73	860	608	71	546	359	66
	TOT	1650	1094	66	1615	983	61	957	620	65
Kirkcaldy	NBOC	825	598	72	596	391	66	402	248	62
	NBYC	825	698	85	694	499	72	516	350	68
	NBTOT	1650	1296	79	1290	890	69	918	598	65
	BOC	–	-	–	162	94	58	65	58	89
	BYC	–	-	–	159	93	58	86	77	90
	BTOT	–	-	–	321	187	58	151	135	89
	OC	825	598	72	758	485	64	467	306	66
	YC	825	698	85	853	592	69	602	427	71
	TOT	1650	1296	79	1611	1077	67	1069	733	69
	OC	3330	2177	65	3124	1757	56	1802	1169	65
	YC	3370	2653	79	3557	2377	67	2354	1583	67
	Total	6700	4830	72	6681	4134	62	4156	2752	66

NB = non-boost sample   B = boost sample   OC = older cohort
YC = younger cohort   a = target sample   b = obtained sample,
c = response rate (100b/a)%

Table A1.2   Sample characteristics: sex, cohort and social class by area (%)

	Wave 1					Wave 2					Wave 3				
	Sw	Sh	Li	Ki	Tot	Sw	Sh	Li	Ki	Tot	Sw	Sh	Li	Ki	Tot
Sex															
Female	51	52	54	49	51	51	53	54	51	52	52	56	59	54	55
Male	49	48	46	51	49	49	47	46	49	48	48	44	41	46	45
Cohort															
Older	46	43	45	46	45	45	42	43	44	44	43	43	41	42	42
Younger	54	57	55	54	55	55	58	58	56	57	47	57	59	58	58
Social class															
Professional	6	6	3	6	5	7	7	3	7	6	9	8	4	8	7
Intermediate	23	19	17	19	20	25	19	18	22	21	25	19	20	22	22
Skilled NM	13	9	16	10	12	13	9	14	11	12	13	9	16	12	12
Skilled M	38	41	28	42	38	36	42	34	40	38	34	43	31	39	37
Semi-skilled	16	18	24	16	18	16	17	22	15	17	16	15	21	15	16
Unskilled	4	7	12	6	7	4	7	9	5	6	4	6	9	5	6

Sw = Swindon   Li = Liverpool   NM = Non-manual
Sh = Sheffield   Ki = Kirkcaldy   M = Manual

Table A1.3   Significant differences

With percentages in the range of 40–60% a percentage difference to be significant at the 0.05 level must exceed:

N_1, N_2	Difference (%)
100	14
200	10
300	8
400	7
500	6

With a standard deviation of 5 for a difference in means to be significant at the 0.05 level it must exceed:

N_1, N_2	Mean diff	For example
100	1.4	20 & 21.4
200	1.0	20 & 21
300	0.8	20 & 20.8
400	0.7	20 & 20.7
500	0.6	20 & 20.6

Table A1.3   *continued*

For a product moment a correlation to be significant at the 0.05 level it must exceed:

N_1	Correlation (r)
100	0.20
200	0.14
300	0.12
400	0.10
500	0.08

Note: The above figures are approximate guidelines; they rest on the assumption of equal interval measurement scales for the variables involved and normal distribution of sampling errors.

Appendix 2 COMPOSITE ATTITUDE AND BEHAVIOUR SCALES

With the exception of scales 13 and 14, the composite scales were formed by summing and averaging the scores on the individual attitude statements (items) comprising the scales as set out below. So for the first scale, 'support for new technology', each of the four constituent items had a five-point scale response scale: strongly agree, agree, can't decide, disagree, strongly disagree. The responses were scored from 1 to 5 depending on the direction of the scale. Thus the first item 'I think a technical training will help me in future', gained a score of 5 for strongly agree and a score of 1 for strongly disagree. The alpha reliabilities of the scales are given in Table A2.1

Table A2.1 Alpha reliabilities of composite variables

Scale	W1	W2	W3
1	0.66	0.65	0.68
2	0.62	–	0.62
3	0.58	0.59	–
4	0.44	0.48	0.54
5	0.60	0.61	0.63
6	0.73	0.78	0.81
7	0.72	–	0.72
8	0.64	0.64	0.63
9	–	0.66	0.63
10	–	–	0.51
11	–	0.73	–
12	0.58	0.58	–
13	0.67	0.73	–
14	0.45	0.55	–
15	–	–	0.37
16	–	–	0.39
17	–	–	0.57
18	–	–	0.49

Key:
W1 = Wave 1, W2 = Wave 2, W3 = Wave 3.
A = Strongly agree, agree, uncertain, disagree, strongly disagree
B = Very much, quite a lot, not sure, not much, not at all
C = Yes, no
R = Reverse scoring

1 Support for new technology (W1, W2, W3)

No.	Item	Scale
1	I think a technical training will help me in the future	A
2	It is not worth the effort to learn about new technology	A R
3	I don't think I need to learn more about how to use computers	A R
4	I would like to have a job involving new technology	A

2 Employment commitment (W1, W3)

No.	Item	Scale
1	A person must have a job to feel a full member of society	A
2	Having almost any job is better than being unemployed	A
3	Once you've got a job it's important to hang on to it even if you don't really like it	A
4	If I didn't like a job I'd pack it in, even if there was no other job to go to	A R
5	A person can get satisfaction out of life without having a job	A R

3 Support for training (W1,W2)

No.	Item	Scale
1	It is much better to get some kind of training than to go straight into a paid job	A
2	Youth training schemes are just slave labour	A R
3	Youth training schemes are better than the dole	A
4	Going on YTS is the best way now for 16- and 17-year-olds to eventually get a job	A

4 Belief in an internal economic locus of control (W1, W2, W3)

No.	Item	Scale
1	Getting a job depends on your ability	A
2	Getting a job today is just a matter of chance	A R
3	It depends on where you live as to whether you get a job or not	A R
4	People who are poor usually have themselves to blame	A
5	It is bad luck that causes people to be poor	A R

No.	Item	Scale
6	Poor people have the system to blame for their poverty	A R
7	People who are successful in their work usually deserve it	A
8	Being successful at work is just a matter of luck	A R
9	Getting on at work really depends on other people	A R

5 Self-efficacy (W1, W2, W3)

No.	Item	Scale
1	If I can't do a job the first time I keep trying until I can	A
2	I avoid trying to learn new things when they look too difficult for me	A R
3	I give up easily	A R
4	I seem to be capable of dealing with most problems that come up in life	A
5	I find it easy to make new friends	A
6	I do not know how to handle social gatherings	A R

6 Estrangement (W1, W2, W3)

No.	Item	Scale
1	I feel unsure of most things in life	A
2	If I could, I would be a very different person from the one I am now	A
3	I find it difficult to know what is going on in the world	A
4	I am happy to be the person I am	A R
5	I sometimes cannot help but wonder if anything is worthwhile	A
6	I am often troubled by emptiness in my life	A
7	I feel that I am as worthwhile as anybody else	A R

7 Opposition to authority (W1, W3)

No.	Item	Scale
1	It can be okay to do something which is against the law if it is to help a friend	A
2	People in authority, like teachers, always pick on me	A
3 *	Most of the rules in places like schools are stupid and petty	A
4 *	School has been a waste of time for me	A
5	Defying people in authority is all right if you can get away with it	A
6	The police are often unnecessarily brutal to people	A
7	If I saw someone make a break in I would tell the police about it	A R
8	Most police officers are honest	A R

* Not asked in Wave 3

8 Support for sex equality (W1, W2, W3)

No.	Item	Scale
1	There should be more women bosses in important jobs in business and industry	A
2	Men and women should do the same jobs around the house	A
3	Men and women should all have the chance to do the same kind of work	A
4	Girls should have the same chance as boys to get some training or have a career	A

9 Belief in traditional maternal role (W2, W3)

No.	Item	Scale
1	If a child is ill and both parents are working it should usually be the mother who takes time off to look after the child	A
2	It is less important for a woman to go out to work than it is for a man	A

10 Sexual conservatism (W3)

No.	Item	Scale
1	Because of AIDS, people should stick to one sexual partner	A
2	It is all right to have sex with someone if you have been going out with them for a few weeks	A R
3	One way to know if you want to marry someone is by living with them first	A R

11 Support for race equality (W2)

No.	Item	Scale
1	It is OK for people from different races to get married	A
2	I would not mind working with people from other races	A
3	I would not want a person from another race to be my boss	A R
4	It is OK for people from different races to live together	A

12 Political cynicism (W1, W2)

No.	Item	Scale
1	Politicians are mainly in politics for their own benefit and not for the benefit of the community	A
2	It does not really make much difference which political party is in power in Britain	A

No.	Item	Scale
3	None of the political parties would do anything to benefit me	A

13 Political activity (communicative) (W1, W2)

No.	Item	Scale
1	Discussed politics with your parents	C
2	Watched a party political broadcast	C
3	Discussed politics with your friends	C

14 Political participation (action) (W1, W2)

No.	Item	Scale
1	Attended a public meeting or rally or gone on a march or demonstration	C
2	Written to an MP	C
3	Handed out leaflets	C
4	Helped to organise any public meeting or event	C

15 Political conservatism (W3)

No.	Item	Scale
1	The time has come to stop relying on the National Health Service, and for everyone to arrange their own private Health Care	B
2	Welfare benefits should only be paid to people who can prove they are very poor	B
3	The government should give the police greater powers	B

16 Political socialism (W3)

No.	Item	Scale
1	Industries like British Gas and British Rail should be owned and controlled by the government, not by shareholders	B
2	The government should pay benefit to unemployed 16- and 17-year-olds	B
3	Private schools should be abolished	B

17 Concern for the environment (W3)

No.	Item	Scale
1	We should tackle problems in the environment even if this means slower economic growth and fewer jobs	A
2	Problems in the environment are not as serious as people claim	A R

No.	Item	Scale
3	Preserving the environment is more important than any other political issue today	A

18 Left–right ideology (W3)

No.	Item	Scale
1	The time has come to stop relying on the National Health Service, and for everyone to arrange their own private Health Care	B
2	Welfare benefits should only be paid to people who can prove they are very poor	B
3	The government should give the police greater powers	B
4	Industries like British Gas and British Rail should be owned and controlled by the government, not by shareholders	B R
5	The government should pay benefit to unemployed 16- and 17-year-olds	B R
6	Private schools should be abolished	B R

Appendix 3 16–19 INITIATIVE OCCASIONAL PAPERS

1. K. Roberts and G. Parsell (1988) *Opportunity structures and career trajectories from age 16–19.*
2. Michael Banks (1988) *Beliefs about economic success.*
3. Angela Dale (1988) *Part-time work among young people in Britain.*
4. John Bynner (1988) *Transition to work: results from a longitudinal study of young people in four British labour markets.*
5. Inge Bates (1988) *Culture, curriculum and caring: an exploration of economic socialisation of YTS girls*
6. Glynis Breakwell (1989) *Psychological and social characteristics of those who have children in adolescence.*
7. N. Emler and D. Abrams (1989) *The sexual distribution of benefits and burdens in the household: adolescent experiences and expectations.*
8. K. Roberts, G. Parsell and M. Siwek (1989) *Britain's economic recovery, the new demographic trend and young people's transitions in the labour market.*
9. M. Banks and S. Evans (1989) *Employment and training orientations as a function of gender, careers and labour markets.*
10. K. Roberts, M. Siwek and G. Parsell (1989) *What are Britain's 16–19 year olds learning?*
11. K. Roberts and G. Parsell (1989) *The stratification of youth training.*
12. John Bynner (1989) *The rise of open learning: a UK approach to work-related education and training.*
13. John Bynner (1989) *Prospects, attitudes and identities in contrasting labour markets.*
14. John Bynner and Glynis Breakwell (1989) *New technologies and youth attitudes: British experience.*
15. Helen Corr, Lynn Jamieson and Nils Tomes (1989) *The social context of 'making up your own mind': the decision to leave or stay on at school.*
16. Chris Fife-Schaw and Glynis Breakwell (1989) *Predicting intention not to vote in late teenage: a UK study of 17 and 18 year olds.*
17. Glynis Breakwell and Evanthia Lyons (1989) *Adolescent self-concept in relation to family structure.*

18. R. Derricott (1989) *Orientations to education and training: a consideration of interventionist strategies to vocationalise the curriculum in the United Kingdom.*

19. I. Bates (1989) *'No bleeding, whining minnies': the role of YTS in class and gender reproduction.*

20. J. Gray and N. Sime (1989) *Extended routes and delayed transitions among 16–19 year olds; national trends and local contexts.*

21. K. Evans (1989) *Education and training 16–19: institutional structures and outcomes.*

22. N. Emler and A. St James (1989) *Staying on at school after sixteen: social and psychological correlates.*

23. Inge Bates (1989) *'Designer' careers. An initial analysis focusing on the influence of family background, gender and the vocational track on female careers.*

24. Dominic Abrams (1989) *Political identity; relative deprivation, social identity and the case of Scottish nationalism.*

25. John Bynner and Sheena Ashford (1990) *Youth politics and lifestyle.*

26. K. Roberts and G. Parsell (1990) *The political orientations, interests and activities of Britain's 16 to 18 year olds in the late 1980s.*

27. K. Roberts and G. Parsell (1990) *Young people's routes into UK labour markets in the late 1980s.*

28. R. MacDonald and F. Coffield (1990) *Youth enterprise and business start-up in a depressed area of Britain.*

29. Helen Corr, Lynn Jamieson and Nils Tomes (1990) *Parents and 'talking politics'.*

30. Lynn Jamieson and Helen Corr (1990) *'Earning your keep': self reliance and family obligation.*

31. Stephen T. Evans and Michael H. Banks (1990) *Latent functions of employment: variations according to employment status and labour market.*

32. Claire Wallace, David Dunkerley and Brian Cheal (1990) *Young people and self-employment in the far South-West.*

33. Michelle Connolly and N.P.K. Torkington (1990) *'Black youth and politics in Liverpool'.*

34. Sheena Ashford (1990) *Cycles of disadvantage – parental employment status and labour market entry.*

35. Claire Wallace, David Dunkerley, Brain Cheal and Martyn Wareen (1990) *Young people and the division of labour in farming families.*

36. Karen Evans and Alan Brown (1990) *Progress into skilled employment.*

37. P. Allatt and L. Benson (1991) *Family discourse: political socialisation amongst teenagers and their families.*

38. P. Weinreich (1991) *Adolescent identity: a comparative study of economic and political socialisation.*

39. Debra Roker (1991) *Gaining 'the edge': the education, training and employment of young people in private schools.*

40. Alan Brown and Martina Behrens (1991) *Comparative failures: peripheral workers' in the making in England and Germany.*

41. Debra Roker and Michael Banks (1991) *The political socialisation of youth: the effects of educational experience on political attitudes.*

REFERENCES

Aggleton, P. (1987) *Rebels Without a Cause*, Lewes: Falmer Press.

Ainley, P. (1988) *From School to YTS, Education and Training in England and Wales from 1964–1987*, Milton Keynes, Open University Press.

Ainley, P. and Corney, M. (1990) *Training for the Future: the Rise and Fall of the Manpower Services Commission*, London, Cassell.

Aitken, P.P. and Jahoda, G. (1983) An observational study of young adults' drinking groups. *Alcohol and Alcoholism*, 18, 135–80.

Allatt, P. (1986) The young unemployed: independence and identity, in Pashley, B. (ed.), *Youth Unemployment and the Transition to Adulthood*, Papers in Social Policy and Professional Studies, Hull, University of Hull.

Allatt, P. (1988) 'Time to leave?' *New Society*, 83, 1 April, 1921.

Allatt, P. and Yeandle, S.M. (1986) 'It's not fair is it?' Youth unemployment, family relations and the social contract. In S. Allen *The Experience of Unemployment*, London, Macmillan.

Allatt, P. and Yeandle, S.M. (1991) *Youth Unemployment and the Family: Voices of Disordered Time*, London, Routledge.

Allen, G. (1979) *Friendship and Kinship*, London, George Allen & Unwin.

Ashton, D. and Lowe, G. (1990) *Making their Way: Education, Training and the Labour Market in Canada and Great Britain*, Milton Keynes, Open University Press.

Ashton, D. and Maguire, M. (1983) *The Vanishing Youth Labour Market*, Youthaid Occasional Paper no. 3, London.

Ashton, D. and Maguire, M. (1986) *Young Adults in the Labour Market*, Department of Employment Research Paper no. 85, London.

Ashton, D., Spilsbury, M. and Maguire, M. (1990) *Restructuring the Labour Market: Implications for Youth*, London, Macmillan.

Baethge, M. (1989) Individualization as hope and disaster: a socio-economic perspective. In K. Hurrelmann and U. Engel (eds), *The Social World of Adolescents*, New York, Walter de Gruyter.

Bandura, A, (1977a) *Social Learning Theory*, New York, Prentice-Hall.

Bandura, A, (1977b) Self-efficacy: toward a unifying theory of behavior change. *Psychological Review*, 84, 191–215.

Bandura, A, (1989) Perceived self-efficacy in the exercise of personal agency. *The Psychologist*, 2, 411–24.

Banks, M.H. (1988) Employment and training orientations: The ESRC 16–19 Initiative, *Cambridge Journal of Education*, 18, 365–75.

Banks, M.H. and Davies, J.B. (1991) *Motivation, Unemployment and Employment Department Programmes*, Department of Employment Research Paper Series, in press.

Banks, M. and Ullah, P. (1987a) *Youth Unemployment: Social and Psychological Perspectives*, Department of Employment Research Paper no. 61, London.

Banks, M.H. and Ullah, P. (1987b) Political attitudes and voting among unemployed and employed youth, *Journal of Adolescence*, 10, 201–16.

Banks, M.H. and Ullah, P. (1988) *Youth Unemployment in the 1980s: Its Psychological Effects*, Beckenham, Croom Helm.

Bates, I. (1984) Schooling for the Dole?: Historical Perspectives on Careers Education. In I. Bates, J. Clarke, P. Cohen, D. Finn, R. Moore and P. Willis, *Schooling for the Dole? The New Vocationalism*, London, Macmillan.

Bates, I., Clarke, J., Cohen, P., Finn, D., Moore, R. and Willis, P. (1984) *Schooling for the Dole?* London, Macmillan.

Bates, I. (1990) 'No bleeding whining minnies': The role of YTS in class and gender reproduction, *British Journal of Education and Work*, 3, 91–110.

Bates, I. (1991a) 'No roughs and no really brainy ones'. The interaction between family background, gender and vocational training on a BTEC design course, *British Journal of Education and Work*, 4, 79–90.

Bates, I. (1991b) Closely observed training: an exploration of the links between social structures, training and identity, *International Journal of the Sociology of Education* (in press).

Bates, I. (ed.) (forthcoming) *Youth in a Classless Society?*, Buckingham, Open University Press.

Becker, H.S., Geer, B. and Hughes, E.C. (1968) *Making the Grade*, Lawrence, Kansas University Press.

Beloff, H. (ed.) (1986) *Getting into Life*, London, Methuen.

Berger, P. and Berger, B. (1972) *Sociology: A Biographical Approach*, New York, Basic Books.

Billig, M. (1986) Very ordinary lives and the Young Conservatives. In H. Beloff (ed.), *Getting into Life*, London, Methuen.

Bowles, S. and Gintis, H. (1976) *Schooling in Capitalist America*, London, Routledge and Kegan Paul.

Brake, M (1985) *Comparative Youth Cultures*, London, Routledge and Kegan Paul.

Breakwell, G.M. (1985), *The Quiet Rebel*, London, Century Press.

Breakwell, G.M. (1986a), Identities at work. In H. Beloff (ed.), *Getting into Life*, London, Methuen.

Breakwell, G.M (1986b), *Coping With Threatened Identities*, London, Methuen.

Breakwell, G.M. (1987) Identity. In H. Beloff and A. Coleman (eds), *Psychology Survey*, Vol. 6, London, British Psychological Society.

Breakwell, G.M., Collie, A., Harrison, B. and Propper, C. (1984) Attitudes towards the unemployed: effects of threatened Identity. *British Journal of Social Psychology*, 23, 87–8.

Breakwell, G., Fife-Shaw, C. and Devereaux, J. (1988) Parental influence and teenagers' motivation to train for technological jobs. *Journal of Occupational Psychology*, 61, 77–88.

Brown, P. (1987) *Schooling Ordinary Kids*, London, Tavistock.

Bryant, B. and Trower, P.E. (1974) Social difficulty in a student sample. *British Journal of Education Psychology*, 44, 13–21.

Butler, D. and Stokes, D. (1969) *Political Change in Britain*, London, Macmillan.

Bynner, J.M. (1969) *The Young Smoker*, London, HMSO.

Bynner, J. (1987) Coping with transition: ESRC's new 16–19 Initiative, *Youth and Policy*, 22, 25–48.

Bynner, J. and Ashford, S. (1990) Youth politics and lifestyle. Paper presented to ESRC 16–19 Initiative Workshop on Youth and Politics, University of Liverpool.

Bynner, J.M. and Breakwell, G.M. (1990) New technologies and youth attitudes: British experience. In R. First-Dilic and M. Stefanov (eds), *Youth and New Technologies*, Vienna, Vienna Centre.

Bynner, J., O'Malley, P.M. and Bachman, J.G. (1981) Self-esteem and delinquency revisited, *Journal of Youth and Adolescence*, 10, 407–17.

Bynner, J.M. and Roberts, K. (1991) *Youth and Work: Transition to Employment in England and Germany*, London, Anglo German Foundation.

Central Statistical Office (1988) *Social Trends 18*, London: HMSO.

Clough, E., Drew, D. and Wojciechowski, T. (1984) *Futures in Black and White: two studies of the experiences of young people in Sheffield and Bradford*, University of Sheffield, mimeographed paper, Division of Education.

Clough, E., Gray, J. and Jones, B. (1988) Curricular patterns in post-compulsory education: provisional findings from the Youth Cohort Study. *Research Papers in Education*, 3, 27–41.

Cochrane, R. and Billig, M. (1982a), Youth and politics in the Eighties, *Youth and Policy*, 2, 31–4.

Cochrane, R. and Billig, M. (1982b) Adolescent support for the National Front: a test of three models of political extremism. *New Community*, 10, 86–94.

Cockburn, C. (1987) *Two-Track Training – Sex Inequalities and YTS*, Basingstoke, Macmillan.

Coffield, F., Borrill, C. and Marshall, S. (1986) *Growing Up at the Margins: Young Adults in the North East of England*, Milton Keynes, Open University Press.

Coleman, J.C. (1974) *Relationships in Adolescence*, London, Routledge and Kegan Paul.

Coleman, J.C. and Hendry, L. (1990) *The Nature of Adolescence*, London, Routledge.

Coles, R. (ed.) (1988) *Young Careers*, Milton Keynes, Open University Press.

Collins, J.C. (1982) Self-efficacy and ability in achievement and behaviour. Paper given at the Annual Meeting of the American Educational Research Association, New York.

Confederation of British Industry (1989) *Towards a Skills Revolution: Report of the Vocational Education and Training Taskforce*, CBI, London.

Corrigan, P. (1979) *Schooling the Smash Street Kids*, London, Macmillan.

Courtenay, G. (1988) *England and Wales, Youth Cohort Study Report on Cohort 1*, Sheffield, Manpower Services Commission.

Crewe, I. (1989), The decline of labour and the decline of Labour, *Essex Papers in Government and Politics*, 65, University of Essex.

Cusack, S. and Roll, J. (1985) *Families Rent Apart: A Study of Young Peoples' contributions to their parents' housing costs*, Child Poverty Action Group, London.

Dale, A. (1989) *Part-time Work among Young People in Britain*, ESRC 16–19 Initiative Occasional Paper No. 3, City University, London.

Davies, L. (1984) *Pupil Power*, Lewes, Falmer Press.

Deem, R. (1986) *All Work and No Play: The Sociology of Women and Leisure*, Milton Keynes, Open University Press.

Department of Education and Science (1988) *Education and Economic Activity of Young People aged 16 to 18 years in England from 1975 to 1988*, Statistical Bulletin, 14/88, London, HMSO.

Department of Education and Science (1990) *International Statistical Comparisons of the Education and Training of 16 to 18 year olds*, Statistical Bulletin, 1/90, London, HMSO.

Department of Employment (1986) *Working Together – Education and Training*, Cmnd 9823, London, HMSO.

Department of Employment (1988) *Employment for the 1990s*, Cm, 540, London, HMSO.

Dobbs, J. and Marsh, A. (1985) *Smoking among Secondary School Children*, OPCS Report, London, HMSO.

Dowse, R.E. and Hughes, J.A. (1971) The family, the school and the political socialisation process, *Sociology*, 5, 21–45.

Dunleavy, P. (1989) The end of class politics? In A. Cochrane and J. Anderson (eds), *Politics in Transition*, Sage, London.

Easton, D. and Dennis, J. (1969) *Children in the Political System. The Origins of Political Legitimacy*, McGraw-Hill, New York.

Edgel, S. (1980) *Middle Class Couples*, London, George Allen & Unwin.

Edwards, A. (1983) The reconstruction of post-compulsory education and training in England and Wales, *European Journal of Education*, 18, 7–20.

Emler, N. (1990) A social psychology of reputation. In W. Stroebe and M. Hewstone *European Review of Social Psychology*, 1, 173–93.

Emler, N., Reicher, S. and Ross, A. (1987) The social context of delinquent conduct, *Journal of Child Psychology and Psychiatry*, 27, 99–109.

Emler, N., Renwick S. and Malone, B. (1983) The relationship between moral reasoning and political orientations, *Journal of Personality and Social Psychology*, 45, 1073–80.

Erikson, E.H. (1965) *The Challenge of Youth*, New York, Doubleday.

Erikson, E.H, (1968) *Identity, Youth and Crisis*, New York, W.W. Norton and Company.

Evans, K. (1990) Post-16 education, training and employment. *British Journal of Education and Work*, 3, 41–59.

Eysenck, H.J. (1971) Social attitudes and social class. *British Journal of Social and Clinical Psychology*, 10, 201–12.

Farrel, C. (1979) *My Mother Said: A Study of How Young People Learn about Birth Control*. London, Routledge and Kegan Paul.

Federal Republic of Germany (1990) *Education Statistics for the Federal Republic of Germany*. Bonn: Federal Ministry of Education and Science.

Fergusson, L.W. (1939) Primary social attitudes. *Journal of Psychology*, 8, 217–23.

Franklin M.N. (1985), *The Decline of Class Voting in Britain*, Oxford, Clarendon Press.

Frazer, E. (1988) Teenage girls talking about class, *Sociology*, 22, 343–58.

Furlong, A., Campbell, R. and Roberts, K. (1989) Class and gender, divisions among young adults at leisure. Paper presented to the British Sociology Association conference, Plymouth, England.

Furnham, A. (1984) The Protestant work ethic: a review of the psychological literature, *European Journal of Social Psychology*, 14, 87–104.

Furnham, A. and Gunter, B. (1983) Political knowledge and awareness in adolescents, *Journal of Adolescence*, 6, 373–85.

Gallie, D. (1988) *The Social Change and Economical Life Initiative: An Overview*, Working Paper No. 1, Swindon, ESRC.

Garner, C.; Main, G.M. and Raffe, D. (1987) Local variations in school leaver unemployment within a large city, *British Journal of Education and Work*, 1, 67–78.

Glaser, B.G. and Strauss, A.L. (1967) *The Discovery of Grounded Theory*, London, Weidenfeld and Nicolson.

Gleeson, D. (1989) *The Paradox of Training: Making Progress Out of Crisis*, Milton Keynes, Open University Press.

Goffman, E. (1961) *Asylums*, Harmondsworth: Penguin.

Goodwin, M. (1989) *The Politics of Locality*. In A. Cochrane and J. Anderson (eds), *Politics in Transition*, London, Sage.

Grant, P. (1987) *Youth Employment and Technological Change*, Aldershot, Avebury.

Gray, J., Jesson, D., Pattie, C. and Sime, N.C. (1989) Youth Cohort Study, *Education and Training Opportunities in the Inner City*, Sheffield, Training Agency.

Green, S. (1986) A critical assessment of RVQ, *Personnel Management*, July, 24–7.

Greenstein, F.I. (1969) *Children and Politics*, New Haven, Conn., Yale University Press.

Griffin, C. (1985) *Typical Girls? Young Women from School to the Full-time Job Market*, London, Routledge and Kegan Paul.

Griffiths, V. (1988) Adolescent girls: transition from girlfriends to boyfriends. In P. Allatt, T. Keil, B. Bryman and B. Blytheway (eds), *Women and the Life-Cycle: Transitions and Turning Points*, Basingstoke, Macmillan.

Hammersley, M. (1987) From ethnography to theory: A programme and paradigm in the sociology of education, *Sociology*, 19, 244–59.

Hammond, S, (1988) The meaning and measurement of adolescent estrangement. Unpublished PhD thesis, University of Surrey.

Hargreaves, D. (1967) *Social Relations in Secondary School*, London, Routledge and Kegan Paul.

Heath, A., Jowell, R. and Curtice, J. (1985), *How Britain Votes*, Oxford, Pergamon Press.

Heath, D. and Topf, R. (1987), Political culture in British social attitudes. In R. Jowell, S. Witherspoon and L. Brock (eds), *British Social Attitudes Survey: the 1987 Report*, Aldershot, Gower.

Heinz, W.R. (1987a) The future of work. In *The Factory and the Future of Work*, Cedefop Training Bulletin, No. 1. Berlin, Cedefop.

Heinz, W.R. (1987b) The transition from school to work in crisis: coping with threatening unemployment, *Journal of Adolescent Research*, 2, 127–41.

Hendry, L. (1976) Early school leavers, sports and leisure, *Scottish Education Studies*, 8, 48–51.

Hendry, L. (1983) *Growing Up and Going Out: Adolescents and Leisure*, Aberdeen, Aberdeen University Press.

Hendry, L.B. (1989) The influence of adolescents and peers on adolescent lifestyles and leisure-styles. In K. Hurrelmann and U. Engel (eds.), *The Social World of Adolescents*, New York, Walter de Gruyter.

Hendry, L.B. and Raymond, M. (1986) Psychological/sociological aspects of youth unemployment, *Journal of Adolescence*, 9, 355–66.

Himmelweit, H. and Swift, B. (1971), *Social and Personality Factors in the Development of Adult Attitudes towards Self and Society*, London, Social Science Research Council.

Himmelweit, H.T., Humphrey, P., Jaeger, M. and Katz, M. (1985) *How Voters Decide*, Milton Keynes, Open University Press.

Horn, M.E. and Rudolph, M. (1987) An investigation of verbal interaction, knowledge of sexual behaviour and self-concept in adolescent mothers. *Adolescence*, 87, 591–8.

Hurrelmann, K. (1988) *Social Structure and Personality Development*, Cambridge, Cambridge University Press.

Hutson, S. and Jenkins, R. (1989) *Taking the Strain: Families, Unemployment and the Transition to Adulthood*, Milton Keynes, Open University Press.

Inglehart, R. (1977) *The Silent Revolution – Changing Values and Political Styles among Western Publics*, Princeton, NJ, Princeton University Press.

Inner London Education Authority (1984) *Improving Secondary Schools*, Report of the Committee on the Curriculum and Organisation of Secondary Schools under the Chairmanship of David Hargreaves, London, ILEA.

Jackson, P.R., Stafford, E.M., Banks, M.H. and Warr, P.B. (1983) Unemployment and psychological distress in young people: The moderating role of employment commitment, *Journal of Applied Psychology*, 68, 525–35.

Jarvis, V. and Prais, S.J. (1988) *Two Nations of Shopkeepers – Training for Retailing in France and Britian*, Discussion Paper No. 1, 140, National Institute of Economic and Social Research London.

Jenkins, R. (1983) *Lads, Citizens and Ordinary Kids: Working Class Youth Styles in Belfast*, London, Routledge and Kegan Paul.

Jennings, M. and Niemi, R.G. (1974), *The Political Character of Adolescence*, Princeton, NJ, Princeton University Press.

Jesson, D. and Gray, J. (1990) *Access, Entry and Potential Demand for Higher Education amongst 18–19 Year Olds in England and Wales*, Sheffield, Training Agency.

Jones, B., Gray, J. and Clough, E. (1987) Finding a post-16 route – the first year's experience. In R. Coles (ed.), *The Search for Jobs and The New Vocationalism*, Aldershot, Gower.

Jones, G. (1986) Leaving the parental home: an analysis of early housing careers, *Journal of Social Policy*, 16, 49–74.

Jones, G. (1988), Integrating process and structure in the concept of youth: a case for secondary analysis, *Sociological Review*, 36, 706–32.

Jones, G. (1991a) Short-term reciprocity in parent–child economic exchanges. In C. Marsh and S. Arber (eds), *Household and Family Divisions and Change*, Basingstoke, Macmillan.

Jones, G. (1991b) The cost of living in the parental home, *Youth and Policy*, January.

Junankar, P.N. (1987) The British youth labour market in crisis, *International Review of Applied Economics*, 1, 48–71.

Kiernan, K. (1980) Teenage motherhood – associated factors and consequences – the experiences of a British birth cohort. *Journal of Biosocial Science*, 12, 393–405.

Kroger, J. (1989) *Identity in Adolescence*, London, Routledge.

Lacey, C. (1990) *Hightown Grammar*, Manchester, Manchester University Press.

Lee, D., Marsden, D., Rickman, P. and Duncombe, J. (1990) *Scheming for Youth: A Study of YTS in the Enterprise Culture*, Milton Keynes, Open University Press.

Lees, S. (1986) *Losing out: Sexuality and Adolescent Girls*, London, Hutchinson.

Lenhardt, G. (1984) Between market and welfare state: the social position of young people in the economic crisis, paper 84/26, *Proceedings of the Standing Conference on the Sociology of Further Education*, Coombe Lodge, Blagdon.

Mahler, F. (1989) Transition and socialisation. In W. Adamski and P. Grootings (eds), *Youth, Education and Work in Europe*, London, Routledge.

Marcia, J.E. (1966) Development and validation of ego-identity status, *Journal of Personality and Social Psychology*, 3, 551–8.

Marsh, A. (1977) *Protest and Political Consciousness*, London, Sage.

Marsh, A. (1990) *Political Action in Europe and the USA*, London, Macmillan.

Marshall, G., Rose, D., Newby, H., and Vogler, C. (1988) *Social Class in Modern Britain*, London, Hutchinson.

Matza, D. (1964) *Delinquency and Drift*, New York, Wiley.

McGurk, H. (1988) *What Next: An Introduction to Research on Young People*, Swindon, ESRC.

McRae, S. (1987) Social and political perspectives found among young unemployed men and women. In M. White (ed.), *The Social World of the Young Unemployed*, London, Policy Studies Institute.

McRobbie, A. (1978) Working Girls and the Culture of Feminity. In Centre for Cultural Studies. In *Women Take Issue*, London, Hutchinson.

Meus, W. (1989) Parental and peer support in adolescence. In K. Hurrelmann and U. Engel (eds), *The Social Life of Adolescents*, New York, Walter de Gruyter.

Moscovici, S. (1981) On Social Representation. In J. Forgas (ed.), *Social Cognition: Perspectives on Everyday Understanding*, London, Academic Press.

Neugarten, B.L. and Datan, N. (1973) Sociological perspectives on the life cycle. In P.B. Baltes and K.W. Schaie (eds), *Life-span Development Psychology: Personality and Socialization*, New York, Academic Press.

Neugarten, B.L., Moore, J. and Lowe, J.C. (1965) Age norms, age contraints, and adult socialization. *American Journal of Sociology*, 70, 710–17.

Parker, H. (1974) *View from the Boys: A Sociology of Down Town Adolescents*, Newton Abbot, David and Charles.

Patten, M. (1981) Self-concept and self-esteem: factors in adolescent pregnancy, *Adolescence*, 65, 73–80.

Pearson, G., Gilman, M. and McIver, S. (1987) *Young People and Heroin*, Aldershot, Gower.

Penhale, B. (1989) *Association between Unemployment and Fertility among Young Women in the Early 1980s*. Working Paper 60, Social Statistics Research Unit, City University, London.

Pollert, A. (1981) *Girls, Wives, Factory Lives*, London, Macmillan.

Prandy, K. (1990) ,The revised Cambridge Scale of Occupations, *Sociology*, 24, 629–55.

Quicke, J. (1990) Moral career continuities and partial transformations. Paper presented to ESRC 16–19 Initiative Workshop on Youth and Politics, Liverpool University.

Quicke, J. C. (1991) Social background, identity and emergent political consciousness in the sixth form, *Cambridge Journal of Education*, 21, 5–8.

Raffe, D. (1987) The context of the Youth Training Scheme: An analysis of its strategy and development, *British Journal of Education and Work*, 1, 1–31.

Raffe, D. (1990) Beyond the 'mixed model': social research and the case for reform of 16–18s education in Britain, Centre for Educational Sociology, University of Edinburgh (mimeo).

Raffe, D. and Courtenay, G. (1988) 16–18 on both sides of the border. In D. Raffe (ed.), *Education and the Youth Labour Market: Schooling over Scheming*, Lewes, Falmer Press.

Raffe, D. and Smith, P. (1987) Young people's attitudes to YTS: the first two years, *British Educational Research Journal,* 13, 241–60.

Raffe, D. and Willms, J.D. (1989) Schooling the discouraged worker: Local labour market effects on educational participation, *Sociology,* 23, 559–81.

Ragin, C.C. (1987) *The Comparative Method: Moving beyond Qualitative and Quantitative Strategies,* Berkeley, University of California Press.

Reicher, S. and Emler, N. (1985) Delinquent behaviour and attitudes to formal authority. *British Journal of Social Psychology,* 3, 161–8.

Redpath, B. and Harvey, B. (1987) *Young People's Intentions to Enter Higher Education,* OPCS Report, London, HMSO.

Ridley, F.F. (1981) View from a disaster area: unemployed youth in Merseyside, *Political Quarterly,* 52, 16–27.

Riseborough, G.F. (1992a) 'The cream team': An ethnography of a BTEC course in hotel management and catering, *British Journal of Sociology of Education,* in press.

Riseborough, G.F. (1992b) 'We're the YTS Boys': An ethnography of a construction YTS', *Qualitative Studies in Education,* in press.

Roberts, K. (1968) The entry into employment: an approach towards a general theory, *Sociological Review,* 16, 168–84.

Roberts, K. (1984) *School-leavers and Their Prospects,* Milton Keynes, Open University Press.

Roberts, K. (1987) ESRC young people in society, *Youth and Policy,* 22, 15–24.

Roberts, K., Campbell, R. and Furlong, A. (1990) Class and gender divisions among young adults at leisure. In C. Wallace and M. Cross (eds), *Youth in Transition: The Sociology and Youth Policy,* Lewes, Falmer Press.

Roberts, K., Dench, S. and Richardson, D. (1987) *The Changing Structure of the Youth Labour Market,* Department of Employment, Research Paper no. 59, London.

Roberts, K. and Parsell G. (1988), The political orientations, interests and activities of Britain's 16 to 18 year olds in the late 1980s. Paper presented to ESRC 16–19 Initiative Workshop, Harrogate.

Robertson, D. (1984), *Class and the British Electorate,* Oxford, Blackwell.

Robins, L. (1988) Political socialization in British schools: some political and sociological approaches, *Teaching Politics,* 17, 19–41.

Roker, D. (1991) Private education and political socialization. In G. Walford (ed.), *Private Schooling of Girls: Past and Present,* London, Frank Cass/Woburn Press, in press

Roll, J. (1990) *Young People Growing Up in the Welfare State,* Family Policy Studies Centre, Occasional Paper No. 10, London.

Rosenberg, M. (1965) *Society and the Adolescent Self-image* Princeton, NJ, Princeton University Press.

Rosenberg, M. (1989) *Society and the Adolescent Self-image,* (revised edn), Middletown, Conn., Wesleyan University Press.

Rotter, J.B. (1966) Generalised expectances for internal versus external control of reinforcement, *Psychological Monographs,* 80, 1–28.

Roy, (1973) Banana time: Job satisfaction and informal interaction. In G. Salamon and K. Thompson (eds), *People and Organisation,* London, Longman.

Sarlvik, B. and Crewe, I. (1983) *Decade of Dealignment,* Cambridge, Cambridge University Press.

Saunders, P. (1978) Domestic property and social class, *International Journal of Urban and Social Research*, 2, 202–27.

Saunders, P. (1981) Beyond housing classes: the sociological significance of private property rights in the means of consumption, *International Journal of Urban and Regional Research*, 5, 202–27.

Saunders, P. (1990) *A Nation of Home Owners*, London, Unwin Hyman.

Schaffer, H.R. and Hargreaves, D. (1978) Young people in society: a research initiative by the SSRC. *Bulletin of the British Psychological Society*, 31, 91–4.

Seeman, M. (1959) On the meaning of alienation. *American Sociological Review*, 24, 783–91.

Seeman, M. (1972) Alienation and engagement. In D. Campbell and P. Converse (eds), *The Human Meaning of Social Change*, New York, Russell Sage.

Sherer, M., Maddux, J.E, Mercandante, B., Prentice-Dunn, S., Jacobs, B. and Rogers, R.W. (1982) The self-efficacy scale: construction and validation. *Psychological Reports*, 51, 663–71.

Shiller, P. (1974) A sex attitude modification process for adolescents, *Journal of Clinical Child Psychology*, 3, 50–1.

Sillitoe, K. and Meltzer, H. (1986) *The West Indian School leaver*, Vols I and II, OPCS Report, London, HMSO.

Simmons, R. and Blyth, D.A. (1987) *Moving into Adolescence*, New York, Aldine.

Stacey, B. (1978) *Political Socialisation in Western Society*, London, Edward Arnold.

Stradling, R. (1977) *The Political Awareness of School-leavers*, London, Hansard Society.

Stradling, R. and Zureik, E. (1971), Political and non-political ideals of English primary and secondary schoolchildren, *Sociological Review*, 19, 203–27.

Stuart, A., Prandy, K. and Blackburn, R. (1980) *Social Stratification and Occupations*, London, Macmillan.

Tanner, J.M. (1962) *Growth at Adolescence*, Oxford, Blackwell.

Turner, S. (1984) Bursting the balloon. Paper presented to *British Sociological Association Conference*, Bradford.

Unesco (1981) *Youth in the 1980s*, Paris, Unesco Press.

Wallace, C. (1987) *For Richer or Poorer: Growing Up in and out of Work*, London, Tavistock.

Warr, P., Banks, M., and Ullah, P. (1985) The experience of unemployment among black and white urban teenagers, *British Journal of Psychology*, 76, 75–87.

Weakliem, D. (1989) Class and party in Britain 1964–83, *Sociology*, 23, 285–97.

Weber, M. (1904) *The Protestant Work Ethic and the Spirit of Capitalism*. London, Allen & Unwin.

Werthman, C. (1977) Delinquents in schools: a test for the legitimacy of authority. In B.R. Cosin, I.R. Dale, G.M. Esland, D. Mackinnon and D.F. Swift (eds), *School and Society*, London, Routledge and Kegan Paul.

Willis, P. (1977) *Learning to Labour: How Working Class Kids Get Working Class Jobs*, London, Saxon House.

Wilson, D. (1978) Sexual codes and conduct: a study of teenage girls. In C. Smart and B. Smart (eds), *Women, Sexuality and Social Control*, London, Routledge and Kegan Paul.

Wilson, G.D. (1973) *The Psychology of Conservatism*, New York, Academic Press.

Zureik, E.T. (1974) Party images and partisanship among young Englishmen, *British Journal of Sociology*, 25, 179–200.

Zongker, C. (1977) The self-concept of pregnant adolescent girls, *Adolescence*, 12, 477–88.

INDEX

635273

β